DATA
STRUCTURES
IN JAVA

A Laboratory Course

Sandra Andersen
Concordia College

JONES AND BARTLETT PUBLISHERS

Sudbury, Massachusetts

BOSTON   TORONTO   LONDON   SINGAPORE

World Headquarters
Jones and Bartlett Publishers
40 Tall Pine Drive
Sudbury, MA 01776
978-443-5000
info@jbpub.com
www.jbpub.com

Jones and Bartlett Publishers
Canada
2406 Nikanna Road
Mississauga, ON L5C 2W6
CANADA

Jones and Bartlett Publishers
International
Barb House, Barb Mews
London W6 7PA
UK

Library of Congress Cataloging-in-Publication Data

Andersen, Sandra.
　　Data structures in Java: a laboratory course / Sandra Andersen.
　　　　p. cm.
　　ISBN 0-7637-1816-5
　　　　1. Java (Computer program language)　2. Data structures (Computer science)　I. Title.

QA76.73.J38 A46 2001
005.13'3—dc21　　　　　　　　　　　　　　　　　　　　　　　　2001050446

Editor-in-Chief: J. Michael Stranz
Development and Product Manager: Amy Rose
Production Assistant: Tara McCormick
Composition: Northeast Compositors
Cover Design: Kristin Ohlin
Printing and Binding: Courier Stoughton
Cover printing: Courier Stoughton

This book was typeset in FrameMaker 5.5 on a Macintosh G4. The font families used were Rotis Sans Serif, Rotis Serif, and Prestige Elite.

Printed in the United States of America

05 04 03 02 01　　　10 9 8 7 6 5 4 3 2 1

To my family and friends, for their love and encouragement.

—S.A.

Preface

TO THE STUDENT

Objectives

To learn a subject such as computer science, you need to immerse yourself in it — learning by doing rather than by simply observing. Through the study of several classic data structures and algorithms, you will become a better informed and more knowledgeable computer science student and programmer. To be able to professionally choose the best algorithm and data structure for a particular set of resource constraints takes practice.

An emphasis on learning by doing is used throughout *Data Structures in Java: A Laboratory Course*. In each laboratory, you explore a particular data structure by implementing it. As you create an implementation, you learn how the data structure works and how it can be applied. The resulting implementation is a working piece of software that you can use in later laboratories and programming projects.

Organization of the Laboratories

Each laboratory consists of four parts: Prelab, Bridge, In-lab, and Postlab. The **Prelab** is a homework assignment in which you create an implementation of a data structure using the techniques that your instructor presents in lecture, along with material from your textbook. In the **Bridge** exercise, you test and debug the software you developed in the Prelab. The **In-lab** phase consists of three exercises. The first two exercises apply or extend the concepts introduced in the Prelab. In the third exercise, you apply the data structure you created in the Prelab to the solution of a problem. The last part of each laboratory, the **Postlab**, is a homework assignment in which you analyze a data structure in terms of its efficiency or use.

Your instructor will specify which exercises you need to complete for each laboratory. Be sure to check whether your instructor wants you to complete the Bridge exercise prior to your lab period or during lab. Use the cover sheet provided with the laboratory to keep track of the exercises you have been assigned.

Student Source Code

The Student Source Code that accompanies this manual (which is available at **http://www.oodatastructures.jbpub.com**) contains a set of tools that make it easier for you to create data structure implementations. Each laboratory includes a visualization method called showStructure that displays a given data structure. You can use this method to watch how your routines change the content and organization of the data structure. Each laboratory also includes an interactive test program that you can use to help you test and debug your work.

Additional files containing data, partial solution shells, and other supporting routines also are provided in the source code. The file *Readme.txt* lists the files used in each laboratory.

TO THE INSTRUCTOR

Objective

Laboratories are a way of involving students as active, creative partners in the learning process. By making the laboratories the focal point of the course, students are immersed in the course material. Students are thus challenged to exercise their creativity (in both programming and analysis) and yet receive the structure, feedback, and support that they need to meet the challenge.

Organization of the Laboratories

In this manual, the laboratory framework includes a creative element but shifts the time-intensive aspects outside of the closed laboratory period. Within this structure, each laboratory includes four parts: Prelab, Bridge, In-lab, and Postlab.

Prelab

The Prelab exercise is a homework assignment that links the lecture with the laboratory period. In the Prelab, students explore and create on their own and at their own pace. Their goal is to synthesize the information they learn in lecture with material from their textbook to produce a working piece of software, usually an implementation of an abstract data type (ADT). A Prelab assignment—including a review of the relevant lecture and textbook materials—typically takes an evening to complete (that is, four to five hours).

Bridge

The Bridge exercise asks students to test the software they developed in the Prelab. The students create a test plan that they then use as a framework for evaluating their code. An interactive, command-driven test program is provided for each laboratory, along with a visualization routine (showStructure) that allows students to see changes in the content and organization of a data structure. This assignment provides an opportunity for students to receive feedback on their Prelab work and to resolve any difficulties they might have encountered. It should take students approximately one hour to finish this exercise.

In-lab

The In-lab section takes place during the actual laboratory period (assuming you are using a closed laboratory setting). Each In-lab consists of three exercises, and each exercise has a distinct role. The first two exercises stress programming and provide a capstone to the Prelab. In

Exercise 3, students apply the software they developed in the Prelab to a real-world problem that has been honed to its essentials to fit comfortably within the closed laboratory environment. Exercises 1 and 2 take roughly 45 minutes each to complete. Exercise 3 can be completed in approximately one and one-half hours.

Most students will not be able to complete all the In-lab exercises within a typical closed laboratory period. A range of exercises has been provided so that you can select those that best suit your laboratory environment and your students' needs.

Postlab

The last phase of each laboratory is a homework assignment that is done following the laboratory period. In the Postlab, students analyze the efficiency or utility of a given data structure. Each Postlab exercise should take roughly 20 minutes to complete.

Using the Four-Part Organization in Your Laboratory Environment

Computer science instructors use the term laboratory to denote a broad range of environments. One group of students in a data structures course, for example, might attend a closed two-hour laboratory; at the same time, another group of students might take the class in a televised format and "attend" an open laboratory. This manual has been developed to create a laboratory format suitable for a variety of open and closed laboratory settings. How you use the four-part organization depends on your laboratory environment.

Two-Hour Closed Laboratory

Prelab Students attending a two-hour closed laboratory are expected to make a good-faith effort to complete the Prelab exercise before coming to the lab. Their work need not be perfect, but their effort must be real (roughly 80 percent correct).

Bridge Students are asked to complete the test plans included in the Bridge exercise and to begin testing and debugging their Prelab work prior to coming to lab (as part of the 80 percent correct guideline).

In-lab The first hour of the laboratory period can be used to resolve any problems the students might have experienced in completing the Prelab and Bridge exercises. The intent is to give constructive feedback so that students leave the lab with working Prelab software - a significant accomplishment on their part.

During the second hour, students complete one of the In-lab exercises to reinforce the concepts learned in the Prelab. You can choose the exercise by section or by student, or you can let the students decide which one to complete.

Students leave the lab having received feedback on their Prelab and In-lab work. You need not rigidly enforce the hourly divisions; a mix of activities keeps everyone interested and motivated.

Postlab   After the lab, the students complete one of the Postlab exercises and turn it in during their next lab period.

One-hour Closed Laboratory

Prelab   If there is only one hour for the closed laboratory, students are asked to complete both the Prelab and Bridge exercises before they come to the lab. This work is turned in at the start of the period.

In-lab   During the laboratory period, the students complete one of the In-lab exercises.

Postlab   Again, the students complete one of the Postlab exercises and submit it during their next lab period.

Open Laboratory

In an open laboratory setting, the students are asked to complete the Prelab and Bridge exercises, one of the In-lab exercises, and one of the Postlab exercises. You can stagger the submission of these exercises throughout the week or have students turn in the entire laboratory as a unit.

ADAPTING THE MANUAL TO YOUR COURSE

Student preparation

This manual assumes that students have a background in C, C++, or Java. The first laboratory introduces the use of classes to implement a simple ADT. Succeeding laboratories introduce more complex Java language features (abstract window toolkit, cloning, inheritance, and so forth) in the context of data structures that use these features.

Order of Topics

Each of us covers the course material in the order that we believe best suits our students' needs. To give instructors flexibility in the order of presentation, the individual laboratories have been made as independent of one another as possible. It is recommended that you begin with the following sequence of laboratories.

Laboratory 1 (*Logbook ADT*)

   Introduces the implementation of an ADT using a built-in Java class

Laboratory 2 (*Point List ADT*) **or** Laboratory 3 (*String ADT*)

   Introduces tokenized input and the use of the abstract window toolkit

Laboratory 4 (*Array Implementation of the List ADT*)

   Introduces use of a Java interface

Laboratory 5 (*Stack ADT*)

   Introduces linked lists

You might wonder why the performance evaluation laboratory is near the end of the manual (Laboratory 15). The reason is simple: everyone covers this topic at a different time. Rather than bury it in the middle of the manual, it is near the end so that you can include it where it best serves your and your students' needs (I do it toward the end of the semester, for instance).

Since it is important to introduce students to problems that are broad in scope, Laboratory 16 is a multi-week programming project in which students work in teams to solve a more open-ended problem. This laboratory gives students practice in using widely accepted object-oriented analysis and design techniques. It also gives students some experience with HTML which, like Java, is another common component of web page development. During the first week, each team analyzes a problem in terms of objects and then develops a design for the problem. During the second week, they create and test an implementation based on their design.

Laboratory 16 begins by walking students through the design and implementation of a simple child's calculator program. The software development framework used in this example stresses object-oriented design and programming, iterative code development, and systematic testing. The students then apply this framework to the solution of a more challenging—and more interesting—problem. This laboratory exercise aids in structuring the dynamics of the team software development process; however, it can also be assigned as an individual project simply by giving the students more time to complete the project.

ADT Implementation

The laboratories are designed to complement a variety of approaches to implementing each ADT. All ADT definitions stress the use of data abstraction and generic data elements. As a result, you can adapt them with minimal effort to suit different implementation strategies.

For each ADT, class definitions that frame an implementation of the ADT are given as part of the corresponding Prelab exercise. This definition framework is also used in the visualization method that accompanies the laboratory. Should you elect to adopt a somewhat different implementation strategy, you need only make minor changes to the data members in the class definitions and corresponding modifications to the visualization routine. You do not need to change anything else in either the supplied software or the laboratory text itself.

Differences between the Manual and Your Text

Variations in style between the approaches used in the textbook and the laboratory manual discourage students from simply copying material from the textbook. Having to make changes, however slight, encourages students to examine in more detail how a given implementation works.

Combining the Laboratories with Programming Projects

One goal in the design of these laboratories was to enable students to produce code in the laboratory that they can use again as part of larger, more applications-oriented programming projects. The ADTs the students develop in the Prelab exercises provide a solid foundation for such projects. Reusing the material that they created in a laboratory frees students to focus on the application they are developing. More important, they see in concrete terms—their time and effort—the value of such essential software engineering concepts as code reuse, data abstraction, and object-oriented programming.

The last exercise in each In-lab is an applications problem based on the material covered in the Prelab for that laboratory. These exercises provide an excellent starting point for programming projects. Free-form projects are also possible. The *projects* directory in the Instructor's files contains a set of programming projects based on the ADTs developed in the laboratories.

Student Files

Challenging students is easy; helping them to meet a challenge is not. The Student Source Code for this manual is available at **http://www.oodatastructures.jbpub.com**. It includes a set of software tools that assist students in developing ADT implementations. The tools provide students with the means for testing an ADT implementation using simple keyboard commands and for visualizing the resulting data structure using ASCII text on a standard text display. Additional files containing data, partial solution shells, and other supporting routines are also included at this site.

Instructor's Files

Instructor's support is available on request from Jones and Bartlett Publishers at **http://www.oodatastructures.jbpub.com**. This material contains solutions to all the Prelab and In-lab exercises, as well as a set of programming projects compatible with the laboratories in this manual. Contact your sales representative at 800-832-0034 to obtain a password to this site.

ACKNOWLEDGMENTS

I would like to thank my editors at Jones and Bartlett, Michael Stranz and Amy Rose, for their assistance in guiding this project to completion.

I am also grateful to the students in my Fundamentals of Data Structures II course at Concordia College-Moorhead, MN, who helped me class-test many of these laboratory exercises. Their comments and suggestions have improved the quality of the final version of these laboratories.

Finally, I owe a debt of thanks to my husband Don for his patience and support while I was working on this project.

S.A.

Contents

Laboratory 8   Doubly Linked List Implementation of the List ADT   171

Focus: Circular doubly linked list implementation of a list

Application: Anagram puzzle

Laboratory 9   Ordered List ADT   193

Focus: Array implementation of an ordered list using inheritance

Application: Assembling messages in a packet switching network

Laboratory 10   Recursion with Linked Lists   215

Focus: Using recursion to process and restructure linked lists

Application: Replacing recursion with iteration

Laboratory 15   Performance Evaluation   351

Focus: *Determining execution times*

Application: *Analyzing the execution times of sorting and searching routines*

Laboratory 16   Team Software Development Project   373

Focus: *Object-oriented analysis and design techniques*

Application: *Create a program that generates an HTML noteboard consisting of a set of monthly calendars and associated notes*

Logbook ADT

OBJECTIVES

In this laboratory, you

- examine the components that form an abstract data type (ADT) in Java.
- implement a programmer-defined ADT in Java.
- create a method that displays a logbook in calendar form.
- investigate how to overload methods in Java.

OVERVIEW

Because it is a pure object-oriented programming language, all Java programs contain one or more class (or ADT) definitions. Java defines many built-in classes and hundreds of methods. The purpose of this laboratory is for you to review how you can implement an abstract data type (ADT) of your own design while utilizing some of the built-in ADTs already implemented in Java. We use a monthly logbook as our example ADT. A **monthly logbook** consists of a set of entries, one for each day of the month. Depending on the logbook, these entries might denote a business's daily receipts, the amount of time a person spent exercising, the number of cups of coffee consumed, and so forth. A typical logbook is shown below.

February 2002						
					1 100	**2** 95
3 90	**4** 0	**5** 150	**6** 94	**7** 100	**8** 105	**9** 100
10 100	**11** 50	**12** 110	**13** 110	**14** 100	**15** 125	**16** 110
17 0	**18** 110	**19** 0	**20** 125	**21** 100	**22** 110	**23** 115
24 111	**25** 0	**26** 50	**27** 110	**28** 125		

When specifying an ADT, you begin by describing the **elements** (or attributes) that the ADT consists of. Then you describe how these ADT elements are organized to form the ADT's overall structure. In the case of the monthly logbook abstract data type—or Logbook ADT, for short—the elements are the entries associated with the days of the month and the structure is linear:

the entries are arranged in the same order as the corresponding days. In Java these elements are called the **data members** of the ADT (or class).

Having specified the ADT's data members, you then define its behavior by specifying the **operations** that are associated with the ADT. For each operation, you specify what conditions must be true before the operation can be applied (its requirements or **precondition**) as well as what conditions will be true once the operation has completed (its results or **postcondition**). The Logbook ADT specification below includes operations (or **methods** in Java) that create a logbook for a given month, store/retrieve the logbook entry for a specific day, and provide general information about the month.

Logbook ADT

Elements

A set of integer values for a logbook month and its associated calendar.

Structure

Each integer value is the logbook entry for a given day of the month. The number of logbook entries varies depending on the month for which data is being recorded. We will refer to this month as the **logbook month**. Each logbook month is actually a calendar month for a particular year. Thus each logbook month starts on a particular day of the week and has a fixed number of days in that month based on our Gregorian calendar.

Constructor

```
Logbook ( int month, int year )
```
Precondition:
Month is a valid calendar month between 1 and 12 inclusive.
Postcondition:
Constructor. Creates an empty logbook for the specified month—that is, a logbook in which all the entries are zero. If month is an invalid value, it will default to today's date.

Methods

```
void putEntry ( int day, int value )
```
Precondition:
Day is less than or equal to the number of days in the logbook month.
Postcondition:
Stores the value as the logbook entry for the specified day.

```
int getEntry ( int day )
```
Precondition:
Day is less than or equal to the number of days in the logbook month.
Postcondition:
Returns the logbook entry for the specified day or −1 if there is no such day.

```
int month ( )
```
Precondition:
None.
Postcondition:
Returns the logbook month.

```
int year ( )
```
Precondition:
None.
Postcondition:
Returns the logbook year.

```
int daysInMonth ( )
```
Precondition:
None.
Postcondition:
Returns the number of days in the logbook month.

LABORATORY 1: Cover Sheet

Name

Hour/Period/Section

Date

Place a check mark (✔) in the Assigned column next to the exercises that your instructor has assigned to you. Attach this cover sheet to the front of the packet of materials that you submit for this laboratory.

Exercise	Assigned	Completed
Prelab Exercise	✔	
Bridge Exercise	✔	
In-lab Exercise 1		
In-lab Exercise 2		
In-lab Exercise 3		
Postlab Exercise 1		
Postlab Exercise 2		
Total		

LABORATORY 1: Prelab Exercise

Name _____

Hour/Period/Section _____

Date _____

The Logbook ADT specification provides enough information for you (or other programmers) to design and develop programs that use logbooks. Before you can begin using logbooks in your Java programs, however, you must first create a Java implementation of the Logbook ADT.

You saw in the Overview that an ADT consists of a set of elements and a set of operations that manipulate those elements. A Java **class** usually consists of a set of **data members** (or elements) and a set of **member methods** (or operations) that manipulate the data members. Thus, classes are a natural means for implementing ADTs.

How do you create a definition for a Logbook class from the specification of the Logbook ADT? You begin with the ADT elements and structure. The Logbook ADT specification indicates that you must maintain the following information about each logbook:

- the (month, year) pair that specify a particular logbook month

- the array of logbook entries for the month

- a calendar facility primarily for determining leap years and day-of-week on which the first day of the month falls

This information is stored in the data members of the Logbook class. The month and year are stored as integer values, the entries are stored as an array of integers, and the calendar facility will be based on Java's built-in GregorianCalendar class, which is derived (or inherited) from Java's Calendar class. We won't go into all the details of inheritance at this time, but because the GregorianCalendar class inherits from the Calendar class, an instance of the GregorianCalendar class can use all public and protected methods and variables in the Calendar class. This illustrates one big advantage of object-oriented programming—the ability to reuse existing ADTs instead of always writing your own.

```
class Logbook
{
    // Data members
    private int logMonth,              // Logbook month
            logYear;                   // Logbook year
    private int[] entry = new int[31]; // Array of Logbook entries
    private GregorianCalendar logCalendar;  // Java's built-in Calendar class
}
```

By declaring the data members to be **private**, you prevent nonmember methods—that is, methods that are not members of the Logbook class—from accessing the logbook data directly. This restriction ensures that all references to the logbook data are made using the operations (or methods) in the Logbook ADT.

Having specified how the logbook data is to be stored, you then add definitions for the member methods corresponding to the operations in the Logbook ADT. These methods are declared as **public**. They can be called by any method—either member or nonmember—and provide a **public interface** to the logbook data. An incomplete definition for the Logbook ADT is given below. Note that it lacks implementation code for the class methods.

```
class Logbook
{
    // Data members
    private int logMonth,                       // Logbook month
              logYear;                          // Logbook year
    private int[] entry = new int[31];          // Array of Logbook entries
    private GregorianCalendar logCalendar;      // Java's built-in Calendar class

    // Constructor
    public Logbook ( int month, int year )      // Create a logbook
    {                              }

    // Logbook marking operations/methods
    public void putEntry ( int day, int value ) // Store entry for day
    {                              }
    public int getEntry ( int day )             // Return entry for day
    {                              }

    // General operations/methods
    public int month ( )                        // Return the month
    {                      }
    public int year ( )                         // Return the year
    {                      }
    public int daysInMonth ( )                  // Number of days in month
    {                      }

} // class Logbook
```

You need to know whether a given year is a leap year in order to determine the number of days in the month of February. To determine this information, a **facilitator method** (or helper method) has been added to the definition of the Logbook class. Note that the facilitator method is *not* an operation listed in the specifications for the Logbook ADT. Thus, it is included as a private member method rather than as part of the public interface. This facilitator method leapYear() can be implemented as follows using the built-in GregorianCalendar method for the Logbook class data member logCalendar.

```
return ( logCalendar.isLeapYear(logYear) );
```

Our current version of the incomplete definition for the Logbook class is shown as follows. Notice this version includes Java import statements for each of the built-in packages being used by the Logbook class. This incomplete definition is stored in the file *Logbook.jshl*.

```
import java.io.*;                        // For reading (keyboard) & writing (screen)
import java.util.*;                      // For GregorianCalendar class

class Logbook
{
    // Data members
    private int logMonth,                // Logbook month
            logYear;                     // Logbook year
    private int[] entry = new int[31];   // Array of Logbook entries
    private GregorianCalendar logCalendar; // Java's built-in Calendar class

    // Constructor
    public Logbook ( int month, int year )  // Create a logbook
    {                         }

    // Logbook marking operations/methods
    public void putEntry ( int day, int value )  // Store entry for day
    {                         }
    public int getEntry ( int day )         // Return entry for day
    {                         }

    // General operations/methods
    public int month ( )                    // Return the month
    {                         }
    public int year ( )                     // Return the year
    {                         }
    public int daysInMonth ( )              // Number of days in month
    {                         }

    // Facilitator (helper) method
    private boolean leapYear ( )            // Leap year?
    {                         }

} // class Logbook
```

This incomplete Logbook class definition provides a framework for the Logbook class. You are to fill in the Java code for each of the constructors and methods where the implementation braces are empty, or only partially filled (noted by "add code here ..."). For example, an implementation of the `month()` method is given below.

```
public int month ( )
// Precondition: None.
// Postcondition: Returns the logbook month.
{
    return logMonth;
}
```

As you complete the class definition for the Logbook ADT in the file *Logbook.jshl*, save your implementation of the member methods in the file *Logbook.java*.

The code in the file *Logbook.java* forms a Java implementation of the Logbook ADT. The following applications program uses the Logbook ADT to record and output a set of logbook entries. Note that this program is stored in its own file called *Coffee.java*.

```java
import java.io.*;

class Coffee
{
  // Records coffee intake for January 2002.
  public static void main ( String args[] ) throws IOException
  {
      int day;                    // Day loop counter

      // Coffee intake for January 2002
      Logbook coffee = new Logbook(1, 2002);

      // Record entries for the 1st and 15th of January 2002
      coffee.putEntry(1, 5);
      coffee.putEntry(15, 2);

      // Output the logbook entries.
      System.out.println("Month/Year : " + coffee.month() + "/" + coffee.year());
      for ( day = 1 ; day <= coffee.daysInMonth() ; day++ )
          System.out.println(day + " : " + coffee.getEntry(day));
  } // main( )

} // class Coffee
```

The statement

```java
Logbook coffee = new Logbook(1, 2002);
```

invokes the Logbook class constructor to create a logbook for January 2002. Notice that in Java each instance (or object) of a class is created by using the new operator. In this case coffee is an instance of the Logbook class. As implemented, the constructor begins by verifying that a valid month value has been received. Then the constructor creates a new logCalendar for January 1, 2001 and sets the logMonth to 1 and logYear to 2002. You can use the assignment operator to perform this task, as in the following code fragment.

```java
public Logbook ( int month, int year )
// Constructs an empty logbook for the specified month and year.
// Note:  Unlike mankind, Java's built-in Calendar numbers months
//          from January = 0
{
    int j;   // Loop counter

    // Verify that a valid month value was entered
    // If not, setup logbook for today's date
    ...........
    ...........
    else
    {
        // Assumes a default DAY_OF_MONTH as first day of month
        logCalendar = new GregorianCalendar(year, month -1, 1);
```

```
        logMonth = month;
        logYear = year;
    }

    // Set each entry in the logbook to 0.
    ...........
    ...........
}
```

Note that Java's GregorianCalendar class numbers the months starting with 0 for January through 11 for December. Since people usually number the calendar months starting with 1 for January through 12 for December, during the execution of the coffee program `logMonth` is assigned the value 1 for January, and the month value for the GregorianCalendar constructor is adjusted accordingly by setting the month parameter to `month −1`. Once the constructor has created the `logCalendar` and assigned values to `logMonth` and `logYear`, it sets each element in the `entry` array to 0 and returns.

A side note: In-lab Exercise 2 will provide more information on how to create a logbook that defaults to today's date. For now you may want to simply implement the error-handling part of this constructor (when the month value is not between 1 and 12, inclusive) by picking arbitrary default values for `logMonth` and `logYear`.

Having constructed an empty logbook, the coffee program then uses the `putEntry()` method to record a pair of logbook entries for the first and fifteenth of January. It then outputs the logbook using repeated calls to the `getEntry()` method, with the `month()` and `year()` methods providing output headings.

Step 1: Implement the member methods in the Logbook class. Base your implementation on the incomplete Logbook class definition given earlier (and in the file *Logbook.jshl*).

Step 2: Save your implementation of the Logbook ADT in the file *Logbook.java*. Be sure to document your code.

LABORATORY 1: Bridge Exercise

Name _____

Hour/Period/Section _____

Date _____

Check with your instructor as to whether you are to complete this exercise prior to your lab period or during lab.

Test your implementation of the Logbook ADT using the program in the file *TestLogbook.java*. This program supports the following tests.

Test	Action
1	Tests the constructor and the month, year, and daysInMonth operations.
2	Tests the putEntry and getEntry operations.

Step 1: Complete the test plan for Test 1 by filling in the expected number of days for each month.

Step 2: Test your implementation of the Logbook ADT in the file *Logbook.java* by compiling and running your test program *TestLogbook.java*.

Step 3: Execute the test plan. If you discover mistakes in your implementation of the Logbook ADT, correct them and execute the test plan again.

Test Plan for *Test1* (constructor, month, year, and daysInMonth Operations)

Test case	Logbook month	No. days in month	Checked
Simple month	1 2002	31	
Month in the past	7 1998		
Month in the future	12 2008		
Current month			
February (not leap year)	2 1999		
February (leap year)	2 2000		
An invalid month	13 2002		

Step 4: Complete the test plan for Test 2 by filling in the input data and expected result for each test case. Use a logbook for the current month.

Step 5: Execute the test plan. If you discover mistakes in your implementation of the Logbook ADT, correct them and execute the test plan again.

Test Plan for *Test2* (putEntry and getEntry Operations)

Test case	Logbook entries	Expected result	Checked
Record entries for the first and fifteenth of the month	2 100 15 200		
Record entries for the first and last day of the month			
Record entries for all the Fridays in the month			
Change the entry for the first day	1 100 1 300		

LABORATORY 1: In-lab Exercise 1

Name _____

Hour/Period/Section _____

Date _____

The entries in a logbook store information about a specific month. A calendar provides a natural format for displaying this monthly data. That is why the GregorianCalendar class was conveniently included as a data member in the Logbook class: namely, the data member `logCalendar`.

void displayCalendar ( )
Precondition:
None.
Postcondition:
Outputs a logbook using the calendar format shown below. Note that each calendar entry includes the logbook entry for the corresponding day.

```
                              2 / 2002
Sun        Mon        Tue        Wed        Thu        Fri        Sat
                                                       1 100      2 95

 3 90       4 0        5 150      6 94       7 100      8 105      9 100

10 100     11 50      12 110     13 110     14 100     15 125     16 110

17 0       18 110     19 0       20 125     21 100     22 110     23 115

24 111     25 0       26 50      27 110     28 125
```

In order to produce a calendar for a given month, you need to know on which day of the week the first day of the month occurs. To do so you will need to implement the facilitator method `dayOfWeek()` described below.

int dayOfWeek (int day)
Input parameter:
Day is a specific day in the logbook month.
Returns:
An integer denoting the day of the week on which the specified day occurs, where 0 corresponds to Sunday, 1 to Monday, and so forth.

First, you will need to set the logbook calendar to the day of the month specified by the input parameter for this facilitator method. To do so you may use the following method call for the GregorianCalendar class object (`logCalendar`).

```
logCalendar.set(logYear, logMonth -1, day);
```

Then the day of the week corresponding to the current logbook's `logCalendar` *month/day/year* can be found using the following method.

```
logCalendar.get(Calendar.DAY_OF_WEEK);
```

This method returns a value between 1 (Sunday) and 7 (Saturday). As noted in the description of the `dayOfWeek()` method given above, we would prefer that the value returned be between 0 (Sunday) and 6 (Saturday). So, you will need to adjust the returned value similar to the way the month parameter was adjusted for the creation of `logCalendar` in the Logbook constructor.

Step 1: Implement the facilitator method `dayOfWeek()` described above and add it to the file *Logbook.java*. This method is included in the incomplete definition of the Logbook class in the file *Logbook.jshl*.

Step 2: Implement the `displayCalendar()` method described above and add it to the file *Logbook.java*. This method is included in the incomplete definition of the Logbook class in the file *Logbook.jshl*.

Step 3: Activate Test 3 in the test program *TestLogbook.java* by removing the comment delimiter (and the character "3") from the lines that begin with "//3".

Step 4: Complete the test plan for Test 3 by filling in the day of the week for the first day of the current month.

Step 5: Execute the test plan. If you discover mistakes in your implementation of the displayCalendar operation, correct them and execute the test plan again.

Test Plan for *Test3* (displayCalendar Operation)

Test case	Logbook month	Day of the week of the first day in the month	Checked
Simple month	1 2000	6 (Saturday)	
Month in the past	7 1998	3 (Wednesday)	
Month in the future	12 2008	1 (Monday)	
Current month			
February (not leap year)	2 2002	5 (Friday)	
February (leap year)	2 2000	2 (Tuesday)	

LABORATORY 1: In-lab Exercise 2

Name _____

Hour/Period/Section _____

Date _____

Java allows you to create multiple methods with the same name so long as these methods have different numbers of arguments or different types of arguments—a process referred to as **method overloading**. The following Logbook ADT operations, for example, each shares the same name as an existing operation. They have fewer arguments than the existing operations, however. Instead of using an argument to specify the month/year (or day) to process, they use the current month/year (or day).

```
Logbook ( )
```
Precondition:
None.
Postcondition:
Default constructor. Creates an empty logbook for the current month/year.

```
void putEntry ( int value )
```
Precondition:
Logbook is for the current month/year.
Postcondition:
Stores the value as the logbook entry for today.

The default constructor for the built-in GregorianCalendar class creates a Calendar object for today's date. Then using the method *get* as we did in dayOfWeek() we can assign the correct value to logYear as follows.

```
logYear = logCalendar.get(Calendar.YEAR);
```

In a similar manner we can assign the correct value to logMonth using the parameter Calendar.MONTH. Also, Calendar.DAY_OF_MONTH contains today's day value for use in the overloaded method putEntry().

Step 1: Implement these operations and add them to the file *Logbook.java*. Each method is included in the incomplete definition of the Logbook class in the file *Logbook.jshl*.

Step 2: Activate Test 4 in the test program *TestLogbook.java* by removing the comment delimiter (and the character "4") from the lines that begin with "//4".

Step 3: Complete the test plan for Test 4 by filling in the expected result for each operation.

Step 4: Execute the test plan. If you discover mistakes in your implementation of these operations, correct them and execute the test plan again.

Test Plan for *Test4* (Overloaded Methods)

Test case	Expected result	Checked
Construct a logbook for the current month	Number of days in the current month:	
Record an entry for today	Day on which entry is made:	

LABORATORY 1: In-lab Exercise 3

Name _____

Hour/Period/Section _____

Date _____

What if we want to add the entries in several logbooks together to find a grand total of daily entries for a particular month? For instance, the code fragment on this page illustrates how we might add the daily entries in a logbook of citySales to the entries in a logbook of suburbSales to give us a logbook of daily salesTotals for the month of September, 2002. The following describes a method that will add the corresponding daily entries in two logbooks.

```
void plus ( Logbook rightBook )
```
Precondition:
The logbooks cover the same month/year.
Postcondition:
Adds each entry in rightBook to the corresponding entry in this logbook.

The following code fragment uses this operation to sum a pair of logbooks and then outputs the combined logbook entries.

```
Logbook citySales = new Logbook(9, 2002),     // City sales
        suburbSales = new Logbook(9, 2002),   // Suburban sales
        salesTotals = new Logbook(9, 2002);   // Combined sales for September 2002
int j;                                         // Loop counter

// Read in the city and suburban sales.
...

// Sum the city and suburban sales.
salesTotals.plus( citySales );                 // Include city sales
salesTotals.plus( suburbSales );               // Include suburban sales

// Output the sum.
salesTotals.displayCalendar( );
```

Step 1: Implement the plus( ) operation and add it to the file *Logbook.java*. This method is included in the incomplete definition of the Logbook class in the file *Logbook.jshl*.

Step 2: Activate Test 5 in the test program *TestLogbook.java* by removing the comment delimiter (and the character "5") from the lines that begin with "//5".

Step 3: Complete the test plan for Test 5 by filling in the expected result. Use a logbook for the current month.

Step 4: Execute the test plan. If you discover mistakes in your implementation of the logbook addition operation, correct them and execute the test plan again.

Test Plan for *Test5* (plus Operation)

Test case	Expected result of adding `logDay200` to `logDay100`	Checked
The entries in logbook `logDay100` are equal to (100 * day) and the entries in logbook `logDay200` are equal to (200 * day)		

LABORATORY 1: Postlab Exercise 1

Name _____

Hour/Period/Section _____

Date _____

Part A

In our implementation of Logbook, the facilitator method leapYear( ) uses the built-in GregorianCalendar class method isLeapYear( ). This is possible because the Logbook class contains a data member from the GregorianCalendar class. If there were no GregorianCalendar (logCalendar) data member in the Logbook class, how would you implement Logbook's leapYear( ) method?

```
private boolean leapYear ( )                    // Leap year?
{



}
```

Part B

In terms of time and space, what is the cost of defining the data member logCalendar to implement leapYear( )?

In terms of time and space, what is the cost (or savings) of implementing leapYear( ) without declaring the GregorianCalendar class data member logCalendar?

LABORATORY 1: Postlab Exercise 2

Name

Hour/Period/Section

Date

Part A

In our implementation of Logbook the facilitator method `dayOfWeek( )` uses several built-in GregorianCalendar class methods to return the correct value. This is possible because the Logbook class has a data member from the GregorianCalendar class. If there were no GregorianCalendar (`logCalendar`) data member, how would you implement `dayOfWeek( )`?

```
private int dayOfWeek ( int day )
// Returns the day of the week corresponding to the specified day.
{



}
```

Part B

What is gained/lost by implementing `dayOfWeek( )` without using the GregorianCalendar data member?

Point List ADT

OBJECTIVES

In this laboratory, you

- implement a list of points using an array representation of a list—including development of an iteration scheme that allows you to move through a list element by element.

- use the new operator to dynamically allocate memory and rely on automatic garbage collection to deallocate memory.

- use a Java tokenizer to read data from the keyboard input stream.

- display a curve represented by a point list using Java's AWT (abstract window toolkit).

OVERVIEW

The list is perhaps the most commonly used data structure. Just think how often you make lists of things to do, places to be, and so on. The defining property of a **list** is that the elements are organized linearly—that is, every element has one element immediately before it and another immediately after it (except, of course, the elements at the beginning and end of the list).

In this laboratory, you explore lists in which each element is a two-dimensional point—or (x,y) pair. We refer to this type of list as a **point list**. Point lists are routinely used in computer graphics, computer-aided design (CAD), and computer modeling to represent lines, curves, edges, and so forth.

The Point List ADT described below provides operations that allow you to add points to a list, check the state of a list (Is it empty? or Is it full?), and iterate through the points in a list. Iteration is done using a **cursor** that you move through the list much as you move the cursor in a text editor or word processor. In the following example, the Point List ADT's gotoBeginning operation is used to move the cursor to the beginning of the list. The cursor is then moved through the list point by point, by repeated applications of the gotoNext operation. Note that the point marked by the cursor is shown in bold.

After gotoBeginning: **(0,0)** (1,1) (2,2) (3,3)

After gotoNext: (0,0) **(1,1)** (2,2) (3,3)

After gotoNext: (0,0) (1,1) **(2,2)** (3,3)

After gotoNext: (0,0) (1,1) (2,2) **(3,3)**

Point List ADT

Elements:

Each element in a point list is of type Point (a built-in Java class) and contains a pair of integers that represent the point's x- and y-coordinates. Once again, since the Point class is built into Java, some of our object-oriented programming has already been done for us.

Structure:

The points form a linear structure in which points follow one after the other, from the beginning of the list to its end. The ordering of the points is determined by the order in which they were appended to the list. At any moment in time, one point in any nonempty list is marked using the list's cursor. You travel through the list using operations that change the position of the cursor.

Constructors and their Helper Method

```
PointList ( )
```
Precondition:
None.
Postcondition:
Default Constructor. Calls setup, which creates an empty list. Allocates enough memory for a list containing DEF_MAX_LIST_SIZE (a constant value) points.

```
PointList ( int maxNumber )
```
Precondition:
maxNumber > 0.
Postcondition:
Constructor. Creates an empty list. Allocates enough memory for a list containing maxNumber points.

```
void setup(int size)
```
Precondition:
size > 0. A helper method for the constructors. Is declared private since only point list constructors should call this method.
Postcondition:
Creates an empty point list of a specific size based on the value of size received from the constructor.

Methods

```
void append ( Point newPoint )
```
Precondition:
List is not full.
Postcondition:
Adds newPoint to the end of a list. If the list is empty, then adds newPoint as the first (and only) point in the list. Moves the cursor to newPoint.

```
void clear ()
```
Precondition:
None.
Postcondition:
Removes all the points in a list.

```
boolean isEmpty ( )
```
Precondition:
None.
Postcondition:
Returns true if a list is empty. Otherwise, returns false.

```
boolean isFull ( )
```
Precondition:
None.
Postcondition:
Returns true if a list is full. Otherwise, returns false.

```
boolean gotoBeginning ( )
```
Precondition:
None.
Postcondition:
If a list is not empty, then moves the cursor to the point at the beginning of the list and returns true. Otherwise, returns false.

```
boolean gotoEnd ( )
```
Precondition:
None.
Postcondition:
If a list is not empty, then moves the cursor to the point at the end of the list and returns true. Otherwise, returns false.

```
boolean gotoNext ( )
```
Precondition:
List is not empty.
Postcondition:
If the cursor is not at the end of a list, then moves the cursor to the next point in the list and returns true. Otherwise, returns false.

```
boolean gotoPrior ( )
```
Precondition:

List is not empty.

Postcondition:

If the cursor is not at the beginning of a list, then moves the cursor to the preceding point in the list and returns true. Otherwise, returns false.

```
Point getCursor ( )
```
Precondition:

List is not empty.

Postcondition:

Returns a copy of the point marked by the cursor.

```
void showStructure ( )
```
Precondition:

None.

Postcondition:

Outputs the points in a list. If the list is empty, outputs "Empty list". Note that this operation is intended for testing/debugging purposes only.

LABORATORY 2: Cover Sheet

Name _____

Hour/Period/Section _____

Date _____

Place a check mark (✔) in the Assigned column next to the exercises that your instructor has assigned to you. Attach this cover sheet to the front of the packet of materials that you submit for this laboratory.

Exercise	Assigned	Completed
Prelab Exercise	✔	
Bridge Exercise	✔	
In-lab Exercise 1		
In-lab Exercise 2		
In-lab Exercise 3		
Postlab Exercise 1		
Postlab Exercise 2		
Total		

LABORATORY 2: Prelab Exercise

Name _____

Hour/Period/Section _____

Date _____

You can implement a list in many ways. Given that a list is linear and that all the list elements are of the same type (in this case, the built-in class Point), an array seems a natural choice. You could declare the size of the array at compile-time (as you did with the logbook array in Laboratory 1), but your Point List ADT will be more flexible if you specify the size of the array at runtime and dynamically allocate the memory required to store it.

Memory allocation for the array is done by the constructor. The Point constructor is invoked during the execution of the program. Once called, the PointList constructor allocates an array of points using Java's new operator. The statement below, for example, allocates memory for an array of maxSize points. The variable name ptlist is the reference through which we have access to this array of points.

```
Point ptlist = new Point[maxSize];
```

During program execution a variable reference can become inaccessible. Whenever a point (ptlist) reference goes out of scope—that is, whenever the method containing the corresponding variable declaration terminates—the ptlist variable is no longer accessible. In other words, the program can no longer use the ptlist variable because it has gone out of scope. The memory allocated for ptlist may also become inaccessible through reassignment such as:

```
ptlist = new Point[10];              // First assignment
   ......
   ......
ptlist = new Point[8];               // Reassignment; first instance is inaccessible
```

When all references to a memory location have been lost, the memory location no longer serves any useful purpose and is called **garbage**.

What happens to memory that was allocated for an instance variable such as the ptlist array when all references to that memory location have been lost? Unlike object-oriented programming languages such as C++ where the programmer must explicitly manage memory deallocation, Java has a built-in mechanism that finds unused memory and makes that memory available for use to store new instances of other program variables. This process of returning inaccessible memory to the available-memory (or free-storage) list is called **garbage collection**. Since garbage collection is built-in and not directly controlled by the programmer, we say Java has **automatic garbage collection**.

There are tradeoffs between Java's automatic garbage collection and programmer-controlled memory deallocation that is used in other object-oriented programming languages. Automatic garbage collection is slower, but it is less prone to programming errors and frees the programmer to focus on the implementation details of the problem at hand. However, garbage collection actually occurs infrequently (if at all) during the execution of your Java program. In other words, garbage collection does not occur the instant one or more objects become inaccessible.

Step 1: Implement the operations in the Point List ADT using an array to store the list of points. Arrays have a limited capacity, which the programmer might store in a separate variable such as maxSize. An important characteristic of arrays in Java is that the size of the array is held in a constant called length in the array object. Therefore, in Java a separate variable (such as maxSize) is not necessary, since the maximum number of elements our point list can hold can be determined by referencing length–more specifically in our case, by referencing ptlist.length. Lists change in size, therefore you need to store the actual number of points in the list (size), along with the points themselves (ptlist). You also need to keep track of the cursor array index (cursor). Base your implementation on the following incomplete definitions from the built-in class Point and the file *PointList.jshl*.

```
//---------------------------- sketch of built-in class Point -------------------- //
//--------- (only the Point methods used in this Laboratory are shown here) -------- //
class Point
{
    // Data members
    // Point coordinates (can be accessed directly)
    public int x,
              y;

    // Constructors
    public Point ( )
    // Default Constructor
    {
        x = 0;
        y = 0;
    }

    public Point ( int x0, int y0 )
    // Constructor
    {
        x = x0;
        y = y0;
    }

} // built-in class Point

// -------------------------------PointList.jshl ---------------------------- //
class PointList
{
    // Default maximum list size — a constant
    public static final int DEF_MAX_LIST_SIZE = 10;
```

```
// Data members
private int size,                          // Actual number of points in the list
          cursor;                          // Cursor index
private Point ptlist[];                    // Array containing the points

// Constructors and helper method setup
public PointList ( )                       // Constructor: default size
{              }
public PointList ( int maxNumber )         // Constructor: specific size
{              }

// Class  methods
private void setup(int size)               // Called by constructors only
{              }

// List manipulation operations/methods
public void append ( Point newPoint )      // Append point to list
{              }
public void clear ( )                      // Clear list
{              }

// List status operations/methods
public boolean isEmpty ( )                 // Is list empty?
{              }
public boolean isFull ( )                  // Is list full?
{              }

// List iteration operations
public boolean gotoBeginning ( )           // Go to beginning
{              }
public boolean gotoEnd ( )                 // Go to end
{              }
public boolean gotoNext ( )                // Go to next point
{              }
public boolean gotoPrior ( )               // Go to prior point
{              }
public Point getCursor ( )                 // Return point
{              }

// Output the list structure—used in testing/debugging
public void showStructure ( )
{              }

} // class PointList
```

Step 2: Save your implementation of the Point List ADT in the file *PointList.java*. Be sure to document your code.

The following code fragment (in the file *SampPtList.java*) reads data input from the keyboard and uses the operations in the Point List ADT. The operations in the Point List ADT are used to help construct a list of points as well as iterate through the list from beginning to end, outputting each point along the way.

```java
import java.io.*;

class SampPtList
{
    public static void main ( String args[] ) throws IOException
    {
        // Set of vertices for a polygon
        PointList polygon = new PointList( );
        Point vertex;                  // Vertex

        //----------------------------------------------------------------
        // Initialize reader and tokenizer for the input stream -
        //    for reading 'tokens' (namely point values)
        //    input from the keyboard.
        //
        // Initialize reader - To read a character at a time
        InputStreamReader reader = new InputStreamReader(System.in);

        // Initialize the tokenizer -
        //    To read tokens (words and numbers separated by whitespace)
        StreamTokenizer tokens = new StreamTokenizer(reader);

        // Note: Use the tokenizer's  nextToken( )  method
        //    to step through a stream of tokens.
        //        Use the tokenizer's instance variable  nval
        //    to obtain the number read.
        //        Since nval is of type double, cast it to an int
        //    when reading points x and y     (int)tokens.nval

        // Read in the polygon's vertices.
        System.out.print("Enter the polygon's vertices (end with eof) : ");

        // Keep reading as long as text (the word eof) has not been entered
        while ( tokens.nextToken( ) != tokens.TT_WORD )
        {
            vertex = new Point( );             // Create new Point
            vertex.x = (int)tokens.nval;       // Assign x value of the point
            tokens.nextToken( );
            vertex.y = (int)tokens.nval;       // Assign y value of the point
            polygon.append(vertex);            // Add to PointList's array of Points
        }

        // Output the vertices one per line.
        if ( polygon.gotoBeginning( ) )        // Go to beginning of list
            do
            {
                vertex = polygon.getCursor( );
                System.out.println("(" + vertex.x + "," + vertex.y + ")");
            } while ( polygon.gotoNext( ) ); // Go to next point (if any)
    }

} // class SampPtList
```

Using the code fragment above let's review the set of Java statements needed to read data from an input stream such as the keyboard. (A similar set of statements was also provided for you in the file *TestLogbook.java* for Laboratory 1.) In Java the standard input stream—the keyboard—is associated with the variable System.in. The following statement will create an InputStreamReader connected to the keyboard input stream (System.in):

```
InputStreamReader reader = new InputStreamReader(System.in);
```

Next, insert a StreamTokenizer between this InputStreamReader and the program so that not just a single character but an entire number or word can be read. To do so use a statement similar to the following:

```
StreamTokenizer tokens = new StreamTokenizer(reader);
```

The StreamTokenizer treats whitespace characters as delimiters that divide character sequences into tokens. The StreamTokenizer class has a nextToken method that returns the next token (number or word) in the stream. Thus, use the following statement to read the next token in the input stream:

```
tokens.nextToken( );
```

The method nextToken returns the constant TT_WORD if the token of data read is a word of text, or it returns the constant TT_NUMBER if the token read is numeric. The StreamTokenizer instance provides two public data members, nval and sval. The data member nval contains the number read if nextToken returned TT_NUMBER. If nextToken returned TT_WORD, the data member sval contains the word read.

Our program keeps reading (numbers) until the user enters eof. Since the data to be processed is numeric, the following statement reads the next token and checks to see if the user entered text (or eof).

```
// Keep reading as long as text (the word eof) has not been entered
while ( tokens.nextToken( ) != tokens.TT_WORD )
```

If nextToken does not return TT_WORD, then the (otherwise) numeric value is assigned to vertex.x as follows:

```
vertex.x = (int)tokens.nval;
```

Since nval is of type double and vertex.x is an int, we cast nval to an int in the above statement. In like manner we read and assign a value to vertex.y as follows:

```
tokens.nextToken( );
vertex.y = (int)tokens.nval;
```

This series of statements for reading keyboard input can generally be used for reading keyboard input in any Java program. You will be asked later in this laboratory to use commands similar to these in your own program.

LABORATORY 2: Bridge Exercise

Name _____

Hour/Period/Section _____

Date _____

Check with your instructor as to whether you are to complete this exercise prior to your lab period or during lab.

The test program that you used in Laboratory 1 consisted of a series of tests that were hard-coded into the program. Adding a new test case to this style of test program requires changing the test program itself. In this laboratory, you use a more flexible kind of test program to evaluate your ADT implementation, one in which you specify a test case using commands, rather than code. This interactive, command-driven test program allows you to check a new test case by simply entering a series of keyboard commands and observing the results.

The test program in the file *TestPointList.java* supports the following commands.

Command	Action
+ x y	Append point (x,y) to the end of the list.
@	Display the point marked by the cursor.
N	Go to the next point.
P	Go to the prior point.
<	Go to the beginning of the list.
>	Go to the end of the list.
E	Report whether the list is empty.
F	Report whether the list is full.
C	Clear the list.
Q	Quit the test program.

Suppose you wish to confirm that your array implementation of the Point List ADT successfully constructs a point list storing the vertices of a square. You can test this case by entering the following sequence of keyboard commands.

Command	+ 1 1	+ 1 2	+ 2 2	+ 2 1	Q
Action	Append (1,1)	Append (1,2)	Append (2,2)	Append (2,1)	Quit

It is easy to see how this interactive test program allows you to rapidly examine a variety of test cases. This speed comes with a price, however. You must be careful not to violate the preconditions required by the operations that you are testing. For instance, the commands

Command	C	@
Action	Clear list	Error

cause the test program to fail during the call to the getCursor operation. The source of the failure does not lie in the implementation of the Point List ADT, nor is the test program flawed. The failure occurs because this sequence of operations creates a state that violates the preconditions of the getCursor operation (the list must *not* be empty when the getCursor operation is invoked). The speed with which you can create and evaluate test cases using an interactive, command-driven test program makes it very easy to produce this kind of error. It is very tempting to just sit down and start entering commands. A much better strategy, however, is to create a test plan listing the test cases you wish to check and then to write out command sequences that generate these test cases.

Step 1: Complete the test plan below by adding test cases that check whether your implementation of the Point List ADT correctly handles the following tasks:

• appending points to a list that has been cleared

• filling a list to its maximum size

• determining whether a list is empty

• determining whether a list is full

Assume that the output of one test case is used as the input to the following test case and note that, although expected results are listed for the final command in each command sequence, you should confirm that *each* command produces a correct result.

Step 2: Test your implementation of the Point List ADT by compiling and running your test program *TestPointList.java*.

Step 3: Execute your test plan. If you discover mistakes in your implementation of the Point List ADT, correct them and execute your test plan again.

Test Plan for the *Operations in the Point List ADT*

Test case	Commands	Expected result	Checked
Append a series of points	+ 1 2 + 3 4 + 5 6 + 7 8	(1,2) (3,4) (5,6) **(7,8)**	
Iterate from the beginning	< N N	(1,2) (3,4) **(5,6)** (7,8)	
Iterate from the end	> P P	(1,2) **(3,4)** (5,6) (7,8)	
Display the point marked by the cursor	@	(3,4)	
Clear the list	C	Empty list	

Note: The point marked by the cursor is shown in **bold**.

LABORATORY 2: In-lab Exercise 1

Name _____

Hour/Period/Section _____

Date _____

As we noted in the Overview, point lists are commonly used in computer graphics to represent curves. Rather than storing all the points required to display a curve at a given level of detail—an approach that would require massive amounts of storage—only selected points are stored in the list. These points are then connected by line segments when the curve is displayed (as in the "connect the dots" game). The figure below shows a circle centered at (2, 2) with radius 1, its point list representation, and the resulting display.

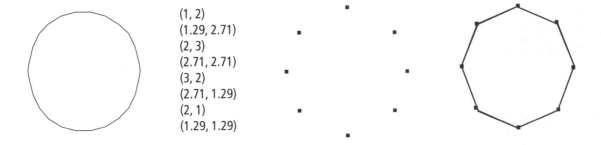

(1, 2)
(1.29, 2.71)
(2, 3)
(2.71, 2.71)
(3, 2)
(2.71, 1.29)
(2, 1)
(1.29, 1.29)

Note that we have sacrificed some of the smoothness of the circle by approximating it using only nine points (with one point repeated so that the curve is closed). We could produce a much smoother circle by dividing the circle into smaller pieces.

Step 1: Using the shell in the file *DrawCurv.jshl* as a basis, create a program that displays the points in a point list. (Segments that are commented with the label 'graphics:' are NOT to be implemented until In-lab 2.) Your program need only display the points themselves, *not* the lines connecting them. Call the `makeSquare()` method to generate the point list for a square. Call the `makeDragon()` method to generate the point list for a dragon curve. Save your implementation in the file *DrawCurv.java*. Be sure to document your code.

Step 2: Using the test plan below, test your program using a square.

Step 3: Similarly test your program using a dragon curve. Note that the point lists for dragon curves grow quite large as the recursion depth is increased.

Step 4: If you discover mistakes in your implementation of *DrawCurv.java*, correct them and execute your test plan again.

Test Plan for the *Curve Drawing Program*

Test case	Expected result	Checked
Square (center (100, 100), length 150)	(25, 25) (175, 25) (175, 175) (25, 175) (25, 25)	
Dragon curve (start pt (50, 50), length 100, angle 70, recursion depth 2)	(96, 33) (113, 79) (67, 96) (84, 142) (84, 142)	
Dragon curve (recursion depth 5)		

LABORATORY 2: In-lab Exercise 2

Name _____

Hour/Period/Section _____

Date _____

It is preferable to see the graphical form of the curve represented by the point list created in *DrawCurv.java* rather than just have a list of points that would become a square (or dragon curve) if we "connected the dots." Each point in our Point List ADT for a square or a dragon curve represents the location of a pixel in our graphic display. On the computer screen a pixel (or picture element) is a tiny dot that represents a very small piece of a picture. Today's computer screens typically have a resolution of 1024 by 768 pixels or greater. Each computer system and programming language defines a coordinate system that allows us to refer to a pixel location on the screen. Fortunately, Java has a vast graphics library, officially called the **abstract window toolkit** (AWT), to help you create and manage your graphic display.

For the most part two revisions to the DrawCurv program are needed to display a graphic drawing in a simple window: (1) additions to the default constructor and (2) definition of a new subclass of the Canvas class. Among the AWT classes used for this graphic display are the Frame class, the Canvas class, the WindowAdapter class, and the Graphics class.

Every graphical program in Java consists of one or more frame windows. Therefore, begin by defining the DrawCurvFrame class so that it extends Java's Frame class as follows.

```
class DrawCurvFrame extends Frame
```

The default constructor for DrawCurvFrame has purposely been designed to define the runtime environment and initiate the processing for the DrawCurv program. To convert this console application (where the display is confined to a single terminal window) to a graphical application (that is capable of displaying both text and graphics) requires definition of a graphical runtime environment. To initialize the window frame for this graphical application, add the code fragments (as illustrated below) to the default constructor for DrawCurvFrame.

```
class DrawCurvFrame extends Frame
{
    ......
    ......
    // Create area/Canvas for drawings
    CurvCanvas cBoard = new CurvCanvas( );
```

```
        // Default constructor
        public DrawCurvFrame( ) throws IOException
        {
            ......
            // Set up graphics windows -- Frame & added Canvas
            // Initialize the basic window Frame
            setTitle("Curve Drawing - Laboratory 2"); // window title
            setSize(500, 400);                          // window size

            // Define how the window responds to click on close button
            addWindowListener(new MyLocalWindowAdapter( ));
            ......
            // Add area/Canvas for drawings
            add(cBoard);
            ......
            if ( dispPts == 'Y' || dispPts == 'y')
            {
                // Iterate through the PointList
                ......
                // Make Canvas invisible
                cBoard.setVisible(false);
            }
            else
            {
                // Show window display of curve - make frame visible
                setVisible(true);
            }
        } // default constructor: DrawCurvFrame( )

        // Define MyLocalWindowAdapter
        private class MyLocalWindowAdapter extends WindowAdapter
        {
        public void windowClosing(WindowEvent event)
        {
            dispose( );
            System.exit(0);
        }
    } // Inner class MyLocalWindowAdapter
        ......
        ......
    }// class DrawCurvFrame
```

This code fragment gives the window/frame the title "Curve Drawing—Laboratory 2," establishes its initial size at 500 by 400 pixels, and then adds a WindowListener for programming the desired response when the user clicks on the close button and a Canvas board in which the drawing will actually appear. In the if-clause, the setVisible method determines whether a particular component will be visible (setVisible(true)) or invisible (setVisible(false)). Also included is an inner class definition that allows us to override the windowClosing method in Java's WindowAdapter class. (An inner class is a class definition embedded inside another class.) When the user clicks on the window's close button, our windowClosing method in this inner class MyLocalWindowAdapter first calls dispose, which releases all associated graphics resources and causes the window display to close; then the program itself terminates (System.exit(0)).

Finally, create a class definition for CurvCanvas that extends Java's Canvas class as follows:

```
class CurvCanvas extends Canvas
{
    // Paint is the inherited method we override
    //  in order to draw our own image in an AWT window
    public void paint(Graphics g)
    {
        Point pt;                       // Point on curve
        int   startX,                   // (x, y) points for drawLine
              startY;

        // Display the curve by iterating through the PointList (drawPts)
        if ( DrawCurvFrame.drawPts.gotoBeginning( ) )
        {


            // Call g.drawLine( int p1, int p2, int p3, int p4 )


        }

    } // class CurvCanvas
```

In Java a canvas is used to provide a dedicated drawing area for graphics. The `paint` method given above overrides the `paint` method in Java's Canvas class. The `paint` method in *DrawCurv.java* will contain the code for drawing a square or dragon curve on the computer screen—it will allow us to "connect the dots."

The coordinate system on the computer screen is slightly different from the traditional two-dimensional coordinate system. As illustrated below, the origin (0, 0) is in the upper-left corner of the computer window and all coordinates are positive. The *x*-axis increases horizontally from left to right. And (most notable) the *y*-axis increases (not decreases) vertically from top to bottom.

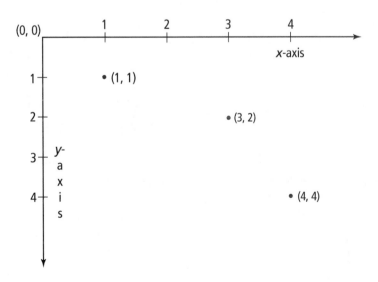

In the `paint` method the statement `g.drawLine(startX, startY, endX, endY)` is used to draw a line from point A (`startX`, `startY`) to point B (`endX`, `endY`) where `g` is the Graphics parameter passed to the `paint` method. In other words, the following statement would draw a line between points (1, 1) and (3, 2).

```
g.drawLine(1, 1, 3, 2);
```

These points without the drawn line are illustrated above.

Step 1: Modify your DrawCurv program (*DrawCurve.java*) so it produces a graphic display of the line segment connecting each pair of points in a point list. Segments where the comments are labeled 'graphics:' in the *DrawCurve.jshl* file are to be implemented at this time.

Step 2: Test your modified program using a square and a dragon curve. A test plan is given below.

Step 3: If you discover mistakes in your graphics implementation of *DrawCurv.java*, correct them and execute your test plan again.

Test Plan for the *Curve Drawing Program*

Test case	Expected curves	Checked
Square		
Dragon curve (recursion depth 2)		
Dragon curve (recursion depth 7)		

LABORATORY 2: In-lab Exercise 3

Name _____

Hour/Period/Section _____

Date _____

Inserting points at the beginning of a point list is a little bit trickier—and more time consuming—than adding them at the end.

```
void insertBeginning ( Point newPoint )
```
Precondition:
List is not full.
Postcondition:
Inserts newPoint at the beginning of a list. If the list is empty, then inserts newPoint as the first (and only) point in the list. In either case, moves the cursor to newPoint.

Step 1: Implement this method and add it to the file *PointList.java*. An incomplete definition for this method is included in the definition of the PointList class in the file *PointList.jshl*.

Step 2: Complete the following test plan by adding test cases that check whether your implementation of the insertBeginning method correctly inserts points into an empty list.

Step 3: Activate the "#" (insert at beginning) command in the test program *TestPointList.java* by removing the comment delimiter (and the character "#") from the lines beginning with "//#".

Step 4: Execute your test plan. If you discover mistakes in your implementation of the `insertBeginning` method, correct them and execute your test plan again.

Test Plan for the *insertBeginning Operation*

Test case	Commands	Expected result	Checked
Insert a series of points at the beginning of the list	+ 1 2 + 3 4 + 5 6 + 7 8	**(7,8)** (5,6) (3,4) (1,2)	

Note: The point marked by the cursor is shown in **bold**.

LABORATORY 2: Postlab Exercise 1

Name _____

Hour/Period/Section _____

Date _____

In In-lab Exercise 2 you used Java's AWT to create a basic graphic display of the point list for a square and a dragon curve. As stated earlier, Java has a vast graphics library or AWT to help you create and manage your graphic display. Obviously, there are many other AWT commands in addition to the ones discussed in In-Lab Exercise 2 that could have been used to give your graphic display a little more "pizzaz."

For example, the background color is white by default. Explain how you could have made the background color in your graphics window blue or green instead of white. Explain what other AWT library facilities you might have used to further enhance your graphic display of a square or a dragon curve.

LABORATORY 2: Postlab Exercise 2

Name _____

Hour/Period/Section _____

Date _____

In this lab, you allocated the array used to store a point list dynamically. What is the advantage of allocating an array dynamically? Why was dynamic allocation not needed for the logbook array in Laboratory 1?

String ADT

OBJECTIVES

In this laboratory, you

- examine some of the shortcomings in Java's built-in String class.

- create a program that performs lexical analysis using Java's built-in String data type.

- create an efficient program involving several modifications to the same String.

- develop an AWT implementation that manipulates Strings.

OVERVIEW

When computers were first introduced, they were popularly characterized as giant calculating machines. This characterization ignores the fact that computers are equally adept at manipulating other forms of information, including alphanumeric characters.

Java supports the manipulation of character data through the primitive data type char and the associated operations for the input, output, assignment, and comparison of characters. Most applications of character data require character sequences—or strings—rather than individual characters. In Java a string is represented by the built-in class String. However, manipulating a String data type in Java is quite different from manipulating a set (or array) of characters. For example,

- Strings are compared using methods that have very different calling conventions from the familiar relational operators (==, <, >, and so forth).

- Java Strings are immutable. That is, once a String is set up, it cannot be changed. Therefore, each time we modify a String in any way, the Java system makes a new String object and the old one becomes subject to garbage collection. This can be very inefficient if a lot of changes are made to a String.

- When significant modifications to a String will be necessary, another built-in class, called a StringBuffer, is usually a better choice for the implementation.

The Java API (application programming interface) defines hundreds of classes and methods. It is important to be familiar with several of these built-in classes, especially with some of the classes and methods that the Java programmer will use on a day-to-day basis. Strings are among the most used data types in programming. Therefore, in this Laboratory we will take a side trip from the usual development of your own ADT to more closely examine Java's built-in String ADT (class) and some other classes that can be useful for manipulating alphanumeric data or strings.

Although most Java classes require use of the `new` operator to instantiate an object of that data type, a Java String can be declared and initialized without using the `new` operator. For instance,

```
String fname = "Sandy";
```

assigns the string literal "Sandy" to the variable fname. Wherever a string literal appears, a String object is created. That is, for String objects, the explicit use of the `new` operator and the call to the constructor can be replaced with this shortcut notation.

You can assign a different string to the variable fname as follows:

```
fname = "Jim";
```

Remember Java String objects are immutable. That is, once a String object is created, its value cannot be lengthened or shortened, nor can any of its characters be changed. So, the statement above represents the creation of a new String object. The memory location that held the old `fname` object with the string "Sandy" becomes garbage.

The class String provides the method `length( )`, which returns as an `int` value the number of characters in the String object. For example, in the following statement `len` will equal 3 assuming the String variable `fname` still contains the string "Jim".

```
int len = fname.length( );
```

The empty string, a string containing no characters, is written as `""` and has a length of 0.

Java String position numbers start at 0. For example, here are the position numbers in the String "Hello World!":

0	1	2	3	4	5	6	7	8	9	10	11
H	e	l	l	o		W	o	r	l	d	!

The length of this String is 12. The position number of the last character in the String (11 for the String "Hello World!") is always 1 less than the length of the String.

Some of the more commonly used methods of the String class along with a brief description of what that method does are given next. This is not a complete list of all the String methods available in Java. For uniformity, the format used to describe the built-in String class is similar to the format used in all other laboratories when describing programmer-defined ADTs. For brevity, whenever the Preconditions are None, the Precondition information has been omitted.

STRING ADT (a built-in class)

Elements

A (possibly empty) set of characters.

Structure

The characters in a string are in sequential (or linear) order—that is, the characters follow one after the other from the beginning of a string to its end. The character positions are numbered beginning with zero. A word, phrase, or sentence are some examples of strings.

CONSTRUCTORS (some of the more commonly used String constructors)

```
String ( )
```
Postcondition:
Default constructor. Creates an empty String object.

```
String ( char[ ] charSeq )
```
Postcondition:
Creates a new String object with a character sequence identical to the character array charSeq.

```
String ( String str )
```
Postcondition:
Creates a new String object whose contents are equivalent to String str. The newly created String object is an exact but separate copy of the String str.

METHODS (some of the more commonly used String methods)

```
char charAt ( int n )
```
Precondition:
n must be a valid String index less than the length of the String.
Postcondition:
Returns the nth character in a string. Can throw a StringIndexOutOfBoundsException.

```
int compareTo ( String str )
```
Precondition:
str is not null.
Postcondition:
Returns a value indicating if the invoking String object is lexically before (returns a negative value), equal to (returns 0), or after (returns a positive value) the String str. Can throw a NullPointerException.

```
boolean equals ( String rightString )
```
Postcondition:
Returns true if the invoking String object and rightString have the same value.

```
boolean equalsIgnoreCase ( String rightString )
```
Postcondition:
Returns true if the invoking String object and rightString have the same value independent of the case (uppercase or lowercase) of each character. Otherwise, returns false.

```
int indexOf ( int ch )
```
Postcondition:
Returns the position within the invoking String object at which the first (the leftmost) occurrence of the character ch is located. If ch is not found, -1 is returned.

```
int indexOf ( int ch, int start )
```
Postcondition:
Returns the position within the invoking String object at which the first (the leftmost) occurrence of the character ch is located, with start specifying the position at which to begin the search. If ch is not found, -1 is returned.

```
int indexOf ( String str )
```
Precondition:
str is not null.
Postcondition:
Returns the position within the invoking String object at which the first (the leftmost) occurrence of the String str is located. If str is not found, -1 is returned. Can throw a NullPointerException.

```
int length ( )
```
Postcondition:
Returns the number of characters in the String object.

```
String substring ( int start )
```
Precondition:
start must be a nonnegative String index not greater than the length of the String.
Postcondition:
Returns a new String object containing the substring starting at position start and continuing until the end of the invoking object. Can throw a StringIndexOutOfBoundsException.

`String substring ( int start, int end )`
Precondition:
start and end must be nonnegative String indices not greater than the length of the String and start must not be greater than end.
Postcondition:
Returns a new String object containing the substring starting at position start through position `end - 1` of the invoking String object. A total of `end - start` characters are copied into the new String object. Can throw a StringIndexOutOfBoundsException.

`String toLowerCase ( )`
Postcondition:
Returns the invoking String object if all its characters are already lowercase. Otherwise, returns a new String object in which all characters have been converted to lowercase.

`String toUpperCase ( )`
Postcondition:
Returns the invoking String object if all its characters are already uppercase. Otherwise, returns a new String object in which all characters have been converted to uppercase.

LABORATORY 3: Cover Sheet

Name

Hour/Period/Section

Date

Place a check mark (✔) in the Assigned column next to the exercises that your instructor has assigned to you. Attach this cover sheet to the front of the packet of materials that you submit for this laboratory.

Exercise	Assigned	Completed
Prelab Exercise	✔	
Bridge Exercise	✔	
In-lab Exercise 1		
In-lab Exercise 2		
In-lab Exercise 3		
Postlab Exercise 1		
Postlab Exercise 2		
Total		

LABORATORY 3: Prelab Exercise

Name _____

Hour/Period/Section _____

Date _____

There are many useful methods built into Java's String class. As a Java programmer, taking some time to practice (or review) the use of several of these String methods will help make them a part of the Java operations you use on a day-to-day basis. In this PreLab exercise you will be asked to implement six different operations that utilize methods in the String class: showStructure, lessThan, gtrThan, strCharCount, findSubstring, and firstLtrWord.

The characters in a String can be manipulated one at a time with the use of the charAt method. A printout of the representation of a String in a fashion similar to our earlier illustration of the String "Hello World!" (minus, of course, the boxes around each letter) could be used to illustrate the relationship between each character in a given String and the numbered position of that character within the String. Part of the showStructure method is given below.

```
static void showStructure (String str)
{
    int j;   // Loop counter
    for ( j = 0 ; j < str.length( ); j++ )
        System.out.print(j + "\t");
    System.out.println( );
    ...
    ...
}
```

Recall that the keyword static in the method header means it may be accessed without the use of an invoking object. When completing the implementation of the showStructure method remember that the charAt method can throw a StringIndexOutOfBoundsException.

Most applications that use strings will at some point sort the string data into alphabetical order, either to make their output easier to read or to improve program performance. In order to sort strings, you first must develop relational operations that compare strings with one another. The String class provides the method equals, which is the equivalent of comparing two characters using the relational operator ==. However, there is no defined counterpart for the greater than (>) or less than (<) relational operators. To implement these relational operators a programmer might create the following method headers for these method definitions:

```
static boolean lessThan ( String leftString, String rightString )
static boolean gtrThan ( String leftString, String rightString )
```

These methods use the String class method `compareTo` to determine if the `leftString` is less than (or greater than) the `rightString`.

An example of the method header for the definition of the `strCharCount` method is given below.

```
static int strCharCount ( String inputString, char ch )
```

This method uses the String method `indexOf` to return a count of the number of times the character `ch` occurs in the String `inputString`.

An alternate approach from the one used in the `substring` method in the String class might involve the String position at which to start and (instead of the stopping position) the number of characters to be extracted from the original String. An example of the `findSubstring` method header is given below.

```
static String findSubstring ( String testStr1, int start, int count )
```

This method uses `substring` and `length` and returns a substring of `testStr1` starting at position `start` and extracting `count` characters if that many characters exist in the String `testStr1`. While implementing the `findSubstring` method, remember that the `substring` method can throw a StringIndexOutOfBoundsException.

Last, a combination of `length`, `charAt`, `substring`, and `indexOf` can be used to find the first letter, the first word, and the last letter in a given sentence or phrase. An example of the `firstLtrWord` method header is given below.

```
static void firstLtrWord ( String inStr )
```

This method prints the following lines of information.

```
String is:
The string's length is:
The first letter is:
The last letter is:
The first word is:
```

If the String is empty, this method prints

```
String is:
The string's length is: 0
The string is empty! No more data to print.
```

This method should not throw an exception if there is only one word or letter in the String `inStr`.

Step 1: Implement the six operations described above: `showStructure`, `lessThan`, `gtrThan`, `strCharCount`, `findSubstring`, and `firstLtrWord`. Each method implementation is to utilize one or more of the methods in the built-in String class. Base your implementation on the incomplete class definition provided in the file *Test3.jshl*.

Step 2: Save your method implementations in the file *Test3.java*. Be sure to document your code.

LABORATORY 3: Bridge Exercise

Name

Hour/Period/Section

Date

Check with your instructor as to whether you are to complete this exercise prior to your lab period or during lab.

Test your implementations in the file *Test3.java*. This program supports the following tests.

Test	Action
1	Tests showStructure operation.
2	Tests relational operations (lessThan and gtrThan).
3	Tests strCharCount operation.
4	Tests findSubstring operation.
5	Tests firstLtrWord operation.

Step 1: Complete the test plan for Test 1 by filling in the expected result for each String.

Step 2: Compile and run your implementations of these operations in the file *Test3.java*.

Step 3: Execute the test plan. If you discover mistakes in your implementation of the showStructure method, correct them and execute the test plan again.

Test Plan for *Test1* (showStructure Operation)

Test case	String	Expected result	Checked
Simple string	alpha	0 1 2 3 4 a l p h a	
Longer string	epsilon		
Single-character string	a		
Empty string	*empty*		

Step 4: Complete the test plan for Test 2 by filling in the expected result for each pair of strings.

Step 5: Execute the test plan. If you discover mistakes in your implementation of the relational operations, correct them and execute the test plan again.

Test Plan for *Test2* (lessThan and gtrThan Operations)

Test case	Pair of Strings	Expected result < == >	Checked
Second string greater	alpha epsilon		
First string greater	epsilon alpha		
Identical strings	alpha alpha		
First string embedded in second	alp alpha		
Second string embedded in first	alpha alp		
First string is a single character	a alpha		
Second string is a single character	alpha a		
First string is empty	*empty* alpha		
Second string is empty	alpha *empty*		
Both strings are empty	*empty empty*		

Step 6: Complete the test plan for Test 3 by filling in the character count for each String.

Step 7: Execute the test plan. If you discover mistakes in your implementation of the strCharCount method, correct them and execute the test plan again.

Test Plan for *Test3* (strCharCount Operation)

Test case	Character to find	Expected count	Checked
a	z	0	
a	a		
mississippi	i		
Empty string	*empty*		

Step 8: Complete the test plan for Test 4 by filling in the expected result for each String, start, count combination.

Step 9: Execute the test plan. If you discover mistakes in your implementation of the findSubstring method, correct them and execute the test plan again.

Test Plan for *Test4* (findSubstring Operation)

Test case	(String, start, count)	Expected result	Checked
Simple substring	("alpha", 0, 3)	alp	
Single character string and negative start index	("a", -1, 1)	a	
Start greater than String length	("test", 5, 1)		
Count greater than String length	("test", 0, 8)		
Start and count greater than String length	("test", 8, 8)		

Step 10: Complete the test plan for Test 5 by filling in the output printed by the `firstLtrWord` operation.

Step 11: Execute the test plan. If you discover mistakes in your implementation of the *firstLtrWord* method, correct them and execute the test plan again.

Test Plan for *Test5* (firstLtrWord Operation)

Test case	Line(s) printed	Expected result	Checked
Simple phrase "Begin and end"	String is: The string's length is: The first letter is: The last letter is: The first word is:	Begin and end 13 B d Begin	
Single word "Begin"	String is: The string's length is: The first letter is: The last letter is: The first word is:	Begin 5 B n Begin	
Single character string "A"			
Empty String			

LABORATORY 3: In-lab Exercise 1

Name _____

Hour/Period/Section _____

Date _____

A compiler begins the compilation process by dividing a program into a set of delimited strings, or **tokens**. This task is referred to as **lexical analysis**. For instance, given the Java statement,

```
if ( j <= 10 ) return -1 ;
```

lexical analysis by a Java compiler produces the following nine tokens.

```
"if"  "("  "j"  "<="  "10"  ")"  "return"  "-1"  ";"
```

Before you can perform lexical analysis, you need operations that support the input (or reading) of strings. Classes that let us define input streams are found in the *java.io* package of Java's standard library. The PreLab Exercise in Laboratory 2 provided a review of how to instantiate a basic reader for reading data from the keyboard:

```
// Initialize reader  connected to the standard input stream
InputStreamReader reader = new InputStreamReader( System.in );
```

For top efficiency when reading larger amounts of data, instead of using the statement above consider buffering the input stream as follows:

```
// For efficiency, use a BufferedReader connected to the standard input stream.
BufferedReader bufReader =
              new BufferedReader( new InputStreamReader( System.in ) );
```

Since input can come from a file as well as from the keyboard, Java's InputStreamReader can also be connected to a file. To create an InputStream object connected to a file, first create an instance of the FileInputStream class for a specific file. For example, the following creates a FileInputStream called `inFile` that is attached to the file "`progsamp.dat`" (where `String filename = `"`progsamp.dat`" and `FileInputStream inFile` have been declared):

```
// catch FileNotFoundException
try
{
    // Initialize the FileInputStream
    inFile = new FileInputStream( filename );
}
catch (FileNotFoundException e)
{
    System.out.print("Error opening file " + filename);
    return;                                 // Can't continue execution
}
```

Because the FileInputStream constructor can throw a FileNotFoundException, the FileInputStream constructor statement above is enclosed in try (and catch) blocks. Also, remember it is good programming practice to always close the file when it is no longer needed:

```
infile.close( );
```

To create a BufferedReader for an InputStreamReader connected to this FileInputStream, simply replace `System.in` (the keyboard reference) in the BufferedReader statement above with the FileInputStream object `inFile` as follows:

```
BufferedReader bufFinReader =
            new BufferedReader( new InputStreamReader( inFile ) );
```

Since a program implementation might read from both the keyboard and a file, the code fragment above also includes a revised variable name which uses the prefix 'Fin' (for file input) to distinguish it from the keyboard input stream variable (`bufReader`) that was declared earlier.

There are two reading methods in the BufferedReader class: `read` and `readLine`. The `read` method reads a character at a time. Because the `read` method returns an `int`, it must be cast to a `char` as follows.

```
char ch = (char)bufFinReader.read( );
```

The `readLine` method returns a String object containing the sequence of characters in the entire line of text up to, but excluding, the line terminator character (newline and/or carriage return). When the end of the file is encountered, `readLine` returns a null reference.

In Laboratory 2 a StreamTokenizer was inserted between the InputStreamReader and the program to read a line of words (a string) separated by whitespace characters. The StreamTokenizer's `nexttoken` method returns the constant `TT_EOF` when the end of the stream is encountered.

Another class in the Java standard class library, called StringTokenizer, will also tokenize a line of text. The StringTokenizer class is in the *java.util* package. The default delimiters used by the StringTokenizer class are the tab, space, newline, and carriage return characters—usually referred to as the whitespace characters. Some common methods of the StringTokenizer class are listed below.

CONSTRUCTOR (The more commonly used StringTokenizer constructor)

```
StringTokenizer ( String str )
```
Postcondition:
Creates a new StringTokenizer object that will separate the String str into individual tokens using the default delimiters (space, tab, newline, and carriage return).

METHODS (some of the more commonly used StringTokenizer methods)

```
int countTokens ( )
```
Postcondition:
Using the current set of delimiters, returns the number of tokens left to be extracted from the String.

```
boolean hasMoreTokens ( )
```
Postcondition:
Returns true if there are more tokens to be extracted from the String.

```
String nextToken ( )
```
Precondition:
Another token remains in the String.
Postcondition:
Returns the next token as a String. Can throw a NoSuchElementException.

Step 1: Create a program that uses the operations in the String class and a tokenizer class to perform lexical analysis on a text file containing a short Java program. Your program should read the tokens in this file and output each token to the screen using the following format.

```
1 : [1stToken]
2 : [2ndToken]
      . . .
```

This format requires that your program maintain a running count of the number of tokens that have been read from the text file. Assume that the tokens in the text file are delimited by whitespace characters—an assumption that is not true for Java programs in general. Save your program as *Lexical.java*. Be sure to document your code.

Step 2:   Test your lexical analysis program using the Java program in the file *progsamp.dat*.

Test Plan for the *Lexical Analysis Program*

Test case	Expected result	Checked
Program in the file *progsamp.dat*		

LABORATORY 3: In-lab Exercise 2

Name _____

Hour/Period/Section _____

Date _____

String class objects are immutable or unchangeable. Therefore, Java provides a separate String-Buffer class for String objects that must be modified several times during the execution of a program. The reasoning behind this dichotomy is that providing the flexibility for dynamically changing a string requires substantial overhead (more computer memory and greater coding complexity). Thus, the simpler String class is preferred when String modification will be infrequent or nonexistent.

The code fragment

```
StringBuffer strBuf = new StringBuffer(15);
```

illustrates an essential distinction between StringBuffer objects and String objects. StringBuffer objects can have unused character positions; String objects cannot. The string in this String-Buffer is filled with 15 null characters. (Remember the null character in Java indicates that it refers to no object at all.)

The **capacity** of the StringBuffer—the amount of space allocated for character storage—is changed automatically whenever the current capacity is not sufficient to hold all the characters to be added to the current StringBuffer object. However, it is best to initialize the object with sufficient starting capacity since dynamically changing the capacity of a StringBuffer means the entire object has to be restructured and reallocated computer memory. If this costly overhead is not avoided, the advantages of using a StringBuffer versus frequently modifying an immutable String object are diminished.

Listed below are some common methods in the built-in StringBuffer class. Notice that several of these methods (such as substring, length, and charAt) are very similar to the methods with an identical method header in the String class.

CONSTRUCTOR (some of the more commonly used StringBuffer constructors)

```
StringBufferer ( )
```
Postcondition:
Creates a new StringBuffer object—default size 16. All 16 character positions are initially null.

```
StringBufferer ( int size )
```
Postcondition:

Creates a new StringBuffer object and explicitly reserves room for size characters. All character positions are initially null. Can throw a NegativeArraySizeException.

```
StringBufferer ( String str )
```
Postcondition:

Creates a new StringBuffer object, sets its initial contents to str and reserves room for 16 additional characters. These additional 16 character positions are initially null.

METHODS (some of the more commonly used StringBuffer methods)

```
StringBuffer append ( String str )
```
Postcondition:

Concatenates the String str to the end of the invoking StringBuffer object.

```
int capacity ( )
```
Postcondition:

Returns the number of character positions the invoking StringBuffer object has been allocated.

```
char charAt ( int n )
```
Precondition:

n must be a nonnegative String index less than the length of the StringBuffer.

Postcondition:

Returns the nth character in the StringBuffer object—where the characters are numbered beginning with zero. Can throw a StringIndexOutOfBoundsException.

```
StringBuffer delete ( int start, int end )
```
Precondition:

start must be a nonnegative String index not greater than the length of the StringBuffer object and start must not be greater than end.

Postcondition:

Removes the substring starting at position start through position `end - 1` of the invoking object or through the end of the StringBuffer if end is greater than the length of the String-Buffer. If start is equal to end, no changes are made. Can throw a StringIndexOutOfBounds-Exception.

```
StringBuffer insert ( int index, String str )
```
Precondition:

index must be a nonnegative String index not greater than the length of the StringBuffer object.

Postcondition:

Inserts the contents of the String str into the invoking StringBuffer object starting at position index. Can throw a StringIndexOutOfBoundsException.

```
int length ( )
```
Postcondition:
Returns the number of non-null characters the invoking StringBuffer object currently contains.

```
StringBuffer reverse ( )
```
Postcondition:
Returns the invoking StringBuffer object but with its character sequence reversed.

```
void setCharAt ( int index, char ch )
```
Precondition:
index must be a nonnegative String index less than the length of the StringBuffer object.
Postcondition:
Replaces the character at position index in the invoking StringBuffer object with the new character value ch. Can throw a StringIndexOutOfBoundsException.

```
String substring ( int start )
```
Precondition:
start must be a nonnegative String index not greater than the length of the StringBuffer object.
Postcondition:
Returns a new String object containing the subsequence of characters starting at position start and extending to the end of the string of non-null characters contained in the invoking StringBuffer object. Can throw a StringIndexOutOfBoundsException.

```
String substring ( int start, int end )
```
Precondition:
start and end must be nonnegative String indices not greater than the length of the StringBuffer object and start must not be greater than end.
Postcondition:
Returns a new String object containing the substring starting at position start and runs through position `end - 1` of the invoking object. Can throw a StringIndexOutOfBoundsException.

```
String toString ( )
```
Postcondition:
Returns a new String object equivalent to the invoking StringBuffer object.

In this exercise you will use String and StringBuffer objects to create a two-person version of the "Hangman" word-guessing game. The game begins with one player entering a secret word that is scrolled off the screen before the other player sits down to play. A blank guess template then appears on the screen. This template is the same length as the secret word but has dashes in place of the letters in the word.

The player attempting to guess the secret word enters letters one at a time. After each guess, the guess template is updated (if necessary) to show which letters in the secret word match the letter guessed. For example, if the secret word is "scissors", guessing 's' as the first correctly guessed letter results in the following changes in the guess template:

```
Guess a letter: s
s--ss--s
```

This process continues until the guess template matches the secret word. The number of guesses is then output. A sample game is shown below.

```
Enter the secret word: test          (This scrolls off the screen)
----
Guess a letter: a
----
Guess a letter: e
-e--
Guess a letter: n
-e--
Guess a letter: s
-es-
Guess a letter: t
test=test
You guessed the word in 5 guesses.
```

There are three key methods in this Hangman program. Note that because the guess template string will be modified several times, for efficiency it is implemented as a StringBuffer rather than a String. Partial definitions for these methods are given below:

```
static StringBuffer createTemplate ( String secretWord )
// Returns a new StringBuffer object, which is a template
//    containing the same number of dashes as there are letters in the secretWord.

static void updateTemplate ( String secretWord, char guessLetter,
                             StringBuffer guessTemplate )
// Updates the guessTemplate to include the new letter (guessLetter) guessed
//    if it matches a letter in the secretWord. For multiple occurrences of the same
//    letter, all letter matches are added to the guessTemplate.

static boolean matchTemplate ( String secretWord, StringBuffer guessTemplate )
// Returns true if the secretWord and guessTemplate match.
// Otherwise, returns false.
```

Step 1: Create a program that implements the two-person "Hangman" word-guessing game described above. Save your program as *Hangman.java*. Be sure to document your code.

Step 2: Complete the following test plan.

Step 3: Execute the test plan. If you discover mistakes in your implementation of the Hangman game, correct them and execute the test plan again.

Test Plan for the *Hangman Program*

Test case	Sample data	Expected result	Checked

test	a e n s t	```----```
		```----```
		```-e--```
		```-e--```
		```-es-```
		```test=test```
		```You guessed the word in 5 guesses.```	

cryptic	a e i o u y n s t r h c p		
Your secret word			

LABORATORY 3: In-lab Exercise 3

Name _____

Hour/Period/Section _____

Date _____

Strings can also be read and written in a Java GUI. A correct implementation of the DrawCurv program in Laboratory 2 (In-lab 2) generates a simple drawing of a set of points—the program "connects the dots." A more interactive GUI that prints and accepts text will be developed in this lab exercise. In this process the console application of the Hangman program from In-lab 2 will be converted to a frame-based graphical application much like the DrawCurv program in Laboratory 2: In-lab 1 was converted to a graphical application in Laboratory 2: In-lab 2.

First, it will not be necessary in this Hangman graphical application to import *java.io.**, so remove that import statement from your program. In this program it is intended that all I/O will occur in the GUI. Only the *java.awt* import statements used in the DrawCurv program will be needed here.

The data members in the HangmanFrame class will include most of the variables used in the non-GUI Hangman implementation from In-lab 2 such as `secretWord`, `guessLetter`, `numGuesses`, and `guessTemplate` plus the following graphic components:

```
private TextField guessedTxt,          // for input of guessLetter
                  secretTxt;           // for input of secretWord
private Label secretLbl,               // message for secretWord text field
              tempLbl,                 // displays the guessTemplate
              guessLbl;                // message for guessLetter text field
```

These graphic components will be defined and added to the frame in the constructor for the HangmanFrame class.

Several statements need to be included in the HangmanFrame constructor. Along with other basic frame setup statements like `setTitle` and `setSize`, include the `setLayout` method statement and its single argument as illustrated below.

```
// implement a simple layout similar to how text flows on a page
setLayout(new FlowLayout( ));
```

The `setLayout` method governs how multiple components will be arranged in the Hangman frame. The FlowLayout class implements a simple layout style that is similar to the way in which words flow as you type them into a word processor. Flow layout puts as many components in a row as possible. When a component cannot fit in the current row, it is put on the next row. The alignment defaults to center. In this layout the order in which components are added to the frame affects their positioning within the window.

The Label class is used to display a String in a GUI application. It defines three constants that can be used to control the alignment of the String: LEFT, CENTER, and RIGHT. A label is most often used for relaying a message to the program's user. The following code fragment includes a Label declaration for a label that is centered and tells the user to "Enter the secret word":

```
// Add a Label message to get the secret word.
secretLbl = new Label(" Enter the secret word:          ", Label.CENTER);
add(secretLbl);
// A manual 'trick' for moving next component to the next row
toNextRow( );
```

Also included with the code fragment above is a call to toNextRow. This method ensures that the next component appears on the next row in the frame. The code for this method is provided for you in the file *toNextRow.jshl*. Our Hangman GUI has three labels: secretLbl, tempLbl, and guessLbl. In order to reserve adequate space for the tempLbl label, declare it with a dummy string that is large enough to handle the longest template the program is likely to accept.

```
tempLbl = new Label("---------------------------------------", Label.CENTER);
```

Most graphical applications collect keyboard input through text fields. The TextField class creates a single-line of editable text in a GUI program. The text field appears on the screen as a white rectangular box. The program's user can click on the box and type information that can be read by the application. Our Hangman GUI has two text fields, one for accepting the secret word (secretTxt) and one for entering the next letter guessed (guessedTxt). The TextField constructor has one argument—an integer that specifies how many characters can be viewed in the text field. For example, the first text field in our Hangman GUI is declared as:

```
secretTxt = new TextField(15);
```

The user can actually type more than 15 characters, but only 15 characters of a longer string will be visible at one time. As with all components to be included in the window for this GUI, this text field must be added to the frame:

```
add(secretTxt):
```

When the user presses the Enter key inside a text field, the text field generates an action event. To capture each action event an ActionListener can be attached to each text field. For example, the following statement adds an action listener to our text field (secretTxt).

```
secretTxt.addActionListener(new MySecretListener( ));
```

The actionPerformed method in the inner class MySecretListener specifies the actions to be performed when text is entered in text field secretTxt.

```
// An inner listener class for getting the secret word
private class MySecretListener implements ActionListener
{
    public void actionPerformed(ActionEvent event)
```

```
    {
            // Get the secretWord; then clear and later remove it.
            secretWord = secretTxt.getText( );
            secretTxt.setText("");                 // Clear it: set to empty string
            secretLbl.setText("GUESS MY SECRET WORD");
            remove(secretTxt);                      // Remove text box so player can't see it

            // Create the guessTemplate for the secretWord
            ......

            // Enlarge the font for the template for emphasis
            tempLbl.setFont(new Font("Courier", Font.PLAIN, 18));

            // setText in tempLbl to the created guessTemplate
            tempLbl.setText(guessTemplate.toString( ));
            inTxtFld.requestFocus( );               // Place cursor in this TextField
                                                    //  for receiving guessLetter input
    }

} // inner class MySecretListener
```

In this `actionPerformed` method, the `getText` method returns the current contents of the text field as a String object. The `setText` method is used three times in this code fragment to reset the contents of the text field (and labels) to the specified String argument. For instance, `secretTxt.setText("")` clears the text field (or sets its text to the empty string) so that the user has a visual indication that the input has been processed. The `remove(secretTxt)` statement removes the specified component (`secretTxt`) from the invoking object (HangmanFrame) so the Hangman player will never see the `secretWord` text field. For greater emphasis, the method `setFont` is used to enlarge the size of the font for the Hangman template displayed by the Label `tempLbl`. The `setFont` method used above takes one argument of type `Font`, and subsequently the Font constructor takes three parameters: the font face name as the String `Courier`, the style as the Font constant `Font.PLAIN`, and the point size as *18*. Finally, the `requestFocus` method does the user a favor by automatically placing the cursor in the `guessedTxt` text field waiting for the next guessed letter to be entered. The `guessedTxt` text field will also need an action listener that is defined as an inner class that implements the ActionListener along with its `actionPerformed` method.

Step 1: Create a program that implements the two-person Hangman word-guessing game described in In-lab 2 as a graphical application or GUI. If necessary refer to Laboratory 2: In-lab 2, for additional help. Be sure to document your code.

Step 2: Complete the following test plan.

Step 3: Use the test plan you created in In-lab Exercise 2. Execute the test plan. If you discover mistakes in your implementation of the Hangman game, correct them and execute the test plan again.

LABORATORY 3: Postlab Exercise 1

Name _____

Hour/Period/Section _____

Date _____

For many programmers the assignment operator can deliver some unexpected results. For example, in this laboratory you have reviewed two common classes in Java for working with strings, the String class and the StringBuffer class. Now consider the following code fragment:

```
// Using assignment operator with the String class
String str1 = "test";
String str2;
str2 = str1;
str1 = str1 + "s";                          // same as str1 = str1.concat("s")

// versus using assignment operator with the StringBuffer class
StringBuffer bstr1 = new StringBuffer("test");
StringBuffer bstr2;
bstr2 = bstr1;
bstr1.append("s");
```

What is the result of using the assignment operator with objects of either of these classes? Do changes to the String `str1` also affect the state of `str2`? Do changes to the StringBuffer `bstr1` also affect the state of `bstr2`? Is the change phenomenon the same in both cases? Explain why or why not.

LABORATORY 3: Postlab Exercise 2

Name _____

Hour/Period/Section _____

Date _____

In Laboratory 2 and 3 you used Java's AWT (abstract window toolkit) to create a frame-based graphical application. An applet, like a frame, is a component that can hold other components. The Applet class is contained in the *java.applet* package in Java's standard library. Here are a few steps to follow to convert most frame applications to an applet:

1. Add a statement to `import java.applet.Applet`.

2. Remove the definition of the `main` method that shows the frame—an applet calls the `init` method instead of `main`. If nothing else remains in the surrounding class, also drop the class.

3. For code readability, rename the class that extends frame (e.g., `HangmanFrame`) as an applet (e.g., `HangmanApplet`).

4. Define the class as `public` and indicate that it `extends Applet`, not `Frame`.

5. Rename the default constructor in this class (e.g., was `HangmanFrame`) as the `public void init` method.

6. Remove the WindowListener—an applet has no close buttons; hence there is no WindowAdapter subclass and no `windowClosing` method in the Applet classes.

7. Remove the applet call to `setSize` and instead set the size in the applet's HTML page.

8. Remove the applet call to `setTitle`—an applet has no title bar.

9. Save the file under the same name that was assigned to the class that extends Applet (e.g., *HangmanApplet.java*).

In general a Java applet is created to run in a Java-enabled Web browser, such as Netscape Navigator or Microsoft Internet Explorer. Because it runs on a Web browser an applet is always invoked through an HTML page. During development and testing, the **appletviewer** provided as part of the JDK (Java Development Kit from Sun Microsystems) can be used instead of a Web browser. An abbreviated sample HTML document that will run the Hangman applet would look like the following:

```
<HTML>
<BODY>
<P>
<APPLET code = "HangmanApplet.class" width=300 height = 200>
</APPLET>
</P>
</BODY>
</HTML>
```

It is essential that all the HTML tags shown above appear in every HTML document used to run a Java applet. The applet tag portion in the above HTML sample is:

```
<APPLET code = "HangmanApplet.class" width=300 height = 200>
</APPLET>
```

This tag dictates that the bytecode in the file *Hangman.class* should be executed on the computer that is viewing this particular HTML document. To execute the DrawCurvApplet instead of the HangmanApplet, replace the String "HangmanApplet.class" with the String "DrawCurvApplet.class". The size of the applet window can be adjusted by changing the values after width= and height= in the HTML applet tag. In other words, to run a different compiled Java program, insert the name of its *.class* file in place of the "HangmanApplet.class" name given in the sample above and change the width and height of your applet window by resetting those values within that same HTML applet tag.

Experiment with applets by creating the file *HangmanApplet.java* and the HTML document *Hangman.html* discussed above. Compile your program as usual. Run the applet by loading the HTML document into a Web browser or using the JDK appletviewer. Based on your experience what are some advantages and disadvantages of developing and using Java applets? For instance, is it easy to develop applets from scratch? Does your applet look the same in Netscape and Internet Explorer? To permit someone else who knows nothing about Java to run your applet, what file(s) must you give them? What other comments/concerns do you have about Java applets?

Array Implementation of the List ADT

OBJECTIVES

In this laboratory you

- implement the List ADT using an array representation of a list—including development of an iteration scheme that allows you to move through a list element by element.

- use an interface to define a generic set of methods to be implemented by every list data structure.

- create a program that analyzes the genetic content of a DNA sequence.

- analyze the efficiency of your array implementation of the List ADT.

OVERVIEW

The list is one of the most frequently used data structures. Although all programs share the same definition of **list**—a sequence of homogeneous elements—the type of element stored in lists varies from program to program. Some use lists of integers, others use lists of characters, floating-point numbers, points, and so forth.

Fortunately, you do not need to create a different list implementation for each type of list element. Instead, you create a list implementation in terms of list elements of Java's **generic** type Object. The Object class is the root of the class hierarchy in Java. Every class is a subclass of Object, but it is not necessarily a direct subclass.

But what about a list (or array) of int—one of Java's primitive data types? Remember that a primitive variable is *not* an Object, but everything else is. Java provides a wrapper class (Byte, Short, Integer, Long, Character, Float, Double, or Boolean) that encapsulates each of the primitive data types (byte, short, int, long, char, float, double, or boolean, respectively). Note that the class names Character and Integer are not abbreviated like their primitive counterparts char and int. When it is necessary to represent a primitive as an Object, use a wrapper class.

A primitive data type can be converted into an Object and visa versa. Here's an example of how an `int` is placed into an `Integer` (wrapper class) object and taken back out:

```
int i = 55;
int j;
Integer example = new Integer(i);      // Constructor converts int to Integer
                                       // Both have value of 55
j = example.intValue( );               // The Integer method intValue
                                       // converts it back to an int
```

The primitive operations (+, -, <, >=, etc.) are not available in their wrapper class counterparts. For example, the expressions $x + y$ is not valid when x and y are Integer objects. To perform this primitive operation, first convert each Integer to an `int` and then add. The `intValue( )` method in the Integer class can be used to convert x and y to `int` values and then the resulting `int` values can be summed using the primitive operation +.

The following is a table of the eight wrapper classes for the eight primitives along with the constructor and method that provides conversion between the wrapper class and its corresponding primitive.

Wrapper Class	Constructor: Converts Primitive to Wrapper	Method: Converts Wrapper to Primitive
Boolean	Boolean(boolean value)	*boolean booleanValue( )*
Byte	Byte(byte value)	*byte byteValue( )*
Character	Character(char value)	*char charValue( )*
Double	Double(double value)	*double doubleValue( )*
Float	Float(float value)	*float floatValue( )*
Integer	Integer(int value)	*int intValue( )*
Long	Long(long value)	*long longValue( )*
Short	Short(short value)	*short shortValue( )*

Once a list implementation has been created in terms of the generic type Object, the implementation can be customized to produce a list of elements of a specified type by substituting that type for the generic type Object. A list of characters, for example, requires substituting type `Character` or `char` converted to `Character` for the Object parameter in the `insert` method as illustrated in the following code fragment.

```
ListArray testList = new ListArray(8);      // Test ListArray of size 8
char testElement = 'c';                     // A list element, initialized to 'c'
// Insert a char converted to Character—Character is a subclass of Object
testList.insert(new Character(testElement));
```

A similar substitution is required in any other method that takes an Object parameter, such as the `replace` method. For a method that returns the generic Object, the process needs to be reversed in order to get back the `char` that was earlier added to the list. The following code fragment will convert the Object that is returned in the method `getCursor` back to its `char` form.

```
// Get it back again: cast Object to Character, then convert Character to char
testElement = ((Character)testList.getCursor( )).charValue( );
```

If an ADT is to be useful, its operations must be both expressive and intuitive. The List ADT described next provides operations that allow you to insert elements in a list, remove elements from a list, check the state of a list (Is it empty? or Is it full?), and iterate through the elements in a list. Iteration is done using a **cursor** that you move through the list much as you move the cursor in a text editor or word processor. In the following example, the List ADT's `gotoBeginning` operation is used to move the cursor to the beginning of the list. The cursor is then moved through the list element by element, by repeated applications of the `gotoNext` operation. Note that the element marked by the cursor is shown in bold.

After gotoBeginning:	**a** b c d
After gotoNext:	a **b** c d
After gotoNext:	a b **c** d
After gotoNext:	a b c **d**

List ADT

Elements

The elements in a list are of generic type Object.

Structure

The elements form a linear structure in which list elements follow one after the other, from the beginning of the list to its end. The ordering of the elements is determined by when and where each element is inserted into the list and is *not* a function of the data contained in the list elements. At any point in time, one element in any nonempty list is marked using the list's cursor. You travel through the list using operations that change the position of the cursor.

Constructors and their Helper Method

`List ( )`
Precondition:
None.
Postcondition:
Default Constructor. Calls setup, which creates an empty list and allocates enough memory for a list containing DEF_MAX_LIST_SIZE (a constant value) elements.

`List ( int maxNumber )`
Precondition:
maxNumber > 0.
Postcondition:
Constructor. Calls setup, which creates an empty list and allocates enough memory for a list containing maxNumber elements.

```
void setup( int maxNumber )
```
Precondition:
maxNumber > 0. A helper method for the constructors. Is declared private since only list constructors should call this method.
Postcondition:
Creates an empty list of a specific size based on the value of maxNumber received from the constructor.

Methods in the Interface

```
void insert ( Object newElement )
```
Precondition:
List is not full and newElement is not null.
Postcondition:
Inserts newElement into a list after the cursor. If the list is empty, newElement is inserted as the first (and only) element in the list. In either case (empty or not empty), moves the cursor to newElement.

```
void remove ( )
```
Precondition:
List is not empty.
Postcondition:
Removes the element marked by the cursor from a list. If the resulting list is not empty, then moves the cursor to the element that followed the deleted element. If the deleted element was at the end of the list, then moves the cursor to the element at the beginning of the list.

```
void replace ( Object newElement )
```
Precondition:
List is not empty and newElement is not null.
Postcondition:
Replaces the element marked by the cursor with newElement. The cursor remains at newElement.

```
void clear ( )
```
Precondition:
None.
Postcondition:
Removes all the elements in a list.

```
boolean isEmpty ( )
```
Precondition:
None.
Postcondition:
Returns true if a list is empty. Otherwise, returns false.

```
boolean isFull ( )
```
Precondition:
None.
Postcondition:
Returns true if a list is full. Otherwise, returns false.

```
boolean gotoBeginning ( )
```
Precondition:
None.
Postcondition:
If a list is not empty, then moves the cursor to the beginning of the list and returns true. Otherwise, returns false.

```
boolean gotoEnd ( )
```
Precondition:
None.
Postcondition:
If a list is not empty, then moves the cursor to the end of the list and returns true. Otherwise, returns false.

```
boolean gotoNext ( )
```
Precondition:
List is not empty.
Postcondition:
If the cursor is not at the end of a list, then moves the cursor to the next element in the list and returns true. Otherwise, returns false.

```
boolean gotoPrior ( )
```
Precondition:
List is not empty.
Postcondition:
If the cursor is not at the beginning of a list, then moves the cursor to the preceding element in the list and returns true. Otherwise, returns false.

```
Object getCursor ( )
```
Precondition:
List is not empty.
Postcondition:
Returns a copy of the element marked by the cursor.

```
void showStructure ( )
```
Precondition:

None.

Postcondition:

Outputs the elements in a list. If the list is empty, outputs "Empty list". Note that this operation is intended for testing/debugging purposes only.

LABORATORY 4: Cover Sheet

Name _____

Hour/Period/Section _____

Date _____

Place a check mark (✔) in the Assigned column next to the exercises that your instructor has assigned to you. Attach this cover sheet to the front of the packet of materials that you submit for this laboratory.

Exercise	Assigned	Completed
Prelab Exercise	✔	
Bridge Exercise	✔	
In-lab Exercise 1		
In-lab Exercise 2		
In-lab Exercise 3		
Postlab Exercise 1		
Postlab Exercise 2		
Total		

LABORATORY 4: Prelab Exercise

Name _____

Hour/Period/Section _____

Date _____

You can implement a list in many ways. Given that all the elements in a list are of the same type, and that the list structure is linear, an array seems a natural choice.

Arrays have a limited capacity. An important characteristic of arrays in Java is that the size of the array is held in a final public data member called `length` in the array object. Unlike the `length` method in the class String, this is a data member, not a method, so there are no parentheses following `length`. For example, consider the declaration

```
int scores = new int[10];
```

After this declaration, `scores.length` is 10. Note that although `length` is public, its value cannot be changed because is it also declared as `final`.

Valid values for the array index range from 0 through one less than the length of the array. Java safely handles invalid array index references. Trying to access an invalid array index will cause the program to terminate with an ArrayIndexOutOfBoundsException.

The List ADT has a common set of methods that any List implementation should provide. For example, the Point List ADT in Laboratory 2 has a set of commands nearly identical to the List ADT in this laboratory. Some future laboratories will also implement this List ADT.

In Java, one approach to identifying these common methods that may be used for a variety of list implementations is to define an **interface**. An interface definition is similar to a class definition, but

- An interface does not (and cannot) have any data members.

- An interface can specify a set of constants—the modifiers *public static final* need not be specified since they are implicit for constants in an interface.

- All methods are automatically *abstract*—they don't have an implementation. The header of each method, including its parameter list, is simply followed by a semicolon.

- All methods are automatically *public*. Note that the class must explicitly declare the implemented interface method as public, however.

- An interface cannot be instantiated—it is not a class and all its methods are abstract.

The List interface is in the file *List.java* and is defined as follows:

```
interface List                              // Constants & Methods common to List ADTs
{
    // Default maximum list size - a constant
    public static final int DEF_MAX_LIST_SIZE = 10;

    // List manipulation operations
    public void insert(Object newElement);  // Insert Object after cursor
    public void remove( );                  // Remove element at cursor
    public void replace (Object newElement); // Replace element at cursor
    public void clear( );                   // Remove all elements from list

    // List status operations
    public boolean isEmpty( );              // Returns true if list is empty
    public boolean isFull( );               // Returns true if list is full
    public boolean gotoBeginning( );        // Moves cursor to beginning of list
    public boolean gotoEnd( );              // Moves cursor to end of list
    public boolean gotoNext( );             // Moves cursor to next element in list
    public boolean gotoPrior( );            // Moves cursor to preceding element
    public Object getCursor( );             // Returns the element at the cursor
    public void showStructure( );           // Outputs the elements in a list.
                                            // for testing/debugging purposes only

} // interface List
```

Any class that `implements List`, as the class ListArray does in Step 1 below, is required to provide a `public` implementation for *every* method listed in the interface List. The Java compiler will produce errors if any of the methods in the interface are not given a definition in the implementing class.

Step 1: Implement the operations in the List ADT using an array to store the list elements. Lists change in size as elements are added, removed, and the like. Therefore, you need to store the actual number of elements in the list (`size`), along with the list elements themselves (`element`). The maximum number of elements our list can hold can be determined by referencing `length` in the array object—more specifically, in our case, by referencing `element.length`. You also need to keep track of the cursor array index (`cursor`).

Base your implementation on the following incomplete definitions from the file *ListArray.jshl*. You are to fill in the Java code for each of the constructors and methods in which the implementation braces are empty, only partially filled (noted by "add code here ..."), or where an entire method or set of methods from the interface needs to be inserted (noted by "insert method ... here").

```
class ListArray implements List            // Array based list class
{
    // Data Members
    private int size,                       // Actual number of elements in the list
               cursor;                      // Cursor array index
    private Object [] element;              // Array containing the list elements

    // Constructors and helper method setup
    public ListArray( )                     // Constructor: default size
    {                                }
```

```
    public ListArray(int maxNumber)           // Constructor: specific size
    {                                      }

    // Class methods
    private void setUp (int maxNumber)        // Called by constructors only
    {                                      }

    // ------ Insert method implementations for the interface list here ------ //

} // class ListArray
```

Step 2: Save your implementation of the List ADT in the file *ListArray.java*. Be sure to document your code.

The following sample program (in the file *Sample.java*) uses the array implementation of the operations in the List ADT (in the file *ListArray.java*) to read in a list of integer samples and compute their sum. Especially notice how conversions are made between a primitive (int) to an Object (Integer) and back again.

```
import java.io.*;

class Sample
{
    public static void main ( String [] args ) throws IOException
    {
        ListArray samples = new ListArray(100);// Set of samples
        int newSample,                         // Input sample
           total = 0;                          // Sum of the input samples
        //-------------------------------------------------------------
        // Instantiate several classes for processing input.
        BufferedReader reader =
            new BufferedReader(new InputStreamReader(System.in));
        StreamTokenizer tokens = new StreamTokenizer(reader);

        // Read in a set of samples from the keyboard.
        System.out.print("Enter list of samples (end with eof) : ");
        // Keep reading as long as text (the word eof) has not been entered
        while ( tokens.nextToken( ) != tokens.TT_WORD )
        {
            newSample = (int)tokens.nval;
            // insert an Object — an int converted to an Integer
            samples.insert(new Integer(newSample));
        }

        // Sum the samples and output the result.
        if ( samples.gotoBeginning() )        // Go to beginning of list
            // Add element to running sum
            // must cast Object to Integer, then convert Integer to int
            do
                total += ((Integer)samples.getCursor( )).intValue( );
            while ( samples.gotoNext() );     // Go to next element (if any)

        System.out.println("Sum is " + total);
    } // main

} // class Sample
```

LABORATORY 4: Bridge Exercise

Name _____

Hour/Period/Section _____

Date _____

Check with your instructor as to whether you are to complete this exercise prior to your lab period or during lab.

The test programs that you used in Laboratories 1 and 3 consisted of a series of tests that were hardcoded into the programs. Adding a new test case to this style of test program requires changing the test program itself. In this and subsequent laboratories, you use a more flexible kind of test program to evaluate your ADT implementations, one in which you specify a test case using commands, rather than code. These interactive, command-driven test programs allow you to check a new test case by simply entering a series of keyboard commands and observing the results.

The test program in the file *TestListArray.java*, for instance, supports the following commands.

Command	Action
+x	Insert element x after the cursor.
-	Remove the element marked by the cursor.
=x	Replace the element marked by the cursor with element x.
@	Display the element marked by the cursor.
N	Go to the next element.
P	Go to the prior element.
<	Go to the beginning of the list.
>	Go to the end of the list.
E	Report whether the list is empty.
F	Report whether the list is full.
C	Clear the list.
Q	Quit the test program.

Suppose you wish to confirm that your array implementation of the List ADT successfully inserts an element into a list that has been emptied by a series of calls to the remove operation. You can test this case by entering the following sequence of keyboard commands.

Command	+a	+b	-	-	+c	Q
Action	Insert a	Insert b	Remove	Remove	Insert c	Quit

It is easy to see how this interactive test program allows you to rapidly examine a variety of test cases. This speed comes with a price, however. You must be careful not to violate the preconditions required by the operations that you are testing. For instance, the commands

Command	+a	+b	-	-	-
Action	Insert a	Insert b	Remove	Remove	Error

cause the test program to fail during the last call to the remove operation. The source of the failure does not lie in the implementation of the List ADT, nor is the test program flawed. The failure occurs because this sequence of operations creates a state that violates the preconditions of the remove operation (the list must *not* be empty when the remove operation is invoked). The speed with which you can create and evaluate test cases using an interactive, command-driven test program makes it very easy to produce this kind of error. It is very tempting to just sit down and start entering commands. A much better strategy, however, is to create a test plan listing the test cases you wish to check and then to write out command sequences that generate these test cases.

Step 1: Complete the following test plan by adding test cases that check whether your implementation of the List ADT correctly handles the following tasks:

- insertions into a newly emptied list
- insertions that fill a list to its maximum size
- deletions from a full list
- determining whether a list is empty
- determining whether a list is full

Assume that the output of one test case is used as the input to the following test case and note that, although expected results are listed for the final command in each command sequence, you should confirm that *each* command produces a correct result.

Step 2: Compile and run the test program in the file *TestListArray.java*. Note that compiling this program will compile your array implementation of the List ADT (in the file *ListArray.java*) to produce an implementation for a list of characters.

Step 3: Execute your test plan. If you discover mistakes in your implementation of the List ADT, correct them and execute your test plan again.

Test Plan for the *Operations in the List ADT*

Test case	Commands	Expected result	Checked
Insert at end	+a +b +c +d	a b c **d**	
Travel from beginning	< N N	a b **c** d	
Travel from end	> P P	a **b** c d	
Delete middle element	–	a **c** d	
Insert in middle	+e +f +f	a c e f **f** d	
Remove last element	> –	**a** c e f f	
Remove first element	–	**c** e f f	
Display element	@	Returns c	
Replace element	=g	**g** e f f	
Clear the list	C	Empty list	

Note: The element marked by the cursor is shown in **bold**.

Step 4: Change the list in the test program (*TestListArray.java*) from a list of characters to a list of integers (or any other primitive data type—except `char`) by replacing the declaration `testElement` with

```
String testElement = null;          // List element
```

replacing the assignment statement for `testElement` further down in the code with

```
testElement = aToken;
```

and in statements with the words "`new Character`", replacing `Character` with the word `Integer`.

Every wrapper class constructor except the Character class accepts a String argument. Thus, the only change necessary to process a list of (say) doubles instead of the list of integers used in this version of the program is the third replacement above—in statements with the words "`new Integer`", replacing `Integer` with the word `Double`. The `testElement` declaration and assignment statements remain unchanged unless you want to process a list of characters, which is what the initial version of the program did.

Step 5: Replace the character data in your test plan ('a' to 'g') with integer values.

Step 6: Recompile and rerun the test program. Note that recompiling the program will compile your implementation of the List ADT (in the file *ListArray.java*) to produce an implementation for a list of integers.

Step 7: Execute your revised test plan using the revised test program. If you discover mistakes in your implementation of the List ADT, correct them and execute your revised test plan again.

LABORATORY 4: In-lab Exercise 1

Name _____

Hour/Period/Section _____

Date _____

The genetic information encoded in a strand of deoxyribonucleic acid (DNA) is stored in the purine and pyrimidine bases (adenine, guanine, cytosine, and thymine) that form the strand. Biologists are keenly interested in the bases in a DNA sequence because these bases determine what the sequence does.

By convention, DNA sequences are represented using lists containing the letters 'A', 'G', 'C', and 'T' (for adenine, guanine, cytosine, and thymine, respectively). The following method computes one property of a DNA sequence—the number of times each base occurs in the sequence.

```
void countBases ( ListArray dnaSequence )
```
Input:
dnaSequence: contains the bases in a DNA sequence encoded using the characters

'A', 'C', 'T', and 'G'.

Output:
aCount, cCount, tCount, gCount: the number of times the corresponding base appears in the DNA sequence.

Step 1: Implement this method and add it to the program in the file *TestDNA.java*. Your implementation should manipulate the DNA sequence using the operations in the List ADT. An incomplete definition for this method is given in the file *TestDNA.java*.

Step 2: The program in the file *TestDNA.java* reads a DNA sequence from the keyboard, calls the countBases( ) method, and outputs the resulting base counts. Complete the following test plan by adding DNA sequences of different lengths and various combinations of bases.

Step 3: Execute your test plan. If you discover mistakes in your implementation of the `countBases( )` method, correct them and execute your test plan again.

Test Plan for the *countBases() Method*

Test case	DNA sequence	Expected result	Checked
Sequence with 10 bases	AGTACATGTA	aCount = 4 cCount = 1 tCount = 3 gCount = 2	

LABORATORY 4: In-lab Exercise 2

Name _____

Hour/Period/Section _____

Date _____

In many applications, the ordering of the elements in a list changes over time. Not only are new elements added and existing ones removed, but elements are repositioned within the list. The following List ADT operation moves an element to a new position in a list.

```
void moveToNth ( int n )
```
Precondition:
List contains at least $n + 1$ elements.
Postcondition:
Removes the element marked by the cursor from a list and reinserts it as the nth element in the list, where the elements are numbered from beginning to end, starting with zero. Moves the cursor to the moved element.

Step 1: Implement this operation and add it to the file *ListArray.java*. An incomplete definition of this operation is included in the definition of the ListArray class in the file *ListArray.jshl*.

Step 2: Complete the following test plan by adding test cases that check whether your implementation of the moveToNth operation correctly processes moves within full and single-element lists.

Step 3: Activate the "M" (move) command in the test program *TestListArray.java* by removing the comment delimiter (and the character "M") from the lines that begin with "//M".

Step 4: Execute your test plan. If you discover mistakes in your implementation of the `moveToNth` operation, correct them and execute your test plan again.

Test Plan for the *moveToNth Operation*

Test case	Commands	Expected result	Checked
Set up list	+a +b +c +d	a b c **d**	
Move first element	< M2	b c **a** d	
Move element back	M0	**a** b c d	
Move to end of list	M3	b c d **a**	
Move back one	M2	b c **a** d	
Move forward one	M3	b c d **a**	

LABORATORY 4: In-lab Exercise 3

Name _____

Hour/Period/Section _____

Date _____

Finding a particular list element is another very common task. The operation below searches a list for a specified element. The fact that the search begins with the element marked by the cursor—and not at the beginning of the list—means that this operation can be applied iteratively to locate all of the occurrences of a specified element.

```
boolean find ( Object searchElement )
```
Precondition:
List is not empty.
Postcondition:
Searches a list for searchElement. Begins the search with the element marked by the cursor. Moves the cursor through the list until either searchElement is found (returns true) or the end of the list is reached without finding searchElement (returns false). Leaves the cursor at the last element visited during the search.

Step 1: Implement this operation and add it to the file *ListArray.java*. An incomplete definition of this operation is included in the definition of the ListArray class in the file *ListArray.jshl*.

Step 2: Complete the following test plan by adding test cases that check whether your implementation of the find operation correctly conducts searches in full lists, as well as searches that begin with the last element in a list.

Step 3: Activate the "?" (find) command in the test program *TestListArray.java* by removing the comment delimiter (and the character "?") from the lines that begin with "//?".

Step 4: Execute your test plan. If you discover mistakes in your implementation of the find operation, correct them and execute your test plan again.

Test Plan for the *find Operation*

Test case	Commands	Expected result	Checked
Set up list	+a +b +c +a	a b c a	
Successful search	< ?a	Search succeeds **a** b c a	
Search for duplicate	N ?a	Search succeeds a b c **a**	
Successful search	< ?b	Search succeeds a **b** c a	
Search for duplicate	N ?b	Search fails a b c **a**	
Trivial search	?a	Search succeeds a b c **a**	

LABORATORY 4: Postlab Exercise 1

Name

Hour/Period/Section

Date

Given a list containing N elements, develop worst-case, order-of-magnitude estimates of the execution time of the following List ADT operations, assuming they are implemented using an array. Briefly explain your reasoning behind each estimate.

insert	O( )

Explanation:

remove	O( )

Explanation:

gotoNext	O( )

Explanation:

gotoPrior	O( )

Explanation:

LABORATORY 4: Postlab Exercise 2

Name

Hour/Period/Section

Date

Part A

Give the changes that must be made to *TestListArray.java* for a list of floating-point numbers called `echoReadings`. Assume that the list can contain no more than 50 floating-point numbers.

Part B

Give the changes to *TestListArray.java* required for a list of (*x*,*y*,*z*)-coordinates called coords. Assume that *x*, *y*, and *z* are floating-point numbers and that there can be no more than 20 coordinates in the list.

Stack ADT

OBJECTIVES

In this laboratory you

- create two implementations of the Stack ADT—one based on an array representation of a stack and the other based on a singly linked list representation.

- analyze the limitations of using an ordinary assignment statement to duplicate objects versus using a copy constructor or cloning for the singly linked list representation of a stack.

- create a program that evaluates arithmetic expressions in postfix form.

- analyze the kinds of permutations you can produce using a stack.

OVERVIEW

Many applications that use a linear data structure do not require the full range of operations supported by the List ADT. Although you can develop these applications using the List ADT, the resulting programs are likely to be somewhat cumbersome and inefficient. An alternative approach is to define new linear data structures that support more constrained sets of operations. By carefully defining these ADTs, you can produce ADTs that meet the needs of a diverse set of applications, but yield data structures that are easier to apply—and are often more efficient—than the List ADT.

The **stack** is one example of a constrained linear data structure. In a stack, the elements are ordered from most recently added (the **top**) to the least recently added (the **bottom**). All insertions and deletions are performed at the top of the stack. You use the **push** operation to insert an element onto the stack and the **pop** operation to remove the topmost stack element. A sequence of pushes and pops is shown below.

Push a	Push b	Push c	Pop	Pop
		c		
	b	b	b	
a	a	a	a	a
—	—	—	—	—

These constraints on insertion and deletion produce the "last in, first out" (LIFO) behavior that characterizes a stack. Although the stack data structure is narrowly defined, it is used so extensively by systems software that support for a primitive stack is one of the basic elements of most computer architectures.

Stack ADT

Elements

The elements in a stack are of generic type Object.

Structure

The stack elements are linearly ordered from most recently added (the top) to least recently added (the bottom). Elements are inserted onto (pushed) and removed from (popped) the top of the stack.

Constructors and their Helper Method

```
Stack ( )
```
Precondition:
None.
Postcondition:
Default Constructor. Calls setup, which creates an empty stack and (if necessary) allocates enough memory for a stack containing DEF_MAX_STACK_SIZE (a constant value) elements.

```
Stack (int size)
```
Precondition:
size > 0.
Postcondition:
Constructor. Calls setup, which creates an empty stack and (if necessary) allocates enough memory for a stack containing size elements.

```
void setup(int size)
```
Precondition:
size > 0. A helper method for the constructors. Is declared private since only stack constructors should call this method.
Postcondition:
Creates an empty stack of a specific size (where applicable) based on the value of size received from the constructor.

Methods in the Interface

```
void push ( Object newElement )
```
Precondition:
Stack is not full and newElement is not null.
Postcondition:
Inserts newElement onto the top of a stack.

`Object pop ( )`
Precondition:
Stack is not empty.
Postcondition:
Removes the most recently added (top) element from a stack and returns it.

`void clear ( )`
Precondition:
None.
Postcondition:
Removes all the elements in a stack.

`boolean isEmpty ( )`
Precondition:
None.
Postcondition:
Returns true if a stack is empty. Otherwise, returns false.

`boolean isFull ( )`
Precondition:
None.
Postcondition:
Returns true if a stack is full. Otherwise, returns false.

`void showStructure ( )`
Precondition:
None.
Postcondition:
Outputs the elements in a stack. If the stack is empty, outputs "Empty stack". Note that this operation is intended for testing/debugging purposes only.

LABORATORY 5: Cover Sheet

Name

Hour/Period/Section

Date

Place a check mark (✔) in the Assigned column next to the exercises that your instructor has assigned to you. Attach this cover sheet to the front of the packet of materials that you submit for this laboratory.

Exercise	Assigned	Completed
Prelab Exercise	✔	
Bridge Exercise	✔	
In-lab Exercise 1		
In-lab Exercise 2		
In-lab Exercise 3		
Postlab Exercise 1		
Postlab Exercise 2		
Total		

LABORATORY 5: Prelab Exercise

Name _____

Hour/Period/Section _____

Date _____

Multiple implementations of an ADT are necessary if the ADT is to perform efficiently in a variety of operating environments. Depending on the hardware and the application, you may want an implementation that reduces the execution time of some (or all) of the ADT operations, or you may want an implementation that reduces the amount of memory used to store the ADT elements. In this laboratory, you develop two implementations of the Stack ADT. One implementation stores the stack in an array, the other stores each element separately and links the elements together to form a stack.

The Stack ADT has a common set of methods that any Stack implementation should provide. In Java, one approach to identifying these common methods is to define an **interface**. The Stack interface is in the file *Stack.java* and is defined as follows:

```
public interface Stack              // Constants & Methods common to all stack ADTs
{
  // Default maximum stack size
  public static final int DEF_MAX_STACK_SIZE = 10;

  // Stack manipulation operations
  public void push(Object newElement);  // Push Object onto stack
  public Object pop();                   // Pop Object from top of stack
  public void clear();                   // Remove all Objects from stack

  // Stack status operations
  public boolean isEmpty();              // Return true if stack is empty
  public boolean isFull();               // Return true if stack is full
  public void showStructure ();          // Outputs the elements in the stack
                                         // For testing/debugging purposes only
} // interface Stack
```

A Java interface is a collection of constants and abstract methods. An **abstract method** is a method that does not have an implementation, as is evident in the interface for Stack shown above. In a Java interface, the header of each method, including its parameter list, is simply followed by a semicolon. Any class that implements Stack, as the class AStack does in Step 1 below, is required to provide an implementation for *every* method listed in the interface Stack. The Java compiler will produce errors if any of the methods in the interface are not given a definition in the implementing class.

Step 1: Implement the methods in the Stack ADT using an array to store the stack elements. Stacks change in size; therefore, you need to store the array index of the topmost element in the stack (top), along with the stack elements themselves (element). Arrays have a limited capacity. The maximum number of elements our stack can hold can be determined by referencing length in the array object—more specifically, in our case, by referencing element.length.

Base your implementation on the following incomplete class methods from the file *AStack.jshl*. You are to fill in the Java code for each of the constructors and methods where the implementation braces are empty, only partially filled (noted by "add code here ..."), or where an entire method or set of methods from the interface needs to be inserted (noted by "insert method ... here").

```
class AStack implements Stack             // Array based stack class
{
    // Data members
    private int top;                      // Index for the top element
    private Object [ ] element;           // Array containing stack elements

    // Constructors and helper method setup
    public AStack( )                      // Constructor: default size
    {                                     }
    public AStack(int size)               // Constructor: specific size
    {                                     }

    // Class methods
    private void setup(int size)          // Called by constructors only
    {                                     }

    //----- Insert method implementations for the interface Stack here -----//

} // class AStack
```

Step 2: Save your array implementation of the Stack ADT in the file *AStack.java*. Be sure to document your code.

In your array implementation of the Stack ADT, you allocate the memory used to store a stack when the stack is declared (constructed). The resulting array must be large enough to hold the largest stack you might possibly need in a particular application. Unfortunately, most of the time the stack will not actually be this large and the extra memory will go unused.

An alternative approach is to allocate memory element by element as new elements are added to the stack. In this way, you allocate memory only when you actually need it. Because memory is allocated over time, however, the elements do not occupy a contiguous set of memory locations. As a result, you need to link the elements together to form a linked list representation of a stack, as shown in the following figure.

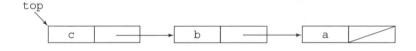

Creating a linked list implementation of the Stack ADT presents a somewhat more challenging programming task than did developing an array implementation. One way to simplify this task is to divide the implementation into two classes: one focusing on the overall stack structure (the LStack class) and another focusing on the individual nodes in the linked list (the StackNode class).

Let's begin with the StackNode class. Each node in the linked list contains a stack element and a reference to the node containing the next element in the list.

Access to the StackNode class is restricted to classes in the Lab5 package (or subdirectory). Classes not in the Lab5 package are blocked from referencing linked list nodes directly because all the members of StackNode do not have an access label (public, private, or protected). These properties are reflected in the following incomplete class definition from the file *StackNode.jshl*.

```
// Facilitator class for the Stack class
class StackNode                              // A singly linked list node
{
  // Data members
  private Object element;                    // Object for this node
  private StackNode next;                    // Reference to next node in list

  // Because there are no access labels (public, private, or protected),
  // access is limited to the package where these methods are declared

  // Constructor
  StackNode(Object newElement, StackNode nextval)
  {                                   }

  // Class methods --
  // Other classes in this package need to know about next and element
  // or set next
  StackNode getNext( )                       // Returns reference to next node
  {                                   }
  Object getElement( )                       // Returns element's value
  {                                   }
  void setNext(StackNode nextVal)            // Sets value of next
  {                                   }

} // class StackNode
```

The StackNode class constructor is used to add nodes to the stack. The statement below, for example, adds a node containing 'd' to a stack of characters. Note that 'd' is a primitive data type (char), which must be converted to an Object by using the wrapper class Character.

```
top = new StackNode(new Character('d'), top);
```

The new operator allocates memory for a linked list node and calls the StackNode constructor, passing both the element to be inserted (new Character('d')) and a reference to the next node in the list (top).

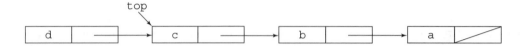

Finally, the assignment operator assigns the reference to the newly allocated node to top, thereby completing the creation and linking of the node.

The methods of the LStack class also implement the operations in the Stack ADT. A reference is maintained to the node at the beginning of the linked list or, equivalently, the top of the stack. The following incomplete definition for the LStack class is given in the file *LStack.jshl*.

```
class LStack implements Stack              // Linked stack class
{
  // Data member
  private StackNode top;                   // Reference to top of stack

  // Constructors and helper method setup
  public LStack( )                         // Default Constructor1
  {                                }
  public LStack(int size)                  // Constructor2: ignore size
                                           // for compatibility with AStack

  {                                }

  // Class methods
  private void setup( )                    // Called by Constructors only
  {                                }

  //----- Insert method implementations for the interface Stack here -----//

} // class LStack
```

Step 3: Implement the operations in the StackNode ADT and the LStack ADT using a singly linked list to store the stack elements. Each node in the linked list should contain a stack element (element) and a reference to the node containing the next element in the stack (next). Your implementation also should maintain a reference to the node containing the topmost element in the stack (top). Base your implementation on the incomplete class definitions in the files *LStack.jshl* and *StackNode.jshl*.

Step 4: Save your linked list implementation of the LStack ADT in the file *LStack.java* and of the StackNode ADT in the file *StackNode.java*. Be sure to document your code.

LABORATORY 5: Bridge Exercise

Name _____

Hour/Period/Section _____

Date _____

Check with your instructor as to whether you are to complete this exercise prior to your lab period or during lab.

The test program in the file *TestAStack.java* allows you to interactively test your implementation of the AStack ADT using the following commands.

Command	Action
+x	Push element x onto the top of the stack.
–	Pop the top element and output it.
E	Report whether the stack is empty.
F	Report whether the stack is full.
C	Clear the stack.
Q	Exit the test program.

Step 1: Complete the following test plan form by adding test cases in which you

• pop an element from a stack containing only one element.

• push an element onto a stack that has been emptied by a series of pops.

• pop an element from a full stack (array implementation).

• clear the stack.

Step 2: Compile and run the test program *TestAStack.java*. Note that compiling this program will compile your array implementation of the Stack ADT (in the file *AStack.java*) to produce an array implementation for a stack of characters.

Step 3: Execute your test plan. If you discover mistakes in your array implementation of the Stack ADT, correct them and execute your test plan again.

Step 4: Modify the test program so that your linked list implementation of the Stack ADT in the file *LStack.java* is used in place of your array implementation. Rename the class TestAStack as TestLStack and then save the file as *TestLStack.java*. Last, modify the code of *TestLStack.java* to instantiate LStack objects instead of AStack objects.

Step 5: Compile and run the test program *TestLStack.java*. Note that this program will compile your linked list implementation of the Stack ADT (in the file *LStack.java*) to produce a linked list implementation for a stack of characters.

Step 6: Use your test plan to check your linked list implementation of the Stack ADT. If you discover mistakes in your implementation, correct them and execute your test plan again.

Test Plan for the *Operations in the Stack ADT*

Test case	Commands	Expected result	Checked
Series of pushes	+a +b +c +d	a b c **d**	
Series of pops	- - -	**a**	
More pushes	+e +f	a e **f**	
More pops	- -	**a**	
Empty? Full?	E F	false false	
Empty the stack	-	Empty stack	
Empty? Full?	E F	true false	

Note: The topmost element is shown in **bold**.

LABORATORY 5: In-lab Exercise 1

Name _____

Hour/Period/Section _____

Date _____

Recall that `length` represents the maximum number of elements an array object in Java can hold. Rather than have the array implementation of a stack grow upward from array entry 0 toward entry `length - 1`, you can just as easily construct an implementation that begins at array entry `length - 1` and grows downward toward entry 0. You could then combine this "downward" array implementation with the "upward" array implementation you created in the Prelab to form an implementation of a Double Stack ADT in which a pair of stacks occupy the same array (assuming that the total number of elements in *both* stacks never exceeds `length`).

Step 1: Create an implementation of the Stack ADT using an array in which the stack grows downward. Base your implementation on the incomplete class definition in the file *AStackDwn.jshl* (these have identical method names as in the file *AStack.jshl*).

Step 2: Save your "downward" array implementation of the Stack ADT in the file *AStackDwn.java*.

Step 3: Modify the test program *TestAStack.java* so that your "downward" array implementation of the Stack ADT in the file *AStackDwn.java* is used in place of your "upward" array implementation. Rename the class TestAStack as TestAStackDwn and then save the file as *TestAStackDwn.java*. Last, modify the code of *TestAStackDwn.java* to instantiate AStackDwn object instead of AStack objects.

Step 4: Use the test plan you created in the Bridge Exercise to check your "downward" array implementation of the Stack ADT. If you discover mistakes in your implementation, correct them and execute your test plan again.

LABORATORY 5: In-lab Exercise 2

Name _____

Hour/Period/Section _____

Date _____

Whenever we set one object (or instance of a class) equal to another in an assignment statement (e.g., stack1 = stack2), both variables (stack1 and stack2) refer to exactly the same object or memory location. In other words, the effect of the assignment statement 'stack1 = stack2' is to make stack1 refer to the same object that stack2 is already referring to. Therefore, changes to either object will also change the other. This situation can cause some unexpected results.

A programmer sometimes needs to make an exact but separate copy of an existing object. Subsequent changes to the copy should not alter the original, nor should subsequent changes to the original alter the copy.

Fortunately, in Java there are two ways to make an exact but separate copy of an object. One approach is to specify exactly how a copy is to be created by including a copy constructor in our Stack class. A copy constructor for the Stack class is described below.

```
Stack ( Stack valueStack )
```
Precondition:
None.
Postcondition:
Copy constructor. Creates an exact but separate copy of valueStack.

Notice that, in the file *TestLStack.java*, the parameter in the call to the copy constructor must be typecast to an LStack in order to call LStack's copy constructor. In particular, this is necessary because the copy constructor for LStack should only copy another LStack (never a different type of Stack such as an AStack). For an example of how this typecasting is done, refer to the code for case '!': in the *TestLStack.java* file.

Another way to make an identical but separate copy of an object is to invoke clone( ) on that object. Because clone( ) is declared in class Object, it is inherited by every Java object. If an object does not implement the Cloneable interface, Object's implementation of clone( ) will throw the CloneNotSupportedException. Otherwise, a new instance of the object will be created with all the fields initialized to values identical to the object being cloned, and a reference to the new object will be returned. However, be aware that the data type of the return value of the `clone` method is actually an Object. Therefore, we must apply a typecast to the `clone` return value, converting it to the intended data type. The `clone` method for the Stack class is described below.

```
Object clone( )
```
Precondition:
None.
Postcondition:
Returns an exact but separate copy of type Object.

Notice that in the file *TestLStack.java* the Stack (`testStack`) must be typecast to a LStack in order to call LStack's `clone` method. In particular, this is necessary because `clone` will only be defined in LStack and is not defined in the Stack interface. Also note that the return value for `clone`, which is an Object, must be typecast to a Stack before it is used. To see how this is done refer to the code for `case '!':` in the *TestLStack.java* file.

To implement the `clone` method for any class, you need to do the following:

1. **Modify the class head** by adding the words "`implements Cloneable`" to the end of the class head. For example, to be able to implement `clone( )` for the class MyStackClass, you would type the following in the head of the definition of the class:

   ```
   class MyStackClass implements Stack, Cloneable
   ```

   Notice that since MyStackClass already `implements Stack`, we simply add a second interface by separating it from the first with a comma.

2. **Use *super.clone* to make a copy.** An implementation of a `clone` method that can be used for the LStack class can be found in the file *clone.txt*. Since Object's `clone` method throws the CloneNotSupportedException, this code includes an example of a `try` block. After the `try` block is a `catch` block that catches and handles the CloneNotSupportedException that may occur in the `try` block. This exception is thrown by the `clone` method from Java's Object class when a programmer tries to call `super.clone( )` without including the `implements Cloneable` clause as part of the class definition.

Be aware that if you wish to clone an object that includes object references as part of its instance data, you may have to do more work in `clone` than just calling `super.clone( )`. In such cases, you may want to consider using the copy constructor or study the use of `clone` in more detail than is presented here.

Step 1: Implement the copy constructor and `clone` operations using the linked list representation of a stack and add it to the file *LStack.java*. An empty method implementation for the copy constructor along with a comment indicating where to insert the `clone` operation from the *clone.txt* file is included in the incomplete definition of the LStack class in the file *LStack.jshl*.

Step 2: Modify the test program *TestLStack.java* as follows: Activate the "!" (call method) command in the test program by removing the comment delimiters (/*! and !*/) from the lines of code for the `case` `'!'` statement and from the lines of code for the dummy method. The definition of the `dummy` method is given at the end of the TestLStack.java file.

Step 3: Complete the following test plan by adding test cases that check whether your implementations of the copy constructor and `clone` correctly copy a single-element stack and an empty stack.

Step 4: Execute your test plan. If you discover mistakes in your implementation of the copy constructor, correct them and execute the test plan again.

Test Plan for the *Copy Constructor and clone Operation*

Test case	Commands	Expected result	Checked
Copy a stack	+a +b +c !	a b **c**	
Copy a larger stack	+a+b+c+d !	a b c **d**	
Copy a smaller stack	+a+b+c+d- - !	a **b**	

Note: The topmost element is shown in **bold**.

LABORATORY 5: In-lab Exercise 3

Name

Hour/Period/Section

Date

We commonly write arithmetic expressions in **infix form**, that is, with each operator placed between its operands, as in the following expression:

$$(3+4)*(5/2)$$

Although we are comfortable writing expressions in this form, infix form has the disadvantage that parentheses must be used to indicate the order in which operators are to be evaluated. These parentheses, in turn, greatly complicate the evaluation process.

Evaluation is much easier if we can simply evaluate operators from left to right. Unfortunately, this left-to-right evaluation strategy will not work with the infix form of arithmetic expressions. However, it will work if the expression is in postfix form. In the **postfix form** of an arithmetic expression, each operator is placed immediately after its operands. The expression above is written below in postfix form as

$$34+52/*$$

Note that both forms place the numbers in the same order (reading from left to right). The order of the operators is different, however, because the operators in the postfix form are positioned in the order that they are evaluated. The resulting postfix expression is hard to read at first, but it is easy to evaluate. All you need is a stack on which to place intermediate results.

Suppose you have an arithmetic expression in postfix form that consists of a sequence of single digit, nonnegative integers and the four basic arithmetic operators (addition, subtraction, multiplication, and division). This expression can be evaluated using the following algorithm in conjunction with a stack of floating-point numbers.

Read in the expression character by character. As each character is read in,

- If the character corresponds to a single digit number (characters '0' to '9'), then push the corresponding floating-point number onto the stack.

- If the character corresponds to one of the arithmetic operators (characters '+', '−', '*', and '/'), then

  ○ Pop a number off of the stack. Call it operand1.
  ○ Pop a number off of the stack. Call it operand2.

○ Combine these operands using the arithmetic operator, as follows

$$result = operand2 \ \text{operator} \ operand1$$

○ Push `result` onto the stack.

• When the end of the expression is reached, pop the remaining number off the stack. This number is the value of the expression.

Applying this algorithm to the arithmetic expression

$$34+52/*$$

yields the following computation:

          `'3'`:   Push 3.0

          `'4'`:   Push 4.0

          `'+'`:   Pop, `operand1` = 4.0

                  Pop, `operand2` = 3.0

                  Combine, `result` = 3.0 + 4.0 = 7.0

                  Push 7.0

          `'5'`:   Push 5.0

          `'2'`:   Push 2.0

          `'/'`:   Pop, `operand1` = 2.0

                  Pop, `operand2` = 5.0

                  Combine, `result` = 5.0 / 2.0 = 2.5

                  Push 2.5

          `'*'`:   Pop, `operand1` = 2.5

                  Pop, `operand2` = 7.0

                  Combine, `result` = 7.0 * 2.5 = 17.5

                  Push 17.5

        `'\n'`: Pop, Value of expression = 17.5

Step 1: Create a program (call it *PostFix.java*) that reads the postfix form of an arithmetic expression, evaluates it, and outputs the result. Assume that the expression consists of single-digit, nonnegative integers ('0' to '9') and the four basic arithmetic operators ('+', '–', '*', and '/'). Further assume that the arithmetic expression is input from the keyboard with all the characters on one line. In *PostFix.java*, values of type `float` will be large enough for our purposes.

Hints: a. Review the code for *TestAStack.java* to recall how to read in characters, deal with whitespace and push an Object onto the stack.

b. To convert from Object to Float and then to the primitive `float` requires a cast and the `Float.floatValue( )` method. For example,

```
float operand1;
operand1 = ((Float)resultStack.pop( )).floatValue( );
```

c. To set precision to two decimal places, `import java.text.DecimalFormat` and use code similar to the following:

```
float outResult;
DecimalFormat fmt = new DecimalFormat("0.##");
System.out.println(fmt.format(outResult));
```

Step 2: Complete the following test plan by filling in the expected result for each arithmetic expression. You may wish to include additional arithmetic expressions in this test plan.

Step 3: Execute the test plan. If you discover mistakes in your program, correct them and execute the test plan again.

Test Plan for the *Postfix Arithmetic Expression Evaluation Program*

Test case	Arithmetic expression	Expected result	Checked
One operator	34+		
Nested operators	34+52/*		
Uneven nesting	93*2+1-		
All operators at end	4675-+*		
Zero dividend	02/		
Single-digit number	7		

LABORATORY 5: Postlab Exercise 1

Name

Hour/Period/Section

Date

Given the input string "abc", determine which permutations of this string can be output by a code fragment consisting of only the statement pairs

```
ch = (char) System.in.read( );
permuteStack.push(new Character(ch));
```

and

```
System.out.print( permuteStack.pop( ));
```

where ch is a character and permuteStack is a stack of characters. Note that each of the statement pairs may be repeated several times within the code fragment and that the statement pairs may be in any order. For instance, the code fragment

```
ch = (char) System.in.read( );
permuteStack.push(new Character(ch));

ch = (char) System.in.read( );
permuteStack.push(new Character(ch));

ch = (char) System.in.read( );
permuteStack.push(new Character(ch));

System.out.print( permuteStack.pop( ));
System.out.print( permuteStack.pop( ));
System.out.print( permuteStack.pop( ));
```

outputs the string "cba".

Part A

For each of the permutations listed below, give a code fragment that outputs the permutation or briefly explain why the permutation cannot be produced.

"abc"	"acb"
"bac"	"bca"
"cab"	"cba"

Part B

Given the input string `"abcd"`, determine which permutations beginning with the character 'd' can be output by a code fragment of the form described above. Why can only these permutations be produced?

LABORATORY 5: Postlab Exercise 2

Name

Hour/Period/Section

Date

In In-lab Exercise 3, you used a stack to evaluate arithmetic expressions. Describe another application in which you might use the Stack ADT. What type of information does your application store in each stack element?

Queue ADT

OBJECTIVES

In this laboratory you

- create two implementations of the Queue ADT—one based on an array representation of a queue, the other based on a singly linked list representation.

- create an array implementation of a deque.

- create a program that simulates the flow of customers through a line.

- analyze the memory requirements of your array and linked list queue representations.

OVERVIEW

This laboratory focuses on another constrained linear data structure, the **queue**. The elements in a queue are ordered from least recently added (the **front**) to most recently added (the **rear**). Insertions are performed at the rear of the queue, and deletions are performed at the front. You use the **enqueue** operation to insert elements and the **dequeue** operation to remove elements. A sequence of enqueues and dequeues is shown below.

Enqueue a	Enqueue b	Enqueue c	Dequeue	Dequeue
a	a b	a b c	b c	c
←front	←front	←front	←front	←front

The movement of elements through a queue reflects the "first in, first out" (FIFO) behavior that is characteristic of the flow of customers in a line or the transmission of information across a data channel. Queues are routinely used to regulate the flow of physical objects, information, and requests for resources (or services) through a system. Operating systems, for example, use queues to control access to system resources such as printers, files, and communications lines. Queues also are widely used in simulations to model the flow of objects or information through a system.

Queue ADT

Elements

The elements in a queue are of generic type Object.

Structure

The queue elements are linearly ordered from least recently added (the front) to most recently added (the rear). Elements are inserted at the rear of the queue (enqueued) and are removed from the front of the queue (dequeued).

Constructors and their Helper Method

```
Queue ( )
```
Precondition:
None.
Postcondition:
Default Constructor. Calls setup, which creates an empty queue and (if necessary) allocates enough memory for a queue containing DEF_MAX_QUEUE_SIZE (a constant value) elements.

```
Queue ( int size )
```
Precondition:
size > 0.
Postcondition:
Constructor. Calls setup, which creates an empty queue and (if necessary) allocates enough memory for a queue containing size elements.

```
void setup ( int size )
```
Precondition:
size > 0. A helper method for the constructors. Is declared private since only queue constructors should call this method.
Postcondition:
Creates an empty queue of a specific size (where applicable) based on the value of size received from the constructor.

Methods in the Interface

```
void enqueue ( Object newElement )
```
Precondition:
Queue is not full and newElement is not null.
Postcondition:
Inserts newElement at the rear of a queue.

```
Object dequeue ( )
```
Precondition:
Queue is not empty.
Postcondition:
Removes the least recently added (front) element from a queue and returns it.

```
void clear ( )
```
Precondition:
None.
Postcondition:
Removes all the elements in a queue.

```
boolean isEmpty ( )
```
Precondition:
None.
Postcondition:
Returns true if a queue is empty. Otherwise, returns false.

```
boolean isFull ( )
```
Precondition:
None.
Postcondition:
Returns true if a queue is full. Otherwise, returns false.

```
void showStructure ( )
```
Precondition:
None.
Postcondition:
Outputs the elements in a queue. If the queue is empty, outputs "Empty queue". Note that this operation is intended for testing/debugging purposes only.

LABORATORY 6: Cover Sheet

Name _____

Hour/Period/Section _____

Date _____

Place a check mark (✔) in the Assigned column next to the exercises that your instructor has assigned to you. Attach this cover sheet to the front of the packet of materials that you submit for this laboratory.

Exercise	Assigned	Completed
Prelab Exercise	✔	
Bridge Exercise	✔	
In-lab Exercise 1		
In-lab Exercise 2		
In-lab Exercise 3		
Postlab Exercise 1		
Postlab Exercise 2		
Total		

LABORATORY 6: Prelab Exercise

Name _____

Hour/Period/Section _____

Date _____

In this laboratory, you create two implementations of the Queue ADT. One of these implementations is based on an array, the other is based on a singly linked list. Just like the Stack ADT (in Laboratory 5), a Queue ADT has a common interface that is in the file *Queue.java* and is defined as follows:

```
public interface Queue                     // Constants & Methods common to queue ADTs
{
    // Default maximum queue size
    public static final int DEF_MAX_QUEUE_SIZE = 10;

    // Queue manipulation operations
    public void enqueue ( Object newElement ); // Enqueue element at rear
    public Object dequeue ( );                 // Dequeue element from front
    public void clear ( );                     // Remove all elements from queue

    // Queue status operations
    public boolean isEmpty ( );                // Is Queue empty?
    public boolean isFull ( );                 // Is Queue full?
    public void showStructure ( );             // Outputs the elements in the stack
                                               // For testing/debugging purposes only

} // interface Queue
```

The array-based queue cannot be efficiently implemented as a simple array. In a simple array-based implementation of a list, all elements of the list must be stored in the first n positions of the array. If we dequeue elements from the front of the array, then the remaining n elements in the list must be shifted forward one position in the array. Shifting every element of the array forward one position after each dequeue operation reduces the efficiency of the queue.

To make the array-based implementation of the queue more efficient, we will still require the elements to be in contiguous array positions, but allow the contents of the queue to drift within the array. Furthermore, we will allow the contents to drift in a circular fashion within the array. Thus, the queue will eventually drift directly from the highest index or position in the array (maxSize - 1) to index 0. This is easily implemented through the use of the modulus operator. In this way, position maxSize -1 immediately precedes position 0 where position 0 is equivalent to position maxSize % maxSize. An array that is used in this way is called a **circular array**.

Step 1: Implement the methods (also called operations) in the Queue ADT using a circular array to store the queue elements. Queues change in size; therefore, you need to store the maximum number of elements the queue can hold (maxSize) and the array index of the elements at the front and rear of the queue (front and rear), along with the queue elements themselves (element). To distinguish an empty queue from a queue with only one element in it, we will set front and rear to an invalid index (such as -1) when the queue is empty. Base your implementation on the incomplete class definition from the file *AQueue.jshl*. You are to fill in the Java code for each of the constructors and methods where the implementation braces are empty, only partially filled (noted by "add code here ... "), or where an entire method or set of methods from the interface needs to be inserted (noted by "insert method ... here").

```
class AQueue implements Queue                  // Array-based queue class
{
    // Data members
    private int maxSize;                       // Maximum number of elements in the queue
    private int front;                         // Index of the front element
    private int rear;                          // Index of the rear element
    private Object [ ] element;                // Array containing the queue elements

    // Constructors and helper method setup
    public AQueue ( )                          // Constructor: default size
    {                              }
    public AQueue ( int size )                 // Constructor: sets size
    {                              }

    // Class methods
    private void setup(int size)               // Called by Constructors only
    {                              }

    //----- Insert method implementations for the interface Queue here -----//

} // class AQueue
```

Step 2: Save your array implementation of the Queue ADT in the file *AQueue.java*. Be sure to document your code.

Step 3: Implement the operations in the Queue ADT using a singly linked list to store the queue elements. Each node in the linked list should contain a queue element (element) and a reference to the node containing the next element in the queue (next). Your implementation also should maintain references to the nodes containing the front and rear elements in the queue (front and rear). In the LQueue constructors these front and rear references should be initialized to null. Base your implementation on the following incomplete class definitions from the file *LQueue.jshl*.

```
    // Facilitator class for the Queue class
    class QueueNode                              // A singly linked list node
    {
        // Data members
        private Object element;                  // Queue element
        private QueueNode next;                  // Pointer to the next element

        // Constructor
        QueueNode ( Object elem, QueueNode nextPtr )
        {                                }

        // Class methods --
        // A client class (such as LQueue)
        //   needs to know about next and element
        //   & must be able to set the nextPtr as needed
        QueueNode getNext ( )
        {                                }
        Object getElement ( )
        {                                }
        void setNext ( QueueNode nextPtr)
        {                                }

    } // Class QueueNode

    //-------------------------------------------------------------------

    class LQueue implements Queue                // Linked list Queue class
    {
        // Data members
        private QueueNode front,                 // Reference to the front element
                        rear;                    // Reference to the rear element

        // Constructors and helper method setup
        public LQueue ( )                        // Constructor: default
        {                                }
        public LQueue ( int size )               // Constructor: ignore size
        {                                }

        // Class methods
        private void setup( )                    // Called by constructor only
        {                                }      // Initializes front and rear to null

        //----- Insert method implementations for the interface Queue here -----//

    } // Class LQueue
```

Step 4: Save your linked list implementation of the Queue ADT in the file *LQueue.java*. Be sure to document your code.

LABORATORY 6: Bridge Exercise

Name

Hour/Period/Section

Date

Check with your instructor as to whether you are to complete this exercise prior to your lab period or during lab.

The test program in the file *TestAQueue.java* allows you to interactively test your implementations of the Queue ADT using the following commands.

Command	Action
+x	Enqueue element x.
−	Dequeue an element and output it.
E	Report whether the queue is empty.
F	Report whether the queue is full.
C	Clear the queue.
Q	Exit the test program.

Step 1: Complete the following test plan form by adding test cases in which you

- enqueue an element onto a queue that has been emptied by a series of dequeues

- combine enqueues and dequeues so that you "go around the end" of the array (array implementation)

- dequeue an element from a full queue (array implementation)

- clear the queue.

Step 2: Compile and run the test program. Note that compiling this program will compile your array implementation of the Queue ADT (in the file *AQueue.java*) to produce an array implementation for a queue of characters.

Step 3: Execute your test plan. If you discover mistakes in your array implementation of the Queue ADT, correct them and execute your test plan again.

Step 4: Modify the test program so that your linked list implementation of the Queue ADT in the file *LQueue.java* is used in place of your array implementation. Rename the class TestAQueue as TestLQueue and then save the file as *TestLQueue.java*. Last, modify the code of *TestLQueue.java* to instantiate LQueue objects instead of AQueue objects.

Step 5: Compile and run the test program *TestLQueue.java*. Note that compiling this program will compile your linked list implementation of the Queue ADT (in the file *LQueue.java*) to produce a linked list implementation for a queue of characters.

Step 6: Use your test plan to check your linked list implementation of the Queue ADT. If you discover mistakes in your implementation, correct them and execute your test plan again.

Test Plan for the *Operations in the Queue ADT*

Test case	Commands	Expected result	Checked
Series of enqueues	+a +b +c +d	**a** b c d	
Series of dequeues	- - -	**d**	
More enqueues	+e +f	**d** e f	
More dequeues	- -	**f**	
Empty? Full?	E F	false false	
Empty the queue	-	Empty queue	
Empty? Full?	E F	true false	

Note: The front element is shown in **bold**.

LABORATORY 6: In-lab Exercise 1

Name _____

Hour/Period/Section _____

Date _____

A **deque** (or double-ended queue) is a linear data structure that allows elements to be inserted and removed at both ends. Adding the operations described below will transform your Queue ADT into a Deque ADT.

```
void putFront ( Object newElement )
```
Precondition:
Queue is not full and newElement is not null.
Postcondition:
Inserts newElement at the front of a queue. The order of the pre-existing elements is left unchanged.

```
Object getRear ( )
```
Precondition:
Queue is not empty.
Postcondition:
Removes the most recently added (rear) element from a queue and returns it. The remainder of the queue is left unchanged.

Step 1: Implement these operations using the array representation of a queue and add them to the file *AQueue.java*. Empty method implementations for these operations are included in the definition of the Queue class in the file *AQueue.jshl*.

Step 2: Activate the ">" (put in front) and "=" (get from rear) commands in the test program *TestAQueue.java* by removing the comment delimiter (and the character ">" or "=") from the lines that begin with "//>" and "//=". Notice that in each of these cases in *TestAQueue.java* testQueue, which is of type Queue, must be typecast to AQueue since the methods putFront, and getRear are not declared in the Queue interface.

Step 3: Complete the following test plan by adding test cases in which you

- insert an element at the front of a newly emptied queue.

- remove an element from the rear of a queue containing only one element.

- "go around the end" of the array using each of these operations.

- mix putFront and getRear with enqueue and dequeue.

Step 4: Execute your test plan. If you discover mistakes in your implementation of these operations, correct them and execute the test plan again.

Test Plan for the *putFront and getRear Operations*

Test case	Commands	Expected result	Checked
Series of calls to *putFront*	>a >b >c >d	**d** c b a	
Series of calls to *getRear*	= = =	**d**	
More calls to *putFront*	>e >f	**f** e d	
More calls to *getRear*	= =	**f**	

Note: The front element is shown in **bold**.

LABORATORY 6: In-lab Exercise 2

Name _____

Hour/Period/Section _____

Date _____

When a queue is used as part of a model or simulation, the modeler is often very interested in how many elements are on the queue at various points in time. This statistic is produced by the following operation.

```
int length ( )
```
Precondition:
None.
Postcondition:
Returns the number of elements in a queue.

Step 1: Create an implementation of this operation using the array representation of a queue and add it to the file *AQueue.java*. An empty method implementation for this operation is included in the definition of the Queue class in the file *AQueue.jshl*.

Step 2: Activate the "#" (`length`) command in the test program *TestAQueue.java* by removing the comment delimiter (and the character "#") from the lines that begin with "//#". As with `putFront` and `getRear`, notice that in this case in *TestAQueue.java* `testQueue`, which is of type Queue, must be typecast to AQueue since the method `length` is not declared in the Queue interface.

Step 3: Complete the following test plan by adding test cases in which you check the length of empty queues and queues that "go around the end" of the array.

Step 4: Execute your test plan. If you discover mistakes in your implementation of the `length` operation, correct them and execute the test plan again.

Test Plan for the *Length Operation*

Test case	Commands	Expected result	Checked
Series of enqueues	+a +b +c +d	**a** b c d	
Length	#	4	
Series of dequeues	- - -	**d**	
Length	#	1	
More enqueues	+e +f	**d** e f	
Length	#	3	

Note: The front element is shown in **bold**.

LABORATORY 6: In-lab Exercise 3

Name _____

Hour/Period/Section _____

Date _____

In this exercise, you use a queue to simulate the flow of customers through a checkout line in a store. In order to create this simulation, you must model both the passage of time and the flow of customers through the line. You can model time using a loop in which each pass corresponds to a set time interval—one minute, for example. You can model the flow of customers using a queue in which each element corresponds to a customer in the line.

In order to complete the simulation, you need to know the rate at which customers join the line, as well as the rate at which they are served and leave the line. Suppose the checkout line has the following properties.

- One customer is served and leaves the line every minute (assuming there is at least one customer waiting to be served during that minute).

- Between zero and two customers join the line every minute, where there is a 50% chance that no customers arrive, a 25% chance that one customer arrives, and a 25% chance that two customers arrive.

You can simulate the flow of customers through the line during a time period n minutes long using the following algorithm.

```
Initialize the queue to empty.
for ( minute = 0 ; minute < n ; minute++ )
{
    If the queue is not empty, then remove the customer at the front of the queue.
    Compute a random number k between 0 and 3.
    If k is 1, then add one customer to the line. If k is 2, then add two customers
       to the line. Otherwise (if k is 0 or 3), do not add any customers to the line.
}
```

Step 1: Using the program shell given in the file *StoreSim.jshl* as a basis, create a program that uses the Queue ADT to implement the model described above. Your program should update the following information during each simulated minute, that is, during each pass through the loop:

- The total number of customers served

- The combined length of time these customers spent waiting in line

- The maximum length of time any of these customers spent waiting in line

In order to compute how long a customer waited to be served, you need to store the "minute" that the customer was added to the queue as part of the queue element corresponding to that customer.

Step 2: Use your program to simulate the flow of customers through the line and complete the following table. Note that the average wait is the combined waiting time divided by the total number of customers served.

Take special note that, in this program shell, the length of the simulation, simLength, is read in as an argument to the program itself. In other words, it is a value assigned to the args parameter of the main method—now you know the use of the args array in the main method of your program. This argument is entered as an additional string when you run your program from the command line prompt. If your Java development system does not allow you to invoke your program from the command line, you will need to determine how this argument is passed in the particular Java development system you are using.

Since each args in main is a String array, args[0] must be converted to an int, which is the data type assigned to the simLength. As illustrated in the statement below (which also appears in the file *StoreSim.jshl*), this conversion is commonly done in Java by using the static method parseInt in the class Integer.

```
simLength = Integer.parseInt( args[0] );
```

Java programmers use this parseInt method on a daily basis as a quick and easy way to convert a String to an int in Java.

Time in minutes	Total number of customers served	Average wait	Longest wait
30			
60			
120			
480			

LABORATORY 6: Postlab Exercise 1

Name

Hour/Period/Section

Date

Part A

Given the following memory requirements

Integer   4 bytes

Address (reference)   4 bytes

and a queue containing 100 Integers, compare the amount of memory used by your array representation of the queue with the amount of memory used by a singly linked list representation. Assume that the array representation allows a queue to contain a maximum of 100 elements.

Part B

Suppose that you have ten queues of Integers. Of these ten queues, four are 50% full, and the remaining six are 10% full. Compare the amount of memory used by your array representation of these queues with the amount of memory used by a singly linked list representation. Assume that the array representation allows a queue to contain a maximum of 100 elements.

LABORATORY 6: Postlab Exercise 2

Name _____

Hour/Period/Section _____

Date _____

In In-lab Exercise 3, you used a queue to simulate the flow of customers through a line. Describe another application where you might use the Queue ADT. What type of information does your application store in each queue element?

Singly Linked List Implementation of the List ADT

OBJECTIVES

In this laboratory you

- implement the List ADT using a singly linked list.

- examine how a fresh perspective on insertion and deletion can produce more efficient linked list implementations of these operations.

- create a program that displays a slide show.

- analyze the efficiency of your singly linked list implementation of the List ADT.

OVERVIEW

In Laboratory 4, you created an implementation of the List ADT using an array to store the list elements. Although this approach is intuitive, it is not terribly efficient either in terms of memory usage or time. It wastes memory by allocating an array that is large enough to store what you estimate to be the maximum number of elements a list will ever hold. In most cases, the list is rarely this large and the extra memory simply goes unused. In addition, the insertion and deletion operations require shifting elements back and forth within the array, a very time-consuming task.

In this laboratory, you implement the List ADT using a singly linked list. This implementation allocates memory element by element as elements are added to the list. Equally important, a linked list can be reconfigured following an insertion or deletion simply by changing one or two links.

List ADT

Elements

The elements in a list are of generic type Object.

Structure

The elements form a linear structure in which list elements follow one after the other, from the beginning of the list to its end. The ordering of the elements is determined by when and where each element is inserted into the list and is *not* a function of the data contained in the list elements. At any point in time, one element in any nonempty list is marked using the list's cursor. You travel through the list using operations that change the position of the cursor.

Constructors and their Helper Method

```
List ( )
```
Precondition:
None.
Postcondition:
Default Constructor. Creates an empty list.

```
List ( int size )
```
Precondition:
None.
Postcondition:
Constructor. Creates an empty list. The argument is provided for call compatibility with the array implementation, so size is ignored here.

```
void setup ( )
```
Precondition:
A helper method for the constructors. Is declared private since only linked list constructors should call this method.
Postcondition:
Creates an empty linked list.

Methods in the Interface

```
void insert ( Object newElement )
```
Precondition:
List is not full, newElement is not null.
Postcondition:
Inserts newElement into a list. If the list is not empty, then inserts newElement after the cursor. Otherwise, inserts newElement as the first (and only) element in the list. In either case, moves the cursor to newElement.

```
void remove ( )
```
Precondition:
List is not empty.
Postcondition:
Removes the element marked by the cursor from a list. If the resulting list is not empty, then moves the cursor to the element that followed the deleted element. If the deleted element was at the end of the list, then moves the cursor to the beginning of the list.

```
void replace ( Object newElement )
```
Precondition:
List is not empty and newElement is not null.
Postcondition:
Replaces the element marked by the cursor with newElement. The cursor remains at newElement.

```
void clear ( )
```
Precondition:
None.
Postcondition:
Removes all the elements in a list.

```
boolean isEmpty ( )
```
Precondition:
None.
Postcondition:
Returns true if a list is empty. Otherwise, returns false.

```
boolean isFull ( )
```
Precondition:
None.
Postcondition:
Returns true if a list is full. Otherwise, returns false.

```
boolean gotoBeginning ( )
```
Precondition:
None.
Postcondition:
If a list is not empty, then moves the cursor to the beginning of the list and returns true. Otherwise, returns false.

```
boolean gotoEnd ( )
```
Precondition:

None.

Postcondition:

If a list is not empty, then moves the cursor to the end of the list and returns true. Otherwise, returns false.

```
boolean gotoNext ( )
```
Precondition:

List is not empty.

Postcondition:

If the cursor is not at the end of a list, then moves the cursor to the next element in the list and returns true. Otherwise, returns false.

```
boolean gotoPrior ( )
```
Precondition:

List is not empty.

Postcondition:

If the cursor is not at the beginning of a list, then moves the cursor to the preceding element in the list and returns true. Otherwise, returns false.

```
Object getCursor ( )
```
Precondition:

List is not empty.

Postcondition:

Returns a copy of the element marked by the cursor.

```
void showStructure ( )
```
Precondition:

None.

Postcondition:

Outputs the elements in a list. If the list is empty, outputs "Empty list". Note that this operation is intended for testing/debugging purposes only.

LABORATORY 7: Cover Sheet

Name _____

Hour/Period/Section _____

Date _____

Place a check mark (✔) in the Assigned column next to the exercises that your instructor has assigned to you. Attach this cover sheet to the front of the packet of materials that you submit for this laboratory.

Exercise	Assigned	Completed
Prelab Exercise	✔	
Bridge Exercise	✔	
In-lab Exercise 1		
In-lab Exercise 2		
In-lab Exercise 3		
Postlab Exercise 1		
Postlab Exercise 2		
Total		

LABORATORY 7: Prelab Exercise

Name _____

Hour/Period/Section _____

Date _____

Your linked list implementation of the List ADT uses a pair of classes, SListNode and SList, to represent individual nodes and the overall list structure, respectively. If you are unfamiliar with this approach to linked lists, read the discussion in Laboratory 5: Prelab Exercise.

Step 1:   Implement the operations in the List ADT using a singly linked list. Each node in the linked list should contain a list element (element) and a reference to the node containing the next element in the list (next). Your implementation also should maintain references to the node at the beginning of the list (head) and the node containing the element marked by the cursor (cursor). Base your implementation on the following class definitions from the files *SListNode.jshl* and *SList.jshl* along with the set of methods that every list is expected to provide (which is defined in the List interface in the file *List.java*).

```
// Facilitator class for the SList class
class SListNode                             // A singly linked list node
{
    // Data members
    private Object element;                 // List element
    private SListNode next;                 // Reference to the next element

    // Constructor
    SListNode(Object elem, SListNode nextPtr)
    {                       }

    // Class Methods used by client class
    SListNode getNext( )                    // Return reference to next element
    {              }
    SListNode setNext( SListNode nextVal )
    // Set reference to next element & return that reference
    {              }
    Object getElement( )                    // Return the element in the current node
    {              }
    void setElement(Object newElem)         // Set current element to newElem
    {                    }

    } // class SListNode

  class SList implements List               // Singly linked list implementation of the
                                            //           List ADT
    {
```

```
// Data members
private SListNode head,            // Reference to the beginning of the list
                cursor;            // Reference to current cursor position

// Constructors & Helper Method
public SList( )                    // Default constructor: Creates an empty list
{                    }
public SList( int size )           // Constructor: Creates an empty list, size is
                                   //              ignored
{                    }

// Class methods
private void setup( )
// Called by constructors only: Creates an empty list
{                    }

//—- Insert method definitions for the interface List here —-//

} // class SList
```

You are to fill in the Java code for each of the constructors and methods where the implementation braces are empty, or an entire method or set of methods from the interface needs to be inserted (noted by "insert method … here").

Step 2: Save your implementation of the List ADT in the files *SListNode.java* and *SList.java*, respectively. Be sure to document your code.

LABORATORY 7: Bridge Exercise

Name

Hour/Period/Section

Date

Check with your instructor as to whether you are to complete this exercise prior to your lab period or during lab.

The test program in the file *TestSList.java* allows you to interactively test your implementation of the List ADT using the following commands.

Command	Action
+x	Insert element x after the cursor.
-	Remove the element marked by the cursor.
=x	Replace the element marked by the cursor with element x.
@	Display the element marked by the cursor.
N	Go to the next element.
P	Go to the prior element.
<	Go to the beginning of the list.
>	Go to the end of the list.
E	Report whether the list is empty.
F	Report whether the list is full.
C	Clear the list.
Q	Quit the test program.

Step 1: Complete the following test plan by adding test cases that check whether your implementation of the List ADT correctly determines whether a list is empty and correctly inserts elements into a newly emptied list.

Step 2: Compile and run the test program. Note that compiling this program will compile your linked list implementation of the List ADT (in the file *SList.java*) to produce an implementation for a list of characters.

Step 3: Execute your test plan. If you discover mistakes in your implementation of the List ADT, correct them and execute your test plan again.

Test Plan for the *Operations in the List ADT*

Test case	Commands	Expected result	Checked
Insert at end	+a +b +c +d	a b c **d**	
Travel from beginning	< N N	a b **c** d	
Travel from end	> P P	a **b** c d	
Delete middle element	–	a **c** d	
Insert in middle	+e +f +f	a c e f **f** d	
Remove last element	> –	**a** c e f f	
Remove first element	–	**c** e f f	
Display element	@	Returns c	
Replace element	=g	**g** e f f	
Clear the list	C	Empty list	

Note: The element marked by the cursor is shown in **bold**.

Step 4: Change the list in the test program (*TestSList.java*) from a list of characters to a list of integers (or any other primitive data type—except `char`) by replacing the declaration `testElement` with

```
String testElement = null;          // List element
```

replacing the assignment statement for `testElement` further down in the code with

```
testElement = aToken;
```

and in statements with the words 'new `Character`', replacing `Character` with the word `Integer`.

Every wrapper class constructor except the Character class accepts a String argument. Thus, the only change necessary to process a list of (say) doubles instead of the list of integers used in this version of the program is the third replacement above—in statements with the words 'new `Integer`', replacing `Integer` with the word `Double`. The `testElement` declaration and assignment statements would remain unchanged unless you want to process a list of characters, which is what the initial version of the program did.

Step 5: Replace the character data (`'a'` to `'g'`) in your test plan with integer values.

Step 6: Recompile and rerun the test program. Note that recompiling this program will compile your implementation of the List ADT to produce an implementation for a list of integers.

Step 7: Execute your revised test plan using the revised test program. If you discover mistakes in your implementation of the List ADT, correct them and execute your revised test plan again.

LABORATORY 7: In-lab Exercise 1

Name

Hour/Period/Section

Date

In many applications, the order of the elements in a list changes over time. Not only are new elements added and existing ones removed, but elements are repositioned within the list. The following List ADT operation moves an element to the beginning of a list.

```
void moveToBeginning ( )
```
Precondition:
List is not empty.
Postcondition:
Removes the element marked by the cursor from a list and reinserts the element at the beginning of the list. Moves the cursor to the beginning of the list.

Step 1: Implement this operation and add it to the file *SList.java*. An incomplete implementation for this operation is included in the definition of the SList class in the file *SList.jshl*.

Step 2: Activate the "M" (move) command in the test program in the file *TestSList.java* by removing the comment delimiter (and the character "M") from the lines beginning with "//M".

Step 3: Complete the following test plan by adding test cases that check whether your implementation of the moveToBeginning operation correctly processes attempts to move the first element in a list as well as moves within a single-element list.

Step 4: Execute your test plan. If you discover mistakes in your implementation of the moveToBeginning operation, correct them and execute your test plan again.

Test Plan for the *moveToBeginning Operation*

Test case	Commands	Expected result	Checked
Set up list	+a +b +c +d	a b c **d**	
Move last element	M	**d** a b c	
Move second element	N M	**a** d b c	
Move third element	N N M	**b** a d c	

Note: The element marked by the cursor is shown in **bold**.

LABORATORY 7: In-lab Exercise 2

Name _____

Hour/Period/Section _____

Date _____

Sometimes a more effective approach to a problem can be found by looking at the problem a little differently. Consider the following List ADT operation.

```
void insertBefore ( Object newElement )
```
Precondition:
List is not full.
Postcondition:
Inserts newElement into a list. If the list is not empty, then inserts newElement immediately before the cursor. Otherwise, inserts newElement as the first (and only) element in the list. In either case, moves the cursor to newElement.

You can implement this operation using a singly linked list in two very different ways. The obvious approach is to iterate through the list from its beginning until you reach the node immediately before the cursor and then to insert newElement between this node and the cursor. A more efficient approach is to copy the element referenced by the cursor into a new node, to insert this node after the cursor, and place newElement in the node pointed to by the cursor. This approach is more efficient because it does not require you to iterate through the list searching for the element immediately before the cursor.

Step 1: Implement the insertBefore operation using the second (more efficient) approach and add it to the file *SList.java*. An incomplete implementation for this operation is included in the definition of the SList class in the file *SList.jshl*.

Step 2: Activate the "#" (insert before) command in the test program in the file *TestSList.java* by removing the comment delimiter (and the character "#") from the lines beginning with "//#".

Step 3: Complete the following test plan by adding test cases that check whether your implementation of the insertBefore operation correctly handles insertions into single-element lists and empty lists.

Step 4: Execute your test plan. If you discover mistakes in your implementation of the `insertBefore` operation, correct them and execute your test plan again.

Test Plan for the *insertBefore Operation*

Test case	Commands	Expected result	Checked
Set up list	+a +b +c	a b **c**	
Insert in middle	#d	a b **d** c	
Cascade inserts	#e	a b **e** d c	
Insert after head	P #f	a **f** b e d c	
Insert as head	P #g	**g** a f b e c	

Note: The element marked by the cursor is shown in **bold**.

LABORATORY 7: In-lab Exercise 3

Name _____

Hour/Period/Section _____

Date _____

List elements need not be one of Java's built-in data types. Remember *every* class, including a programmer-defined class, is a subclass of Java's Object class. The following code fragment, for example, defines the programmer-defined class Slide. As a subclass of the Object class, a slide is another type of element that can be added to a list. Thus a slide show presentation can be represented as a list of slides.

```
class Slide
{
    // constants
    static final int SLIDE_HEIGHT = 10;            // Slide dimensions
    static final int SLIDE_WIDTH  = 36;

    // Data members
    private String [] image =                      // Slide image
        new String [SLIDE_HEIGHT];
    private long pause;                            // Seconds to pause

    public boolean read ( BufferedReader bufFinReader )
    // Read a slide from the file. Returns false at EOF.
    {                                    }
    public void display ( )                        // Display a slide and pause.
    {                                    }
}
```

Step 1: Using the program shell given in the file *SlideShow.jshl* as a basis, create a program that reads a list of slides from a file and displays the resulting slide show from beginning to end. Your program should pause for the specified length of time after displaying each slide. It then should clear the screen (by scrolling, if necessary) before displaying the next slide.

Assume that the file containing the slide show consists of repetitions of the following slide descriptor,

Time

Row 1

Row 2

...

Row 10

where Time is the length of time to pause after displaying a slide (in seconds) and Rows 1 to 10 form a slide image (each row is 35 characters long).

Note that list elements of type Slide will not cause problems with the routines in your implementation of the List ADT, with the exception of the showStructure operation. Simply choose not to call showStructure in your slide show implementation or inactivate this operation by commenting out the showStructure( ) method.

Step 2: Test your program using the slide show in the file *slides.dat*.

Test Plan for the *Slide Show Program*

Test case	Checked
Slide show in the file *slides.dat*	

LABORATORY 7: Postlab Exercise 1

Name _____

Hour/Period/Section _____

Date _____

Given a list containing N elements, develop worst-case, order-of-magnitude estimates of the execution time of the following List ADT operations, assuming they are implemented using a singly linked list. Briefly explain your reasoning behind each estimate.

insert	O( )

Explanation:

remove	O( )

Explanation:

gotoNext	O( )

Explanation:

remove	O( )

Explanation:

LABORATORY 7: Postlab Exercise 2

Name

Hour/Period/Section

Date

Part A

In-lab Exercise 2 introduces a pair of approaches for implementing an `insertBefore` operation. One approach is straightforward, whereas the other is somewhat less obvious but more efficient. Describe how you might apply the latter approach to the `remove` operation. Use a diagram to illustrate your answer.

Part B

The resulting implementation of the `remove` operation has a worst-case, order-of-magnitude performance estimate of O(N). Does this estimate accurately reflect the performance of this implementation? Explain why or why not.

Doubly Linked List Implementation of the List ADT

OBJECTIVES

In this laboratory you

- implement the List ADT using a doubly linked list.
- create an anagram puzzle program.
- reverse a linked list.
- analyze the efficiency of your doubly linked list implementation of the List ADT.

OVERVIEW

The singly linked list implementation of the List ADT (like the one created in Laboratory 7) is quite efficient when it comes to insertion and movement from one node to the next. It is not nearly so efficient, however, when it comes to deletion and movement backward through the list. In this laboratory, you will create an implementation of the List ADT using a circular, doubly linked list. This implementation performs most of the List ADT operations in constant time.

LIST ADT

Elements

The elements in a list are of generic type Object.

Structure

The elements form a linear structure in which list elements follow one after the other, from the beginning of the list to its end. The ordering of the elements is determined by when and where each element is inserted into the list and is *not* a function of the data contained in the list elements. At any point in time, one element in any nonempty list is marked using the list's cursor. You travel through the list using operations that change the position of the cursor.

Constructors and their Helper Method

`List ( )`
Precondition:
None.
Postcondition:
Default Constructor. Creates an empty list.

`List ( int size )`
Precondition:
None.
Postcondition:
Constructor. Creates an empty list. The argument is provided for call compatibility with the array implementation, so size is ignored here.

`void setup ( )`
Precondition:
A helper method for the constructors. Is declared private since only linked list constructors should call this method.
Postcondition:
Creates an empty linked list.

Methods in the Interface

`void insert ( Object newElement )`
Precondition:
List is not full, newElement is not null.
Postcondition:
Inserts newElement into a list. If the list is not empty, then inserts newElement after the cursor. Otherwise, inserts newElement as the first (and only) element in the list. In either case, moves the cursor to newElement.

`void remove ( )`
Precondition:
List is not empty.
Postcondition:
Removes the element marked by the cursor from a list. If the resulting list is not empty, then moves the cursor to the element that followed the deleted element. If the deleted element was at the end of the list, then moves the cursor to the beginning of the list.

`void replace ( Object newElement )`
Precondition:
List is not empty and newElement is not null.
Postcondition:
Replaces the element marked by the cursor with newElement. The cursor remains at newElement.

```
void clear ( )
```
Precondition:

None.

Postcondition:

Removes all the elements in a list.

```
boolean isEmpty ( )
```
Precondition:

None.

Postcondition:

Returns true if a list is empty. Otherwise, returns false.

```
boolean isFull ( )
```
Precondition:

None.

Postcondition:

Returns true if a list is full. Otherwise, returns false.

```
boolean gotoBeginning ( )
```
Precondition:

None.

Postcondition:

If a list is not empty, then moves the cursor to the beginning of the list and returns true. Otherwise, returns false.

```
boolean gotoEnd ( )
```
Precondition:

None.

Postcondition:

If a list is not empty, then moves the cursor to the end of the list and returns true. Otherwise, returns false.

```
boolean gotoNext ( )
```
Precondition:

List is not empty.

Postcondition:

If the cursor is not at the end of a list, then moves the cursor to the next element in the list and returns true. Otherwise, returns false.

```
boolean gotoPrior ( )
```
Precondition:

List is not empty.

Postcondition:

If the cursor is not at the beginning of a list, then moves the cursor to the preceding element in the list and returns true. Otherwise, returns false.

```
Object getCursor ( )
```
Precondition:

List is not empty.

Postcondition:

Returns a copy of the element marked by the cursor.

```
void showStructure ( )
```
Precondition:

None.

Postcondition:

Outputs the elements in a list. If the list is empty, outputs "Empty list". Note that this operation is intended for testing/debugging purposes only.

LABORATORY 8: Cover Sheet

Name

Hour/Period/Section

Date

Place a check mark (✔) in the Assigned column next to the exercises that your instructor has assigned to you. Attach this cover sheet to the front of the packet of materials that you submit for this laboratory.

Exercise	Assigned	Completed
Prelab Exercise	✔	
Bridge Exercise	✔	
In-lab Exercise 1		
In-lab Exercise 2		
In-lab Exercise 3		
Postlab Exercise 1		
Postlab Exercise 2		
Total		

LABORATORY 8: Prelab Exercise

Name

Hour/Period/Section

Date

Each node in a doubly linked list contains a pair of references. One reference points to the node that precedes the node (prior) and the other points to the node that follows the node (next). The resulting DListNode class is similar to the SListNode class you used in Laboratory 7.

```
// Facilitator class for the DList class
class DListNode                              // A doubly linked list node
{
    // Data members
    private Object element;                  // List element
    private DListNode prior,                 // Reference to the previous element
                      next;                  // Reference to the next element

    // Constructor
    DListNode(Object elem, DListNode priorPtr, DListNode nextPtr)
    {                      }

    // Class Methods used by client class
    DListNode getNext( )                     // Return reference to next element
    {                 }
    DListNode setNext( DListNode nextVal )
    // Set reference to next element & return that reference
    {                 }
    DListNode getPrior( )                    // Return reference to prior element
    {                 }
    DListNode setPrior( DListNode priorVal )
    // Set reference to prior element & return that reference
    {                 }
    Object getElement( )                     // Return the element in the current node
    {                 }
    void setElement(Object elem)
    // Set value of the element in the current node
    {                      }

} // class DListNode
```

In a circular, doubly linked list, the nodes at the beginning and end of the list are linked together. The next reference of the node at the end of the list points to the node at the beginning, and the prior reference of the node at the beginning points to the node at the end. Using a circular, doubly linked list simplifies the implementation. The next, prior, head, or cursor references are null only when the list is empty and there is no extra tail reference to keep track of when inserting or removing elements.

Step 1: Implement the methods in the List ADT using a circular, doubly linked list. Base your implementation on the incomplete class definition in the file *DList.jshl* and the interface for the List ADT in the file *List.java*. You are to fill in the Java code for each of the constructors and methods where the implementation braces are empty, or where an entire method or set of methods from the interface needs to be inserted (noted by "insert method ... here").

Step 2: Save your implementation of the List ADT in the file *DList.java*. Be sure to document your code.

LABORATORY 8: Bridge Exercise

Name

Hour/Period/Section

Date

Check with your instructor as to whether you are to complete this exercise prior to your lab period or during lab.

The test program is in the file *TestDList.java*. Please note that, as in some previous laboratory exercises, eventually there will be several methods in this laboratory that are defined in the class DList (and later DList2) that are not declared in the List interface. To compensate for this discrepancy, in this case the test variable (testList) has been instantiated as a DList instead of the more generic type List. The test program (*TestDList.java*) allows you to interactively test your implementation of the List ADT using the following commands.

Command	Action
+x	Insert element x after the cursor.
-	Remove the element marked by the cursor.
=x	Replace the element marked by the cursor with element x.
@	Display the element marked by the cursor.
N	Go to the next element.
P	Go to the prior element.
<	Go to the beginning of the list.
>	Go to the end of the list.
E	Report whether the list is empty.
F	Report whether the list is full.
C	Clear the list.
Q	Quit the test program.

Step 1: Prepare a test plan for your implementation of the List ADT. Your test plan should cover the application of each operation to elements at the beginning, middle, and end of lists (where appropriate). A test plan form follows.

Step 2: Execute your test plan. If you discover mistakes in your implementation of the List ADT, correct them and execute your test plan again.

Test Plan for the *Operations in the List ADT*

Test case	Commands	Expected result	Checked

LABORATORY 8: In-lab Exercise 1

Name _____

Hour/Period/Section _____

Date _____

A list can be reversed in two ways: either you can relink the nodes in the list into a new (reversed) order, or you can leave the node structure intact and exchange elements between pairs of nodes. Use one of these strategies to implement the following List ADT operation.

```
void reverse ( )
```
Precondition:
None.
Postcondition:
Reverses the order of the elements in a list.

Step 1: Implement this operation and add it to the file *DList.java*. An incomplete implementation for this operation is included in the definition of the DList class in the file *DList.jshl*.

Step 2: Activate the "R" (reverse) command in the test program in the file *TestDList.java* by removing the comment delimiter (and the character "R") from the lines that begin with "//R".

Step 3: Prepare a test plan for the reverse operation that covers lists of various lengths, including lists containing a single element. A test plan form follows.

Step 4: Execute your test plan. If you discover mistakes in your implementation of the reverse operation, correct them and execute your test plan again.

Test Plan for the *reverse Operation*

Test case	Commands	Expected result	Checked

LABORATORY 8: In-lab Exercise 2

Name

Hour/Period/Section

Date

In many list applications, you need to know the number of elements in a list and the relative position of the cursor. Rather than computing these attributes each time they are requested, you can store this information in a pair of data members that you update whenever you insert elements, remove elements, or move the cursor.

Step 1: Add the following data members (both are of type `int`) to the DList class definition in the file *DList.java*. Rename the class DList2 and save the result in the file *DList2.java*.

`size :` The number of elements in a list.

`pos :` The numeric position of the cursor, where the list elements are numbered from beginning to end, starting with 0.

Step 2: Modify the methods in your circular, doubly linked list implementation of the DList2 ADT so that they update these data members whenever necessary. Save your modified implementation in the file *DList2.java*.

Step 3: If you are to reference the `size` and `pos` data members within application programs, you must have DList2 ADT operations that return these values. Add the following operations to the DList2 class definition in the file *DList2.java*.

```
int length ( )
```
Precondition:
None.
Postcondition:
Returns the number of elements in a list.

```
int position ( )
```
Precondition:
List is not empty.
Postcondition:
Returns the position of the cursor, where the list elements are numbered from beginning to end, starting with 0.

Step 4: Implement these operations in the file *DList2.java*.

Step 5: Modify the test program in the file *TestDList.java* so that the routines that incorporate your changes (in *DList2.java*) are used in place of those you created in the Prelab. Save the file as *TestDList2.java*.

Step 6: Activate the "#" (length and position) command by removing the comment delimiter (and the character "#") from the lines that begin with "//#".

Step 7: Prepare a test plan for these operations that checks the length of various lists (including the empty list) and the numeric position of elements at the beginning, middle, and end of lists. A test plan form follows.

Step 8: Execute your test plan. If you discover mistakes in your implementation of these operations, correct them and execute your test plan again.

Test Plan for the *length and position Operations*

Test case	Commands	Expected result	Checked

LABORATORY 8: In-lab Exercise 3

Name _____

Hour/Period/Section _____

Date _____

Lists can be used as data members in other classes. In this exercise, you create an implementation of the Anagram Puzzle ADT described below using lists of characters to store both the solution to the puzzle and the current puzzle configuration.

Anagram Puzzle ADT

Elements

Alphabetic characters.

Structure

The characters are arranged linearly. If rearranged properly they spell a specified English word.

Constructor and Methods

```
AnagramPuzzle ( String answ, String init )
```
Precondition:
Strings answ and init are nonempty and contain the same letters (but in a different order).
Postcondition:
Constructor. Creates an anagram puzzle. String answ is the solution to the puzzle and string init is the initial scrambled letter sequence. *Hint:* Use String.charAt(int j) to insert a new Character into the DList. A variation of what was done in the call to insert in *TestDList.java*.

```
void shiftLeft ( )
```
Precondition:
None.
Postcondition:
Shifts the letters in a puzzle left one position. The leftmost letter is moved to the right end of the puzzle.

```
void swapEnds ( )
```
Precondition:

None.

Postcondition:

Swaps the letters at the left and right ends of a puzzle.

```
void display ( )
```
Precondition:

None.

Postcondition:

Displays an anagram puzzle. Shows both the puzzle's target word (goal or solution) and the current state of its scrambled word (puzzle).

```
boolean solved ( )
```
Precondition:

None.

Postcondition:

Returns true if a puzzle is solved. Otherwise returns false.

The code fragment below declares a puzzle in which the word "yes" is scrambled as "yse". It then shows how the puzzle is unscrambled to form "yes".

```
String str1 = new String("yes");
String str2 = new String("yse");

AnagramPuzzle enigma = new AnagramPuzzle(str1, str2); // Word is "yes", start w/ "yse"
enigma.shiftLeft( );                                  // Changes puzzle to "sey"
enigma.swapEnds( );                                   // Changes puzzle to "yes"
```

Rather than having the solution to the puzzle encoded in the program, your puzzle program allows the user to solve the puzzle by entering commands from the keyboard.

Step 1: Complete the anagram puzzle program shell given in the file *AnagramPuzzle.jshl* by creating an implementation of the Anagram Puzzle ADT. Base your implementation on the following incomplete class definition.

```
class AnagramPuzzle
{
    // Data members
    private DList solution,          // Solution to puzzle
                 puzzle;             // Current puzzle configuration

    // Constructor
    public AnagramPuzzle( String answ, String init)  // Construct puzzle
    {                        }
```

```
// Class methods
public void shiftLeft( )                    // Shift letter left
{                    }
public void swapEnds( )                     // Swap end letters
{                    }
public void display( )                      // Display puzzle
{                    }
public boolean solved( )                    // Puzzle solved?
{                    }

} // class AnagramPuzzle
```

Use your circular, doubly linked list implementation of the List ADT to represent the lists of characters storing the puzzle's solution (solution) and its current configuration (puzzle).

Step 2: Test your anagram puzzle program by compiling the file *TestAnagramPuzzle.java* and using the puzzles given in the following test plan.

Test Plan for the *Anagram Puzzle Program*

Test case	Checked
Puzzle word "yes" scrambled as "yse"	
Puzzle word "right" scrambled as "irtgh"	

LABORATORY 8: Postlab Exercise 1

Name _____

Hour/Period/Section _____

Date _____

Part A

Given a list containing N elements, develop worst-case, order-of-magnitude estimates of the execution time of the following List ADT operations, assuming they are implemented using a circular, doubly linked list. Briefly explain your reasoning behind each estimate.

insert	O( )

Explanation:

remove	O( )

Explanation:

gotoPrior	O( )

Explanation:

remove	O( )

Explanation:

Part B

Would these estimates be the same for an implementation of the DList ADT based on a noncircular, doubly linked list? Explain why or why not.

LABORATORY 8: Postlab Exercise 2

Name _____

Hour/Period/Section _____

Date _____

Assume the following memory requirements

Character	2 bytes
Integer	4 bytes
Address (reference)	4 bytes

Part A

Given a list containing N integers, compare the amount of memory used by your singly linked list representation of the list with the amount of memory used by your circular, doubly linked list representation.

Part B

Suppose the list contains N objects of class Slide whose data members are as follows:

```
class Slide
{
    // Data members
    private char image [slideHeight] [slideWidth];  // Slide image
    private int pause;                              // Seconds to pause

    // Class Constructor & Methods
    ...

} // class Slide
```

Compare the amount of memory used by your singly linked list representation of this list with the amount of memory used by your circular, doubly linked representation.

Ordered List
ADT

OBJECTIVES

In this laboratory you

- implement the Ordered List ADT using an array to store the list elements and a binary search to locate elements.

- use inheritance to derive a new class from an existing one.

- create a program that reassembles a message that has been divided into packets.

- use ordered lists to create efficient merge and subset operations.

- analyze the efficiency of your implementation of the Ordered List ADT.

OVERVIEW

In an **ordered list** the elements are maintained in ascending (or descending) order based on the data contained in the list elements. Typically, the contents of one field are used to determine the ordering. This field is referred to as the **key field**, or the **key**. In this laboratory, we assume that each element in an ordered list has a key that uniquely identifies the element—that is, no two elements in any ordered list have the same key. As a result, you can use an element's key to efficiently retrieve the element from a list.

Ordered List ADT

The Ordered List ADT inherits from an array-based List ADT similar to the one created in Laboratory 4. Therefore, the Ordered List ADT is a specialized version of the array-based List ADT. It inherits all of the public and protected instance variables and methods defined by the array-based List ADT and adds its own unique instance variables and methods as needed.

Elements

The elements in an ordered list are of generic type ListData. Each element has a key that uniquely identifies the element. Elements usually include additional data. Objects in the ordered list must support the six basic relational operators, as well as a method called key() that returns an element's key.

Structure

The list elements are stored in ascending order based on their keys. For each list element E, the element that precedes E has a key that is less than E's key and the element that follows E has a key that is greater than E's key. At any point in time, one element in any nonempty list is marked using the list's cursor. You travel through the list using operations that change the position of the cursor.

Constructors

```
OrdList ( )
```
Precondition:
None.
Postcondition:
Default Constructor. Calls the default constructor of its superclass, which creates an empty list. Allocates enough memory for a list containing DEF_MAX_LIST_SIZE (a constant value) elements.

```
OrdList ( int maxNumber )
```
Precondition:
None.
Postcondition:
Constructor. Calls the corresponding superclass constructor, which creates an empty list. Allocates enough memory for a list containing maxNumber elements.

Methods (Many Override Methods in the Superclass)

```
void insert ( ListData newElement )
```
Precondition:
List is not full.
Postcondition:
Inserts newElement in its appropriate position within a list. If an element with the same key as newElement already exists in the list, then updates that element's nonkey fields with newElement's nonkey fields. Moves the cursor to newElement.

```
ListData retrieve ( int searchKey )
```
Precondition:
None.
Postcondition:
Searches a list for the element with key searchKey. If the element is found, then moves the cursor to the element and returns its value. Otherwise, does not move the cursor and returns null to indicate that searchElement is undefined.

```
void remove ( )
```
Precondition:
List is not empty.
Postcondition:
Removes the element marked by the cursor from a list. If the resulting list is not empty, then moves the cursor to the element that followed the deleted element. If the deleted element was at the end of the list, then moves the cursor to the beginning of the list.

```
void replace ( ListData newElement )
```
Precondition:
List is not empty.
Postcondition:
Replaces the element marked by the cursor with newElement. Note that this entails removing the element and inserting newElement in its correct ordered-list position. Moves the cursor to newElement.

```
void clear ( )
```
Precondition:
None.
Postcondition:
Removes all the elements in a list.

```
boolean isEmpty ( )
```
Precondition:
None.
Postcondition:
Returns true if a list is empty. Otherwise, returns false.

```
boolean isFull ( )
```
Precondition:
None.
Postcondition:
Returns true if a list is full. Otherwise, returns false.

```
boolean gotoBeginning ( )
```
Precondition:
None.
Postcondition:
If a list is not empty, then moves the cursor to the element at the beginning of the list and returns true. Otherwise, returns false.

```
boolean gotoEnd ( )
```
Precondition:

None.

Postcondition:

If a list is not empty, then moves the cursor to the element at the end of the list and returns true. Otherwise, returns false.

```
boolean gotoNext ( )
```
Precondition:

List is not empty.

Postcondition:

If the cursor is not at the end of a list, then moves the cursor to the next element in the list and returns true. Otherwise, returns false.

```
boolean gotoPrior ( )
```
Precondition:

List is not empty.

Postcondition:

If the cursor is not at the beginning of a list, then moves the cursor to the preceding element in the list and returns true. Otherwise, returns false.

```
Object getCursor ( )
```
Precondition:

List is not empty.

Postcondition:

Returns a copy of the element marked by the cursor.

```
void showStructure ( )
```
Precondition:

None.

Postcondition:

Outputs the keys of the elements in a list. If the list is empty, outputs "Empty list". Note that this operation is intended for testing/debugging purposes only. It only supports keys that are one of Java's primitive data types (int, char, and so forth).

LABORATORY 9: Cover Sheet

Name _____

Hour/Period/Section _____

Date _____

Place a check mark (✔) in the Assigned column next to the exercises that your instructor has assigned to you. Attach this cover sheet to the front of the packet of materials that you submit for this laboratory.

Exercise	Assigned	Completed
Prelab Exercise	✔	
Bridge Exercise	✔	
In-lab Exercise 1		
In-lab Exercise 2		
In-lab Exercise 3		
Postlab Exercise 1		
Postlab Exercise 2		
Total		

LABORATORY 9: Prelab Exercise

Name _____

Hour/Period/Section _____

Date _____

There is a great deal of similarity between the Ordered List ADT and the List ADT. In fact, with the exception of the insert, retrieve, and replace operations, these ADTs are identical. Rather than implementing the Ordered List ADT from the ground up, you can take advantage of these similarities by using your array implementation of the List ADT from Laboratory 4 as a foundation for an array implementation of the Ordered List ADT.

A key feature of Java is the ability to derive a new class from an existing one through **inheritance**. The **derived class** (or **subclass**) inherits the public and protected methods and data members of the existing **base class** (or **superclass**) and can have its own methods and data members, as well. The following incomplete definitions from the file *OrdList.jshl* derives a class called OrdList from the ListArray class.

```
class OrdList extends ListArray
{
    // Constructors
    public OrdList( )
    public OrdList( int maxNumber )

    // Modified (or new) list manipulation methods
    public void insert ( ListData newElement )
    public ListData retrieve ( int searchKey )
    public void replace ( ListData newElement )

    // Output the list structure -- used in testing/debugging
    public void showStructure ( )

    // Facilitator method
    // Locates an element (or where it should be) based on its key
    private boolean binarySearch ( int searchKey, int index )

} // class OrdList
```

The declaration

```
class OrdList extends ListArray
```

indicates that OrdList is derived from ListArray.

You want the member methods in OrdList—the `insert()` method, in particular—to be able to refer to ListArray's private data members, so you must change the data members in the ListArray class definition (in Laboratory 4) from private to protected, as follows.

```
class ListArray implements List
{
    // Constants
    // Default maximum list size
    static final int DEF_MAX_LIST_SIZE = 10;

    // Data Members
    protected int size,              // Actual number of elements in the list
                 cursor;             // Cursor array index
    protected Object [] element;     // Array containing the list elements

    ...

}
```

Private ListArray data members can only be accessed by ListArray methods. Protected ListArray data members, on the other hand, can be accessed by the methods in any class that is derived from ListArray—OrdList, in this case.

Through inheritance an OrdList object can call any of the ListArray's public and protected methods, as well as any of its own methods. The OrdList class supplies its own constructor, as well as a pair of new methods: a public member method `retrieve()` that retrieves an element based on its key and a private member facilitator method `binarySearch()` that locates an element in the array using a binary search. The OrdList class also includes its own versions of the `insert()` and `replace()` public methods. In Java, when a method in a subclass has the same name and type signature as a method in the superclass, then the method in the subclass is said to **override** the method in the superclass. When an overridden method is called from inside a subclass, it will always refer to the version of the method defined by the subclass. The version of the method defined by the superclass will be hidden but can be called by prefixing the method name with the keyword `super` followed by the dot operator. For example, the following statement

```
super.insert(newElement);
```

written in a method inside of the OrdList class definitions indicates that you wish to call `insert()` in the ListArray superclass from within the subclass OrdList. As illustrated above, using the word `super` is the way to refer to OrdList's immediate superclass.

An incomplete class definition for the ListArray class containing the changes specified above is given in the file *ListArray.jshl*. The interface for the List class is provided in the file *List.java*.

The following programs for the class ListData and the class TestAccount reads in the account number and balance for a set of accounts and, using the OrdList object `accounts`, outputs the list of accounts in ascending order based on their account numbers. As you review this code, pay special attention to the Java statements that are used to read in values for `acctNum` and `balance` input from the keyboard. Once the account information is correctly read and inserted into the OrdList (`accounts`), printing the list of accounts in ascending order is trivial.

```
class ListData
{
    // Data Members
    public int acctNum;                    // (Key) Account number
    public double balance;                 // Account balance

    // Methods
    public int key ( )
    { return acctNum; }                    // Returns the key

} // class ListData

// ------------------------------------------------------------------------
import java.io.*;

class TestAccount
{

    public static void main(String args[]) throws IOException
    {

        OrdList accounts = new OrdList();    // List of accounts
        ListData acct;                       // A single account
        String str;                          // Line read from msg file

        // Initialize reader and tokenizer for the input stream -
        //    for reading 'tokens' (namely acctNum and balance)
        //    input from the keyboard.
        //
        // Initialize reader - To read a character at a time
        BufferedReader reader =
            new BufferedReader(new InputStreamReader(System.in));

        // Initialize the tokenizer - To read tokens
        StreamTokenizer tokens = new StreamTokenizer(reader);

        // Note: use the nextToken( ) method to step through a stream of tokens.
        //    Use nval with the tokenizer to obtain the number read.
        //    Since nval is of type double, cast it to an int for acctNum.

        // Read in information on set of accounts.
        System.out.println( );
        System.out.println("Enter account information (acctNum balance) " +
                        "-- end with EOF : ");

        // Keep reading as long as a string (the word EOF) has not been entered
        while ( tokens.nextToken( ) != tokens.TT_WORD )
        {
            acct = new ListData( );
            acct.acctNum = (int)tokens.nval;
            tokens.nextToken( );
            acct.balance = tokens.nval;
            accounts.insert(acct);
        }
```

```
// Output the accounts in ascending order based on their account
// numbers.
System.out.println( );
if ( accounts.gotoBeginning( ) )
    do
    {
        acct = (ListData)accounts.getCursor( );
        System.out.println( acct.acctNum + " " + acct.balance);
    }
        while ( accounts.gotoNext( ) );
}

} // class TestAccount
```

The ListData class includes a `key()` method that returns an account's key field—its account number. This method is used by the OrdList class to order the accounts as they are inserted. Insertion is done using the OrdList class `insert()` method, but list traversal is done using the inherited ListArray class `gotoBeginning()` and `gotoNext()` methods.

Step 1: Implement the operations in the Ordered List ADT and the revised array-based List ADT. Base your implementation on the incomplete class definitions from the files *OrdList.jshl* and *ListArray.jshl*. The interface for the List class is provided in the file *List.java*.

Note that you only need to create implementations of the constructors, `insert`, `replace`, and `retrieve` operations for the Ordered List ADT; the remainder of the operations are inherited from your array implementation of the ListArray ADT. Your implementations of the `insert` and `retrieve` operations should use the `binarySearch()` method to locate an element. An implementation of the binary search algorithm and the `showStructure` operation is given in the file *OrdList.jshl*.

If you did not complete Laboratory 4 earlier, then implement each method in the ListArray class according to the method comments given in *ListArray.jshl* along with the descriptions given in this laboratory for the Ordered List ADT methods that are not overridden by the OrdList class. Descriptions for all the OrdList class methods (inherited, overridden, and those unique to OrdList) are given at the beginning of this laboratory.

Step 2: Save your implementation of the Ordered List ADT and the array-based List ADT in the files *OrdList.java* and *ListArray.java*, respectively. Be sure to document your code.

LABORATORY 9: Bridge Exercise

Name

Hour/Period/Section

Date

Check with your instructor as to whether you are to complete this exercise prior to your lab period or during lab.

The test program in the file *TestOrdList.java* allows you to interactively test your implementation of the Ordered List ADT using the following commands.

Command	Action
+key	Insert (or update) the element with the specified key.
?key	Retrieve the element with the specified key and output it.
-	Remove the element marked by the cursor.
@	Display the element marked by the cursor.
=key	Replace the element marked by the cursor.
N	Go to the next element.
P	Go to the prior element.
<	Go to the beginning of the list.
>	Go to the end of the list.
E	Report whether the list is empty.
F	Report whether the list is full.
C	Clear the list.
Q	Quit the test program.

Step 1: Prepare a test plan for your implementation of the Ordered List ADT. Your test plan should cover the application of each operation to elements at the beginning, middle, and end of lists (where appropriate). A test plan form follows.

Step 2: Execute your test plan. If you discover mistakes in your implementation, correct them and execute your test plan again.

Test Plan for the *Operations in the Ordered List ADT*

Test case	Commands	Expected result	Checked

Laboratory 9: In-lab Exercise 1

Name

Hour/Period/Section

Date

Suppose you wish to combine the elements in two ordered lists into one ordered list of a fixed size. You could use repeated calls to the insert operation to insert the elements from one list into the other. However, the resulting process would not be very efficient. A more effective approach is to use a specialized **merge** operation that takes advantage of the fact that the lists are ordered.

```
void merge ( OrdList fromL )
```
Precondition:
The merged elements must fit within the receiving list.
Postcondition:
A single pass merges the elements in fromL with the elements in another ordered list. Does not change fromL. Moves cursor in merged list to the beginning of the list. The final merged list contains no duplicate keys, even if the initial lists had keys in common. When there are duplicate keys, a costly second pass through the merged list is required.

Even before you begin to merge the lists, you already know how much larger the merged list might become. By traversing the lists in parallel, starting with their highest keys and working backward, you can perform the merge in a single pass. Given two ordered lists `alpha` and `beta` containing the keys

```
alpha : a d j t
beta  : b e w
```

the call

```
alpha.merge(beta);
```

produces the following results.

```
alpha : a b d e j t w
beta  : b e w
```

Or when there are common keys in the two lists such as

```
alpha : a d e t
beta  : b e w
```

the call to merge produces the following results.

```
alpha : a b d e t w
beta  : b e w
```

Step 1: Implement this operation and add it to the file *OrdList.java*. An incomplete definition for this operation is included in the definition of the Ordered List class in the file *OrdList.jshl*.

Step 2: Activate the implementation of ListData for In-lab 1 and 2 (in the file *ListData.java*) by removing the comment markings (/* and */) from that definition for the class ListData and by commenting out any other active definition for the class ListData. Only one definition of the ListData class can be active when you run your program.

Activate the "M" (merge) command in the test program in the file *TestOrdList2.java* by removing the comment delimiter (and the character "M") from the lines that begin with "//M".

Step 3: Prepare a test plan for the merge operation that covers lists of various lengths, including empty lists and lists that combine to produce a full list. A test plan form follows.

Step 4: Execute your test plan. If you discover mistakes in your implementation of the merge operation, correct them and execute your test plan again.

Test Plan for the *merge Operation*

Test case	Commands	Expected result	Checked

LABORATORY 9: In-lab Exercise 2

Name _____

Hour/Period/Section _____

Date _____

A set of objects can be represented in many ways. If you use an *unordered* list to represent a set, then performing set operations such as intersection, union, difference, and subset require up to $O(N^2)$ time. By using an ordered list to represent a set, however, you can reduce the execution time for these set operations to $O(N)$, a substantial improvement.

Consider the subset operation described below. If the sets are stored as unordered lists, this operation requires that you traverse the list once for *each* element in subL. But if the sets are stored as ordered lists, only a single traversal is required. The key is to move through the lists in parallel.

```
boolean subset ( OrdList subL )
```
Precondition:
None.
Postcondition:
Uses only a single traversal through the lists and does not change either list including the cursor locations. Returns true if every key in subL is also in the calling list. Otherwise, returns false.

Given three ordered lists `alpha`, `beta`, and `gamma` containing the keys

```
alpha : a b c d
beta  : a c x
gamma : a b
delta : <empty list>
```

the call `alpha.subset(beta)` yields false (`beta` is not a subset of `alpha`), the call `alpha.subset(gamma)` yields true (`gamma` is a subset of `alpha`), and the calls `alpha.subset(delta)` and `beta.subset(delta)` yield true (the empty set is a subset of every set).

Step 1: Implement this operation and add it to the file *OrdList.java*. An incomplete definition for this operation is included in the file *OrdList.jshl*. Uncomment this segment of the Ordered List class definition before implementing it.

Step 2: Activate the "s" (subset) command in the test program in the file *TestOrdList2.java* by removing the comment delimiter (and the character "s") from the lines that begin with "//s".

Step 3: Prepare a test plan for the subset operation that covers lists of various lengths, including empty lists. A test plan form follows.

Step 4: Execute your test plan. If you discover mistakes in your implementation of the subset operation, correct them and execute your test plan again.

Test Plan for the *subset Operation*

Test case	Commands	Expected result	Checked

LABORATORY 9: In-lab Exercise 3

Name

Hour/Period/Section

Date

When a communications site transmits a message through a packet-switching network, it does not send the message as a continuous stream of data. Instead, it divides the message into pieces, called **packets**. These packets are sent through the network to a receiving site, which reassembles the message. Packets may be transmitted to the receiving site along different paths. As a result, they are likely to arrive out of sequence. In order for the receiving site to reassemble the message correctly, each packet must include the relative position of the packet within the message.

For example, if we break the message "A SHORT MESSAGE" into packets five characters long and preface each packet with a number denoting the packet's position in the message, the result is the following set of packets.

```
1 A SHO
2 RT ME
3 SSAGE
```

No matter what order these packets arrive, a receiving site can correctly reassemble the message by placing the packets in ascending order based on their position numbers.

Step 1: Using the file *TestPacket.jshl,* create a program that reassembles the packets contained in a text file and outputs the corresponding message. Your program should use the Ordered List ADT to assist in reassembling the packets in a message. Assume that each packet in the message file contains a position number and five characters from the message (like the packet format shown above). Base your program on the following ListData class definition for each packet available in the file *ListData.java.* Since this file contains various implementations/ definitions for the list element, you will need to comment out other portions of this file and subsequently remove the comment markings (/* and */) from the portion of this file that matches the ListData definition shown below.

```java
class ListData
{
    // Constants
    // Number of characters in a packet
    public static final int PACKET_SIZE = 5;

    // Data Members
    int position;                            // (Key) Packet's position w/in message
    char [] body = new char[PACKET_SIZE];    // Characters in the packet
```

```
        // Methods
        int key ( )
        { return position; }                    // Returns the key field

    } // class ListData
```

Step 2: Test your program using the message in the text file *message.dat*.

Test Plan for the *Message Processing Program*

Test case	Checked
Message in the file *message.dat*	

LABORATORY 9: Postlab Exercise 1

Name

Hour/Period/Section

Date

Part A

Given an ordered list containing N elements, develop worst-case, order-of-magnitude estimates of the execution time of the steps in the insert operation, assuming this operation is implemented using an array in conjunction with a binary search. Briefly explain your reasoning behind each estimate.

Array Implementation of the *insert Operation*

Find the insertion point	O( )
Insert the element	O( )
Entire operation	O( )

Explanation:

Part B

Suppose you had implemented the Ordered List ADT using a singly linked list, rather than an array. Given an ordered list containing N elements, develop worst-case, order-of-magnitude estimates of the execution time of the steps in the insert operation. Briefly explain your reasoning behind each estimate.

Linked List Implementation of the *insert Operation*

Find the insertion point	O(	)
Insert the element	O(	)
Entire operation	O(	)

Explanation:

LABORATORY 9: Postlab Exercise 2

Name

Hour/Period/Section

Date

In specifying the Ordered List ADT, we assumed that no two elements in an ordered list have the same key. What changes would you have to make to your implementation of the Ordered List ADT in order to support ordered lists in which multiple elements have the same key?

Recursion with Linked Lists

OBJECTIVES

In this laboratory you

- examine how recursion can be used to traverse a linked list in either direction.

- use recursion to insert, delete, and move elements in a linked list.

- convert recursive routines to iterative form.

- analyze why a stack is sometimes needed when converting from recursive to iterative form.

OVERVIEW

Recursive methods—methods that call themselves—provide an elegant way of describing and implementing the solutions to a wide range of problems, including problems in mathematics, computer graphics, compiler design, and artificial intelligence. Let's begin by examining how you develop a recursive method definition using the factorial calculation as an example.

You can express the factorial of a positive integer n using the following iterative formula:

$$n! = n \bullet (n-1) \bullet (n-2) \bullet \cdots \bullet 1$$

Applying this formula to 4! yields the product $4 \cdot 3 \cdot 2 \cdot 1$. If you regroup the terms in this product as $4 \cdot (3 \cdot 2 \cdot 1)$ and note that $3! = 3 \cdot 2 \cdot 1$, then you find that 4! can be written as $4 \cdot (3!)$. You can generalize this reasoning to form the following recursive definition of factorial:

$$n! = n \cdot (n-1)!$$

where 0! is defined to be 1. Applying this definition to the evaluation of 4! yields the following sequence of computations.

$$
\begin{aligned}
4! &= 4 \cdot (3!) \\
&= 4 \cdot (3 \cdot (2!)) \\
&= 4 \cdot (3 \cdot (2 \cdot (1!))) \\
&= 4 \cdot (3 \cdot (2 \cdot (1 \cdot (0!)))) \\
&= 4 \cdot (3 \cdot (2 \cdot (1 \cdot (1))))
\end{aligned}
$$

The first four steps in this computation are recursive, with $n!$ being evaluated in terms of $(n - 1)!$. The final step ($0! = 1$) is not recursive, however. The following notation clearly distinguishes between the **recursive step** and the nonrecursive step (or **base case**) in the definition of $n!$.

$$n! = \begin{cases} 1 & \text{if } n = 0 \text{ (base case)} \\ n \cdot (n-1)! & \text{if } n > 0 \text{ (recursive step)} \end{cases}$$

The `factorial()` method below uses recursion to compute the factorial of a number.

```
long factorial ( int n )
// Computes n! using recursion.
{
    long result;                        // Result returned

    if ( n == 0 )
        result = 1;                     // Base case
    else
        result = n * factorial(n-1);    // Recursive step
    return result;
}
```

Let's look at the call `factorial(4)`. Because 4 is not equal to 0 (the condition for the base case), the `factorial()` method issues the recursive call `factorial(3)`. The recursive calls continue until the base case is reached—that is, until n equals 0.

```
factorial(4)
    ↓ recursive step
  4*factorial(3)
        ↓ recursive step
      3*factorial(2)
            ↓ recursive step
          2*factorial(1)
                ↓ recursive step
              1*factorial(0)
                    ↓ base case
                  1
```

The calls to `factorial()` are evaluated in the reverse of the order they are made. The evaluation process continues until the value 24 is returned by the call `factorial(4)`.

```
factorial(4)
      ↑ returns 24
   4*factorial(3)
         ↑ returns 6
      3*factorial(2)
            ↑ returns 2
         2*factorial(1)
               ↑ returns 1
            1*factorial(0)
                  ↑ returns 1
               1
```

Recursion can be used for more than numerical calculations, however. The following pair of methods traverse a linked list, outputting the elements encountered along the way.

```
void write ( )
// Outputs the elements in a list from beginning to end.
{
      System.out.print("List : ");
      writeSub(head);
      System.out.println( );
}


// - - - - - - - - - - - - - - - - - - - - - - - - - - - - - - - - - - - - -

void writeSub ( SListNode p )
// Recursive partner of the write( ) method. Processes the sublist
// that begins with the node referenced by p.
{
      if ( p != null )
      {
          System.out.print(p.getElement( ));   // Output element
          writeSub(p.getNext( ));               // Continue with next node
      }
}
```

The role of the `write()` method is to initiate the recursive process, which is then carried forward by its recursive partner, the `writeSub()` method. Calling `write()` with the linked list of characters

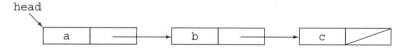

yields the following sequence of calls and outputs "abc".

```
writeSub(head)
        ↓ recursive step
    Output 'a'    writeSub(p.getNext( ))
                      ↓ recursive step
                  Output 'b'    writeSub(p.getNext( ))
                                    ↓ recursive step
                                Output 'c'    writeSub(p.getNext( ))
                                                  ↓ base case
                                              No output
```

Recursion can also be used to add nodes to a linked list. The following pair of methods insert an element at the end of a list.

```
void insertEnd ( Object newElement )
// Inserts newElement at the end of a list. Moves the cursor to
// newElement.
{
    if ( isEmpty( ) )
    {
        head = new SListNode(newElement, null);   // Only node in list
        cursor = head;                            // Move cursor
    }
    else
        insertEndSub(head, newElement);
}

// - - - - - - - - - - - - - - - - - - - - - - - - - - - - - - - - - -

void insertEndSub ( SListNode p, Object newElement )
// Recursive partner of the insertEnd( ) method. Processes the
// sublist that begins with the node referenced by p.getNext( ).
{
    if ( p.getNext( ) != null )
        // Continue searching for end of list
        insertEndSub(p.getNext( ), newElement);
    else
    {
        p.setNext(new SListNode(newElement, null)); // Insert new node
        cursor = p.getNext( );                       // Move cursor
    }
}
```

The `insertEnd()` method initiates the insertion process, with the bulk of the work being done by its recursive partner, the `insertEndSub()` method. Calling `insertEnd()` to insert the character '!' at the end of the following list of characters

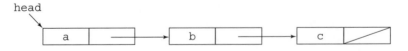

yields the following sequence of calls.

```
insertEndSub(head)
        ↓ recursive step
insertEndSub(p.getNext( ))
        ↓ recursive step
insertEndSub(p.getNext( ))
        ↓ recursive step
insertEndSub(p.getNext( ))
            ↓ base case
```
Create a new node containing '!'

On the last call, `p.getNext( )` is null and the statement

```
p.setNext(new SListNode(newElement, null)); // Insert new node
```

is executed to create a new node containing the character '!'. This assignment sets the `next` reference in the last node in the list ('c') to the new node, thereby producing the list shown below.

Calling `insertEnd()` to insert the character '!' into an empty list results in no call to the `insertEndSub()` method. In this case, `insertEnd()` immediately assigns the address of the newly created node to the list's `head` reference.

LABORATORY 10: Cover Sheet

Name _____

Hour/Period/Section _____

Date _____

Place a check mark (✔) in the Assigned column next to the exercises that your instructor has assigned to you. Attach this cover sheet to the front of the packet of materials that you submit for this laboratory.

Exercise	Assigned	Completed
Prelab Exercise	✔	
Bridge Exercise	✔	
In-lab Exercise 1		
In-lab Exercise 2		
In-lab Exercise 3		
Postlab Exercise 1		
Postlab Exercise 2		
Total		

LABORATORY 10: Prelab Exercise

Name _____

Hour/Period/Section _____

Date _____

In this laboratory you will reuse several files from previous laboratories. You can use Java's import statement to access these files by providing the path to the location of those files but it is probably simpler (especially in the case of the *SList.java* file) to copy each of these files into the package (or subdirectory) for this laboratory. Required files from previous laboratories are:

- *Stack.java* (Laboratory 5)
- *AStack.java* (Laboratory 5)
- *List.java* (Laboratory 7)
- *SListNode.java* (Laboratory 7)
- *SList.java* (Laboratory 7)

We begin by examining a set of recursive methods that perform known tasks. Incomplete implementations of these methods are collected in the file *ListRec.jshl*. The test program for these methods is in the file *Test10.java*.

Part A

Step 1: Revise the singly linked list implementation of the List ADT in the file *SList.java* copied from Laboratory 7 so that the ListRec class for this laboratory can inherit from and use the data members of the SList class. (A similar revision was made to the ListArray class when you implemented the Ordered List ADT in Laboratory 9.)

Step 2: Complete part of the List ADT in the file *ListRec.jshl* by implementing the incomplete methods `write()`, `writeSub()`, `insertEnd()`, and `insertEndSub()` discussed in the Overview section of this laboratory. Incomplete implementations for these methods are included in the definition of the ListRec class in the file *ListRec.jshl*. Save the resulting implementation in the file *ListRec.java*.

Step 3: Activate the calls to the `write()` and `insertEnd()` methods in the test program in the file *Test10.java* by removing the comment delimiter (and the characters "PA") from the lines beginning with "//PA".

Step 4: Execute the `write()` and `insertEnd()` methods using the following list.

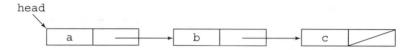

Step 5: What output does `write()` produce?

Step 6: What list does `insertEnd()` produce?

Step 7: Execute these methods using an empty list.

Step 8: What output does `write()` produce?

Step 9: What list does `insertEnd()` produce?

Part B

One of the most common reasons for using recursion with linked lists is to support traversal of a list from its end back to its beginning. The following pair of methods output each list element twice, once as the list is traversed from beginning to end and again as it is traversed from the end back to the beginning.

```
void writeMirror ( )
// Outputs the elements in a list from beginning to end and back
{
    System.out.print("Mirror : ");
    writeMirrorSub(head);
    System.out.println( );
}

// - - - - - - - - - - - - - - - - - - - - - - - - - - - - - - - - - -

void writeMirrorSub ( SListNode p )
// Recursive partner of the writeMirror() method. Processes the
// sublist that begins with the node referenced by p.
{
    if ( p != null )
    {
        System.out.print(p.getElement( )); // Output forward
        writeMirrorSub(p.getNext( ));      // Continue with next node
        System.out.print(p.getElement( )); // Output backward
    }
}
```

Step 1: Complete this part of the List ADT in the file *ListRec.jshl* by implementing the methods `writeMirror()` and `writeMirrorSub()` as described above. Incomplete implementations for these methods are included in the definition of the ListRec class in the file *ListRec.jshl*. Save the resulting implementation in the file *ListRec.java*.

Step 2: Activate the call to the `writeMirror()` method in the test program in the file *Test10.java* by removing the comment delimiter (and the characters "PB") from the lines beginning with "//PB".

Step 3: Execute the `writeMirror()` method using the following list.

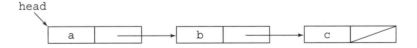

Step 4: What output does `writeMirror()` produce?

Step 5: Describe what each statement in the `writeMirrorSub()` method does during the call in which parameter `p` points to the node containing 'a'.

Step 6: What is the significance of the call to `writeMirrorSub()` in which parameter `p` is null?

Step 7: Describe how the calls to `writeMirrorSub()` combine to produce the "mirrored" output. Use a diagram to illustrate your answer.

Part C

The following pair of methods reverse a list by changing each node's `next` reference. Note that the references are changed on the way back through the list.

```
void reverse ( )
// Reverses the order of the elements in a list.
{
    reverseSub(null, head);
}

// - - - - - - - - - - - - - - - - - - - - - - - - - - - - - - - - - - -

void reverseSub ( SListNode p, SListNode nextP )
// Recursive partner of the reverse() method. Processes the sublist
// that begins with the node referenced by nextP.
{
    if ( nextP != null )
    {
        reverseSub(nextP, nextP.getNext( ));   // Continue with next node
        nextP.setNext( p );                    // Reverse link
    }
    else
        head = p;                              // Move head to end of list
}
```

Step 1: Complete this part of the List ADT in the file *ListRec.jshl* by implementing the incomplete methods `reverse()` and `reverseSub()` as described above. Incomplete implementations for these methods are included in the definition of the ListRec class in the file *ListRec.jshl*. Save the resulting implementation in the file *ListRec.java*.

Step 2: Activate the call to the `reverse()` method in the test program by removing the comment delimiter (and the characters "PC") from the lines beginning with "//PC".

Step 3: Execute the `reverse()` method using the following list.

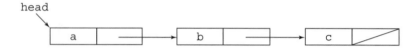

Step 4: What list does `reverse()` produce?

Step 5: Describe what each statement in the `reverseSub()` method does during the call in which parameter `p` references the node containing 'a'. In particular, how are the links to and from this node changed as result of this call?

Step 6: What is the significance of the call to `reverseSub()` in which parameter `p` is null?

Step 7: Describe how the calls to `reverseSub()` combine to reverse the list. Use a diagram to illustrate your answer.

Part D

In the Overview, you saw how you can use recursion to insert a node at the end of a list. The following pair of methods will delete the last node in a list.

```
void deleteEnd ( )
// Deletes the element at the end of a list. Moves the cursor to the
// beginning of the list.
{
    deleteEndSub(head);
    cursor = head;
}

// - - - - - - - - - - - - - - - - - - - - - - - - - - - - - - - - - -

void deleteEndSub ( SListNode p )
// Recursive partner of the deleteEnd( ) method. Processes the
// sublist that begins with the node referenced by p.
{
    if ( p.getNext ( ).getNext ( ) != null )
        deleteEndSub(p.getNext ( ));  // Looking for the last node
    else
    {
        p.setNext(null);              // Set p (link or head) to null
    }
}
```

Step 1: Complete this part of the List ADT in the file *ListRec.jshl* by implementing the methods `deleteEnd()` and `deleteEndSub()` as described above. Incomplete implementations for these methods are included in the definition of the ListRec class in the file *ListRec.jshl*. Save the resulting implementation in the file *ListRec.java*.

Step 2: Activate the call to the `deleteEnd()` method in the test program by removing the comment delimiter (and the characters "PD") from the lines beginning with "`//PD`".

Step 3: Execute the `deleteEnd()` method using the following list.

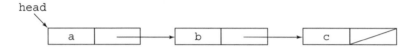

Step 4: What list does `deleteEnd()` produce?

Step 5: What is the significance of the calls to the `deleteEndSub()` method in which `p.getNext( ).getNext( )` is not null?

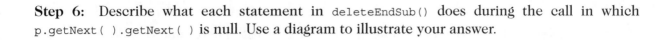

Step 6: Describe what each statement in `deleteEndSub()` does during the call in which `p.getNext( ).getNext( )` is null. Use a diagram to illustrate your answer.

Step 7: What list does `deleteEnd()` produce when called with a list containing one element? Describe how this result is accomplished. Use a diagram to illustrate your answer.

Part E

The following pair of methods determine the length of a list. These methods do not simply count nodes as they move through the list from beginning to end (as an iterative method would). Instead, they use a recursive definition of length in which the length of the list referenced by p is the length of the list referenced to by p.getNext( ) (the remaining nodes in the list) plus one (the node referenced by p).

$$length(p) = \begin{cases} 0 & \text{if } p = 0 \text{ (base case)} \\ length(\text{p.getNext()}) + 1 & \text{if } p \neq 0 \text{ (recursive step)} \end{cases}$$

```
int length ( )

// Returns the number of elements in a list.
{
     return lengthSub(head);
}

// - - - - - - - - - - - - - - - - - - - - - - - - - - - - - - - - - -

int lengthSub ( SListNode p )
// Recursive partner of the length() method. Processes the sublist
// that begins with the node referenced by p.
{
     int result;                              // Result returned

     if ( p == null )
         result = 0;                          // End of list reached
     else
         result = ( lengthSub(p.getNext( )) + 1 );   // Number of nodes
                                              // after this one + 1
     return result;
}
```

Step 1: Activate the call to the `length()` method in the test program by removing the comment delimiter (and the characters "PE") from the lines beginning with "//PE".

Step 2: Execute the `length()` method using the following list.

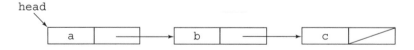

Step 3: What result does `length()` produce?

Step 4: What is the significance of the call to the `lengthSub()` method in which parameter `p` is null?

Step 5: Describe how the calls to `lengthSub()` combine to return the length of the list. Use a diagram to illustrate your answer.

Step 6: What value does the `length()` method return when called with an empty list? Describe how this value is computed. Use a diagram to illustrate your answer.

LABORATORY 10: Bridge Exercise

Name _____

Hour/Period/Section _____

Date _____

Check with your instructor as to whether you are to complete this exercise prior to your lab period or during lab.

Part A

The following pair of methods perform some unspecified action.

```
void unknown1 ( )
// Unknown method 1.
{
      unknown1Sub(head);
      System.out.println( );
}

// - - - - - - - - - - - - - - - - - - - - - - - - - - - - - - - - -

void unknown1Sub ( SListNode p )
// Recursive partner of the unknown1() method.
{
      if ( p != null )
      {
          System.out.print(p.getElement( ));
          if ( p.getNext( ) != null )
          {
              unknown1Sub(p.getNext( ).getNext( ));
              System.out.print(p.getNext( ).getElement( ));
          }
      }
}
```

Step 1:   Activate the call to the `unknown1()` method in the test program in the file *Test10.java* by removing the comment delimiter (and the characters "BA") from the lines beginning with "//BA".

Step 2:   Execute the `unknown1()` method using the following list.

Step 3: What output does `unknown1()` produce?

Step 4: Describe what each statement in the `unknown1Sub()` method does during the call in which parameter `p` references the node containing 'a'.

Step 5: Describe how the calls to `unknown1Sub()` combine to output the list. Use a diagram to illustrate your answer.

Part B

The following pair of methods perform yet another unspecified action.

```
void unknown2 ( )
// Unknown method 2.
{
      unknown2Sub(head);
}

// - - - - - - - - - - - - - - - - - - - - - - - - - - - - - - - - - - - -

void unknown2Sub ( SListNode p )
// Recursive partner of the unknown2() method.
{
      SListNode q;

      if ( p != null  &&  p.getNext( ) != null )
      {
          q = p;
          p = p.getNext( );
          q.setNext( p.getNext( ) );
          p.setNext( q );
          unknown2Sub(q.getNext( ));
      }
}
```

Step 1: Activate the call to the `unknown2()` method in the test program by removing the comment delimiter (and the characters "BB") from the lines beginning with "//BB".

Step 2: Execute the `unknown2()` method using the following list.

Step 3: What list does `unknown2()` produce?

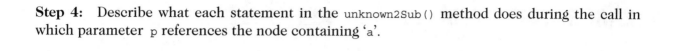
Step 4: Describe what each statement in the `unknown2Sub()` method does during the call in which parameter `p` references the node containing 'a'.

Step 5: Describe how the calls to `unknown2Sub()` combine to restructure the list. Use a diagram to illustrate your answer.

LABORATORY 10: In-lab Exercise 1

Name

Hour/Period/Section

Date

Although recursion can be an intuitive means for expressing algorithms, there are times you may wish to replace recursion with iteration. This replacement is most commonly done when analysis of a program's execution reveals that the overhead associated with a particular recursive routine is too costly, either in terms of time or memory usage.

Part A

Replacing recursion in a routine such as the `length()` method (Prelab Exercise, Part E) is fairly easy. Rather than using recursive calls to move through the list, you move a reference (of type `SListNode`) from node to node. In the case of the `length()` method, this iterative process continues until you reach the end of the list.

The `reverse()` method (Prelab Exercise, Part C) presents a somewhat more challenging problem. The iterative form of this routine moves a set of references through the list in a coordinated manner. As these references move through the list, they reverse the links between pairs of nodes, thereby reversing the list itself.

Step 1: Create an implementation of the `reverse()` method that uses iteration, in conjunction with a small set of references, in place of recursion. Call this method `iterReverse()` and add it to the file *ListRec.java*. An incomplete implementation of this method is included in the definition of the ListRec class in the file *ListRec.jshl*.

Step 2: Activate the call to the `iterReverse()` method in the test program in the file *Test10.java* by removing the comment delimiter (and the characters "1A") from the lines beginning with "`//1A`".

Step 3: Prepare a test plan for the `iterReverse()` method that covers lists of different lengths, including lists containing a single element. A test plan form follows.

Step 4: Execute your test plan. If you discover mistakes in your `iterReverse()` method, correct them and execute your test plan again.

Test Plan for the *iterReverse() Method*

Test case	List	Expected result	Checked

Part B

The `writeMirror()` method (Prelab Exercise, Part B) presents an even greater challenge. The iterative form of this routine uses a stack to store references to the nodes in a list. This stack is used in concert with an iterative process of the following form.

```
Stack tempStack = new AStack(10);          // Stack of references
SListNode p;                               // Iterates through list
System.out.print("Mirror : ");
p = head;
while ( p != null )
{
    System.out.print(p.getElement( ));     // Output element
    tempStack.push(p);                     // Push on stack
    p = p.getNext( );
}
while ( !tempStack.isEmpty( ) )
{
    p = (SListNode)tempStack.pop( );       // Pop off element
    System.out.print( p.getElement( ) );   // Output it
}
System.out.println( );
```

Step 1: Create an implementation of the `writeMirror()` method that uses iteration, in conjunction with a stack, in place of recursion. Call the resulting method `stackWriteMirror()` and add it to the file *ListRec.java*. An incomplete implementation of this method is included in the definition of the ListRec class in the file *ListRec.jshl*. Base your `stackWriteMirror()` method on one of your implementations of the Stack ADT from Laboratory 5.

Step 2: Prepare a test plan for the `stackWriteMirror()` method that covers lists of different lengths, including lists containing a single element. A test plan form follows.

Step 3: Activate the call to the `stackWriteMirror()` method in the test program by removing the comment delimiter (and the characters "1B") from the lines beginning with "//1B".

Step 4: Execute your test plan. If you discover mistakes in your `stackWriteMirror()` method, correct them and execute your test plan again.

Test Plan for the *stackWriteMirror() Method*

Test case	List	Expected result	Checked

LABORATORY 10: In-lab Exercise 2

Name _____

Hour/Period/Section _____

Date _____

You saw in the Prelab that you can use recursion to insert an element at the end of a list. You also can use recursion to add elements at the beginning and middle of lists.

```
void aBeforeb ( )
```
Precondition:
List contains characters.
Postcondition:
Inserts the character 'a' immediately before each occurrence of the character 'b'. Does not move the cursor.

Step 1: Create an implementation of the `aBeforeb()` method that is based on recursion—*not* iteration—and add your implementation to the file *ListRec.java*. An incomplete implementation of this method is included in the definition of the ListRec class in the file *ListRec.jshl*.

Step 2: Prepare a test plan for this method that includes lists containing the character 'b' at the beginning, middle, and end. A test plan form follows.

Step 3: Activate the call to the `aBeforeb()` method in the test program in the file *Test10.java* by removing the comment delimiter (and the character "2") from the lines beginning with "//2".

Step 4: Execute your test plan. If you discover mistakes in your implementation of the aBeforeb() method, correct them and execute your test plan again.

Test Plan for the *aBeforeb() Method*

Test case	List	Expected result	Checked

LABORATORY 10: In-lab Exercise 3

Name

Hour/Period/Section

Date

You saw in the Prelab that you can use recursion to delete the element at the end of a list. You also can use recursion to express the restructuring required following the deletion of elements at the beginning and middle of lists.

```
void cRemove ( )
```
Precondition:
List contains characters.
Postcondition:
Removes all the occurrences of the character 'c' from a list of characters. Moves the cursor to the beginning of the list.

Step 1: Create an implementation of the `cRemove()` method that is based on recursion—*not* iteration—and add it to the file *ListRec.java*. An incomplete implementation of this method is included in the definition of the ListRec class in the file *ListRec.jshl*.

Step 2: Prepare a test plan for this method that includes lists containing the character 'c' at the beginning, middle, and end. A test plan form follows.

Step 3: Activate the call to the `cRemove()` method in the test program in the file *Test10.java* by removing the comment delimiter (and the character "3") from the lines beginning with "//3".

Step 4: Execute your test plan. If you discover mistakes in your implementation of the cRemove() method, correct them and execute your test plan again.

Test Plan for the *cRemove() Method*

Test case	List	Expected result	Checked

LABORATORY 10: Postlab Exercise 1

Name _____

Hour/Period/Section _____

Date _____

One mistake we sometimes make when we first begin writing recursive routines is to use a `while` loop in place of an `if` selection structure. Suppose we replace the `if` statement

```
if ( p != null )
{
    System.out.print( p.getElement( ) );     // Output forward
    writeMirrorSub(p.getNext( ));             // Continue with next node
    System.out.print( p.getElement( ) );     // Output backward
}
```

in the `writeMirrorSub()` method (Prelab Exercise, Part B) with the `while` loop:

```
while ( p != null )
{
    System.out.print( p.getElement( ) );     // Output forward
    writeMirrorSub(p.getNext( ));             // Continue with next node
    System.out.print( p.getElement( ) );     // Output backward
}
```

What would be the consequence of this change?

LABORATORY 10: Postlab Exercise 2

Name

Hour/Period/Section

Date

It is often impossible to convert a recursive routine to iterative form without the use of a stack (see In-lab Exercise 1). Explain why a stack is needed in the iterative form of the `writeMirror()` method.

Expression Tree ADT

OBJECTIVES

In this laboratory you

- create an implementation of the Expression Tree ADT using a linked tree structure.

- develop an implementation of the Logic Expression Tree ADT and use your implementation to model a simple logic circuit.

- create a copy constructor and clone method that make an exact but separate copy of an expression tree ADT.

- analyze how preorder, inorder, and postorder tree traversals are used in your implementation of the Expression Tree ADT.

OVERVIEW

Although you ordinarily write arithmetic expressions in linear form, you treat them as hierarchical entities when you evaluate them. When evaluating the following arithmetic expression, for example,

$$(1+3)*(6-4)$$

you first add 1 and 3, then you subtract 4 from 6. Finally, you multiply these intermediate results together to produce the value of the expression. In performing these calculations, you have implicitly formed a hierarchy in which the multiply operator is built upon a foundation consisting of the addition and subtraction operators. You can represent this hierarchy explicitly using the following binary tree. Trees such as this one are referred to as **expression trees**.

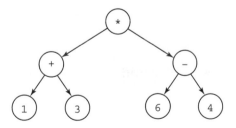

Expression Tree ADT

Elements

Each node in an expression tree contains either an arithmetic operator or a numeric value.

Structure

The nodes form a tree in which each node containing an arithmetic operator has a pair of children. Each child is the root node of a subtree that represents one of the operator's operands. Nodes containing numeric values have no children.

Constructor and Methods

```
ExprTree ( )
```
Precondition:
None.
Postcondition:
Default Constructor. Creates an empty expression tree.

```
void build ( )
```
Precondition:
None.
Postcondition:
Reads an arithmetic expression in prefix form from the keyboard and builds the corresponding expression tree.

```
void expression ( )
```
Precondition:
None.
Postcondition:
Outputs the corresponding arithmetic expression in fully parenthesized infix form.

```
float evaluate ( )
```
Precondition:
Expression tree is not empty.
Postcondition:
Returns the value of the corresponding arithmetic expression.

```
void clear ( )
```
Precondition:

None.

Postcondition:

Removes all the elements in an expression tree.

```
void showStructure ( )
```
Precondition:

None.

Postcondition:

Outputs an expression tree with its branches oriented from left (root) to right (leaves)—that is, the tree is output rotated counterclockwise 90 degrees from its conventional orientation. If the tree is empty, outputs "Empty tree". Note that this operation is intended for testing/debugging purposes only. It assumes that arithmetic expressions contain only single-digit, nonnegative integers and the arithmetic operators for addition, subtraction, multiplication, and division.

We commonly write arithmetic expressions in **infix form**—that is, with each operator placed between its operands, as in the following expression:

$$(1 + 3) * (6 - 4)$$

In this laboratory, you construct an expression tree from the **prefix form** of an arithmetic expression. In prefix form, each operator is placed immediately before its operands. The expression above is written in prefix form as

$$* + 1 3 - 6 4$$

When processing the prefix form of an arithmetic expression from left to right, you will, by definition, encounter each operator followed by its operands. If you know in advance the number of operands that an operator has, you can use the following recursive process to construct the corresponding expression tree.

Read the next arithmetic operator or numeric value.

Create a node containing the operator or numeric value.

`if` the node contains an operator

   `then` Recursively build the subtrees that correspond to the
       operator's operands.

   `else` The node is a leaf node.

If you apply this process to the arithmetic expression

$$*+13-64$$

then construction of the corresponding expression tree proceeds as follows:

Read '*'

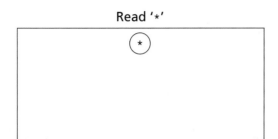

Read '+'

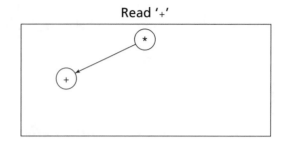

Read '1'

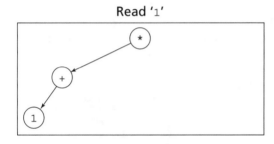

Read '3'

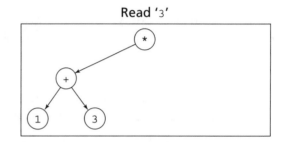

Read '−'

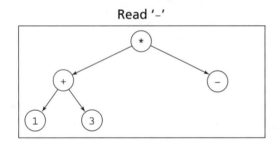

Read '6'

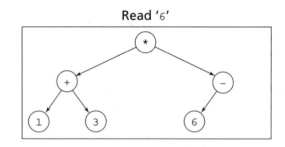

Read '4'

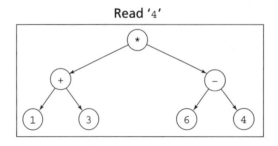

Note that in processing this arithmetic expression we have assumed that all numeric values are single-digit, nonnegative integers, and thus, that all numeric values can be represented as a single character. If we were to generalize this process to include multidigit numbers, we would have to include delimiters in the expression to separate numbers.

LABORATORY 11: Cover Sheet

Name _____

Hour/Period/Section _____

Date _____

Place a check mark (✔) in the Assigned column next to the exercises that your instructor has assigned to you. Attach this cover sheet to the front of the packet of materials that you submit for this laboratory.

Exercise	Assigned	Completed
Prelab Exercise	✔	
Bridge Exercise	✔	
In-lab Exercise 1		
In-lab Exercise 2		
In-lab Exercise 3		
Postlab Exercise 1		
Postlab Exercise 2		
Total		

LABORATORY 11: Prelab Exercise

Name

Hour/Period/Section

Date

In the Overview, you saw how the construction of an expression tree can be described using recursion. In this exercise, you use recursive methods to implement the operations in the Expression Tree ADT.

Step 1: Implement the operations in Expression Tree ADT using a linked tree structure and save them in the file *ExprTree.java*. Assume that an arithmetic expression consists of single-digit, nonnegative integers ('0' to '9') and the four basic arithmetic operators ('+', '−', '*' and '/'). Further assume that each arithmetic expression is input in prefix form from the keyboard with all of the characters on one line.

As with the linear linked structures you developed in prior laboratories, your implementation of the linked tree structure uses a pair of classes: one for the nodes in the tree (ExprTreeNode) and one for the overall tree structure (ExprTree). Each node in the tree should contain a character (element) and a pair of references to the node's children (left and right). Your implementation also should maintain a reference to the tree's root node (root). Since all tree nodes are similar, a TreeNode interface is used. This interface or one very similar to it, will also be used in a future laboratory. The interface TreeNode is in the file *TreeNode.java*. Please note that although there are no access designations in this particular interface file, in Java all methods that implement an interface *must be* declared public.

Base your implementation on the following incomplete definitions from the files *ExprTreeNode.jshl* and *ExprTree.jshl*. You are to fill in the Java code for each of the constructors and methods where the implementation braces are empty, or where an entire method or set of methods from the interface needs to be inserted (noted by "insert method … here").

```java
class ExprTreeNode implements TreeNode
// Facilitator class for the ExprTree and LogiTree class
{
    // Data members
    private char element;              // Expression tree element
    private TreeNode left,             // Reference to the left child
                     right;            // Reference to the right child

    // Constructor
    public ExprTreeNode ( char elem, TreeNode leftPtr,
                          TreeNode rightPtr )
    {                 }
```

```
        // Class Methods used by client class
        // ---Insert method implementations for the interface TreeNode here ---//

} // class ExprTreeNode

class ExprTree
{
    // Data member
    private TreeNode root;                    // Reference to the root node

    // Constructor
    public ExprTree ( )
    {                  }

    // Expression tree manipulation methods
    public void build ( )                     // Build tree from prefix expression
    {                  }
    public void expression ( )                // Output expression in infix form
    {                  }
    public float evaluate ( )                 // Evaluate expression
    {                  }
    public void clear ( )                     // Clear tree
    {                  }

    // Output the tree structure — used in testing/debugging
    public void showStructure ( )
    {                  }

    // Recursive partners of the public member methods
    //   Insert these methods here.
    private void showSub ( TreeNode p, int level )
    {                  }

} // class ExprTree
```

Step 2: The definition of the ExprTree class in the file *ExprTree.jshl* does not include all the recursive private methods needed by your implementation of the Expression Tree ADT. Add these recursive private methods to the file *ExprTree.java*.

Step 3: Complete coding of all the methods and save your implementation of the Expression Tree ADT in the file *ExprTree.java*. Be sure to document your code.

LABORATORY 11: Bridge Exercise

Name _____

Hour/Period/Section _____

Date _____

Check with your instructor as to whether you are to complete this exercise prior to your lab period or during lab.

Test your implementation of the Expression Tree ADT using the test program in the file *TestExprTree.java*.

Step 1: Compile your implementation of the Expression Tree ADT in the file *TestExprTree.java*.

Step 2: Run the Java bytecode files produced by Step 1.

Step 3: Complete the following test plan by filling in the expected result for each arithmetic expression. You may wish to add arithmetic expressions to the test plan.

Step 4: Execute this test plan. If you discover mistakes in your implementation of the Expression Tree ADT, correct them and execute the test plan again.

Test Plan for the *Operations in the Expression Tree ADT*

Test case	Arithmetic expression	Expected result	Checked
One operator	+34		
Nested operators	*+34/52		
All operators at start	-/*9321		
Uneven nesting	*4+6-75		
Zero dividend	/02		
Single-digit number	7		

LABORATORY 11: In-lab Exercise 1

Name _____

Hour/Period/Section _____

Date _____

In Laboratory 5 you created a copy constructor and a clone method for a linked-list data structure. In this exercise, you create a copy constructor and a clone method for your linked tree implementation of the Expression Tree ADT.

```
ExprTree ( ExprTree valueTree )
```
Precondition:
None.
Postcondition:
Copy constructor. Creates an exact but separate copy of valueTree.

```
Object clone( )
```
Precondition:
None.
Postcondition:
Returns an exact but separate copy of type Object.

Remember that to implement the *clone* method for any class you need to do the following:

    a. **Modify the class head** by adding the words "`implements Cloneable`" to the end of the class head.

    b. **Use super.clone to make a copy.** An implementation of a `clone` method that was used for the LStack class in Laboratory 5 can be found in the file *clone.txt* in the Lab5 package/subdirectory.

Remember that if you wish to clone an object that includes object references as part of its instance data, you may have to do more work in `clone` than just calling `super.clone( )`. In such cases, you may want to consider using the copy constructor or study the use of *clone* in more detail than is presented here.

Step 1: Implement these methods and add them to the file *ExprTree.java*. An incomplete definition for these operations is included in the definition of the ExprTree class in the file *ExprTree.jshl*.

Step 2: Activate the test for the copy constructor and `clone` in the test program in the file *TestExprTree.java* by removing the comment delimiter (and the character '1') from the lines that begin with "//1". If you prefer, you may rename the file *TestExprTree2.java*, but remember you need to do more than just change the filename.

Step 3: Prepare a test plan for this operation that includes a variety of expression trees, including empty trees and trees containing a single element. A test plan form follows.

Step 4: Execute your test plan. If you discover mistakes in your implementation of the copy constructor or `clone` method, correct them and execute the test plan again.

Test Plan for the *Copy Constructor and clone Operation*

Test case	Arithmetic expression	Expected result	Checked

LABORATORY 11: In-lab Exercise 2

Name

Hour/Period/Section

Date

Commuting the operators in an arithmetic expression requires restructuring the nodes in the corresponding expression tree. For example, commuting *every* operator in the expression tree

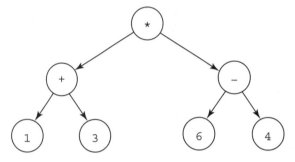

yields the expression tree

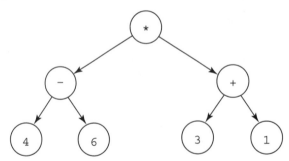

An operation for commuting expression trees is described below.

```
void commute ( )
```
Precondition:
None.
Postcondition:
Commutes the operands for every arithmetic operator in an expression tree.

Step 1: Implement this method and add it to the file *ExprTree.java*. An incomplete definition for this operation is included in the definition of the ExprTree class in the file *ExprTree.jshl*.

Step 2: Activate the test for the `commute` operation in the test program in the file *TestExprTree.java* by removing the comment delimiter (and the character '2') from the lines that begin with "//2". If you prefer, you may rename the file *TestExprTree3.java*, but remember you need to do more than just change the filename.

Step 3: Prepare a test plan for this operation that includes a variety of arithmetic expressions. A test plan form follows.

Step 4: Execute your test plan. If you discover mistakes in your implementation of the `commute` operation, correct them and execute the test plan again.

Test Plan for the *commute Operation*

Test case	Arithmetic Expression	Expected result	Checked

LABORATORY 11: In-lab Exercise 3

Name _____

Hour/Period/Section _____

Date _____

Computers are composed of logic circuits that take a set of boolean input values and produce a boolean output. You can represent this mapping from inputs to output with a logic expression consisting of the boolean logic operators AND, OR, and NOT (defined below) and the boolean values `true` and `false`.

	(NOT)			(AND)	(OR)
A	−A	A	B	A*B	A+B
0	1	0	0	0	0
1	0	0	1	0	1
		1	0	0	1
		1	1	1	1

Just as you can construct an arithmetic expression tree from an arithmetic expression, you can construct a logic expression tree from a logic expression. For example, the following logic expression

$$(1*0)+(1*-0)$$

can be expressed in prefix form as

$$+*10*1-0$$

Applying the expression tree construction process described in the Overview to this expression produces the following logic expression tree.

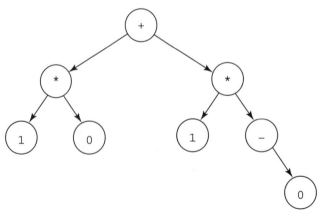

Evaluating this tree yields the boolean value `true`.

Construction of this tree requires processing a unary operator, the boolean operator NOT ('-'). When building a logic expression tree, you should set the right child of any node containing the NOT operator to point to the operand and set the left child to null. Note that you must be careful when performing the remaining operations to avoid traversing these null left children.

Step 1: Modify the `evaluate( )` method in the file *ExprTree.java* so that this method yields an integer value rather than a floating-point number. You may need to modify a related recursive private method as well. Also rename the class (from class ExprTree to class LogiTree) and correspondingly rename the constructor (from ExprTree to LogiTree). Save the resulting class definitions in the file *LogiTree.java*.

Step 2: Further modify various methods in your file *LogiTree.java* to create an implementation of the Expression Tree ADT that supports logic expressions consisting of the boolean values True and False ('1' and '0') and the boolean operators AND, OR, and NOT ('*', '+', and '–'). Be aware that in Java boolean values are *not* equivalent to '1' or '0'. In Java the values of `true` and `false` *cannot* be cast into any numerical representation.

Step 3: Modify the test program in the file *TestExprTree.java* so that your implementation of the Logic Expression Tree ADT in the file *LogiTree.java* is used in place of your (arithmetic) Expression Tree ADT. Rename the class TestExprTree as TestLogiTree and then save the file as *TestLogiTree.java*. Last, modify the code of *TestLogiTree.java* to instantiate LogiTree objects instead of ExprTree objects.

Step 4: Compile and run your implementation of the Logic Expression Tree ADT and the modified test program.

Step 5: Complete the following test plan by filling in the expected result for each logic expression. You may wish to include additional logic expressions in this test plan.

Step 6: Execute this test plan. If you discover mistakes in your implementation of the Logic Expression Tree ADT, correct them and execute the test plan again.

Test Plan for the *Operations in the Logic Expression Tree ADT*

Test case	Arithmetic expression	Expected result	Checked
One operator	+10		
Nested operators	*+10+01		
NOT (Boolean value)	+*10*1-0		
NOT (subexpression)	+-1-*11		
NOT (nested expression)	-*+110		
Double negation	--1		
Boolean value	1		

Having produced a tool that constructs and evaluates logic expression trees, you can use this tool to investigate the use of logic circuits to perform binary arithmetic. Suppose you have two one-bit binary numbers (x and y). You can add these numbers together to produce a one-bit sum (s) and a one-bit carry (c). The results of one-bit binary addition for all combinations of x and y are tabulated below.

	X	Y	C	S
X				
+Y	0	0	0	0
—	0	1	0	1
CS	1	0	0	1
	1	1	1	0

A brief analysis of this table reveals that you can compute the values of outputs s and c from inputs x and y using the following pair of (prefix) logic expressions.

$$C = *XY \qquad S = +*X-Y*-XY$$

Step 7: Using your implementation of the Logic Expression Tree ADT and the modified test program, confirm that these expressions are correct by completing the following table.

X	Y	C = *XY	S = +*X-Y*-XY
0	0	*00 =	+*0-0*-00 =
0	1	*01 =	+*0-1*-01 =
1	0	*10 =	+*1-0*-10 =
1	1	*11 =	+*1-1*-11 =

LABORATORY 11: Postlab Exercise 1

Name _____

Hour/Period/Section _____

Date _____

What type of tree traversal (inorder, preorder, or postorder) serves as the basis of your implementation of each of the following Expression Tree ADT operations? Briefly explain why you used a given traversal to implement a particular operation.

	build
Traversal:	
Explanation:	

	expression
Traversal:	
Explanation:	

	evaluate
Traversal:	

Explanation:

	clear
Traversal:	

Explanation:

LABORATORY 11: Postlab Exercise 2

Name _____

Hour/Period/Section _____

Date _____

Consider the methods `writeSub1()` and `writeSub2()` given below.

```
void writeSub1 ( TreeNode p )
{
    if ( p != null )
    {
        writeSub1(p.getLeft( ));
        System.out.print(p.getElement( ));
        writeSub1(p.getRight( ));
    }
}

void writeSub2 ( TreeNode p )
{
    if ( p.getLeft( ) != null ) writeSub2(p.getLeft( ));
    System.out.print(p.getElement( ));
    if ( p.getRight != null ) writeSub2(p.getRight( ));
}
```

Let `root` be the reference to the root node of a nonempty expression tree. Will the following pair of method calls produce the same output?

```
writeSub1(root);  and  writeSub2(root);
```

If not, why not? If so, how do the methods differ and why might this difference be important?

Binary Search
Tree ADT

OBJECTIVES

In this laboratory you

- create an implementation of the Binary Search Tree ADT using a linked tree structure.

- create operations that compute the height of a tree and output the elements in a tree whose keys are less than a specified key.

- examine how an index can be used to retrieve records from a database file and construct an indexing program for an accounts database.

- analyze the efficiency of your implementation of the Binary Search Tree ADT.

OVERVIEW

In Laboratory 11, you saw how the evaluation of an arithmetic expression can be represented using a hierarchical data structure. In this laboratory, you examine how a binary tree can be used to represent the hierarchical search process embodied in the binary search algorithm.

The binary search algorithm allows you to efficiently locate an element in an array provided that each array element has a unique identifier—called its key—and provided that the array elements are stored in order based on their keys. Given the following array of keys:

Index	0	1	2	3	4	5	6
Key	16	20	31	43	65	72	86

a binary search for the element with key 31 begins by comparing 31 with the key in the middle of the array, 43. Because 31 is less than 43, the element with key 31 must lie in the lower half of the array (entries 0–2). The key in the middle of this subarray is 20. Because 31 is greater than 20, the element with key 31 must lie in the upper half of this subarray (entry 2). This array entry contains the key 31. Thus, the search terminates with success.

Although the comparisons made during a search for a given key depend on the key, the relative order in which comparisons are made is invariant for a given array of elements. For instance, when searching through the previous array, you always compare the key that you are searching for with 43 before you compare it with either 20 or 72. Similarly, you always compare the key with 72 before you compare it with either 65 or 86. The order of comparisons associated with this array is shown below.

Index	0	1	2	3	4	5	6
Key	16	20	31	43	65	72	86
Order compared	3	2	3	1	3	2	3

The hierarchical nature of the comparisons that are performed by the binary search algorithm is reflected in the following tree.

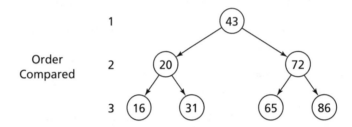

Observe that for each key κ in this tree, all of the keys in κ's left subtree are less than κ and all of the keys in κ's right subtree are greater than κ (or equal to it—if all the keys are not unique). Trees with this property are referred to as **binary search trees**.

When searching for a key in a binary search tree, you begin at the root node and move downward along a branch until either you find the node containing the key or you reach a leaf node without finding the key. Each move along a branch corresponds to an array subdivision in the binary search algorithm. At each node, you move down to the left if the key you are searching for is less than the key stored in the node, or you move down to the right if the key you are searching for is greater than the key stored in the node.

Binary Search Tree ADT

Elements

The elements in a binary search tree are of generic type TreeElem. Each element has a key that uniquely identifies the element. Elements usually include additional data. Objects of type TreeElem must provide a method called *key( )* that returns an element's key. To ensure that TreeElem provides the method *key( )*, it has been defined as an interface in the file *TreeElem.java*. The element's key must support the six basic relational operators.

Structure

The elements form a binary tree. For each element E in the tree, all the elements in E's left subtree have keys that are less than E's key and all the elements in E's right subtree have keys that are greater than E's key.

Constructor and Methods

```
BSTree ( )
```
Precondition:
None.
Postcondition:
Constructor. Creates an empty binary search tree.

```
void insert ( TreeElem newElement )
```
Precondition:
Binary search tree is not full.
Postcondition:
Inserts newElement into a binary search tree. If an element with the same key as newElement already exists in the tree, then updates that element's nonkey fields with newElement's nonkey fields.

```
TreeElem retrieve ( int searchKey )
```
Precondition:
None.
Postcondition:
Searches a binary search tree for the element with key searchKey. If this element is found, then returns the element. Otherwise, returns a null element.

```
void remove ( int deleteKey )
```
Precondition:
None.
Postcondition:
Deletes the element with key deleteKey from a binary search tree.

```
void writeKeys ( )
```
Precondition:
None.
Postcondition:
Outputs the keys of the elements in a binary search tree. The keys are output in ascending order, one per line.

```
void clear ( )
```
Precondition:
None.
Postcondition:
Removes all the elements in a binary search tree.

```
boolean isEmpty ( )
```
Precondition:
None.
Postcondition:
Returns true if a binary search tree is empty. Otherwise, returns false.

```
boolean isFull ( )
```
Precondition:
None.
Postcondition:
Returns true if a binary search tree is full. Otherwise, returns false.

```
void showStructure ( )
```
Precondition:
None.
Postcondition:
Outputs the keys in a binary search tree. The tree is output with its branches oriented from left (root) to right (leaves)—that is, the tree is output rotated counterclockwise 90 degrees from its conventional orientation. If the tree is empty, outputs "Empty tree". Note that this operation is intended for testing/debugging purposes only.

LABORATORY 12: Cover Sheet

Name _____

Hour/Period/Section _____

Date _____

Place a check mark (✔) in the Assigned column next to the exercises that your instructor has assigned to you. Attach this cover sheet to the front of the packet of materials that you submit for this laboratory.

Exercise	Assigned	Completed
Prelab Exercise	✔	
Bridge Exercise	✔	
In-lab Exercise 1		
In-lab Exercise 2		
In-lab Exercise 3		
Postlab Exercise 1		
Postlab Exercise 2		
Total		

Laboratory 12: Prelab Exercise

Name _____

Hour/Period/Section _____

Date _____

Step 1: Implement the operations in Binary Search Tree ADT (in this case, a tree in which all the keys are unique) using a linked tree structure. As with the linear linked structures you developed in prior laboratories, your implementation of the linked tree structure uses a pair of classes: one for the nodes in the tree (BSTreeNode) and one for the overall tree structure (BSTree). Each node in the tree should contain an element (`element`) and a pair of pointers to the node's children (`left` and `right`). Your implementation should also maintain a pointer to the tree's root node (`root`).

The interface TreeNode is in the file *TreeNode.java*. This TreeNode interface is very similar to the one used for the Expression Tree ADT in the previous laboratory. The only difference is that the TreeNode in this laboratory stores (the more generic) elements of type Object instead of the elements of type char that were used in the Expression Tree ADT. This demonstrates that for the most part, the TreeNode interface represents what methods we expect a node in a binary tree to provide, but not how those methods are implemented by the class that uses (implements) the interface. This is the premise behind any interface that a Java programmer creates. Remember that although there are no access designations in the TreeNode interface file, in Java all methods that implement an interface *must be* declared public.

Base your implementation on the following incomplete definitions from the files *BSTreeNode.jshl* and *BSTree.jshl*. You are to fill in the Java code for each of the constructors and methods where the implementation braces are empty, or where an entire method or set of methods from the interface need to be inserted (noted by "insert method ... here"). Save your implementation in the files *BSTreeNode.java* and *BSTree.java*, respectively.

```
class BSTreeNode implements TreeNode
// Facilitator class for the BSTree class
{
    // Data members
    private TreeElem element;          // Binary search tree element
    private TreeNode left,             // Reference to the left child
                     right;            // Reference to the right child

    // Constructor
    public BSTreeNode ( TreeElem elem, TreeNode leftPtr,
                        TreeNode rightPtr )
    {                            }
```

```
        // Class Methods used by client class
        // --- Insert method implementations for the interface TreeNode here --- //

} // class BSTreeNode

class BSTree
{
        // Data member
        private TreeNode root;                          // Reference to the root node

        // Constructor
        public BSTree ( )
        {                       }

        // Binary search tree manipulation methods
        public void insert ( TreeElem newElement )      // Insert element
        {                       }
        public TreeElem retrieve ( int searchKey )      // Retrieve element
        {                       }
        public void remove ( int deleteKey )            // Remove element
        {                       }
        public void writeKeys ( )                       // Output keys
        {                       }
        public void clear ( )                           // Clear tree
        {                       }


        // Binary search tree status methods
        public boolean isEmpty ( )                      // Is tree empty?
        {                       }
        public boolean isFull ( )                       // Is Tree full?
        {                       }


        // Output the tree structure — used in testing/debugging
        public void showStructure ( )
        {                       }

        // Recursive partners of the public member methods
        // ----- Insert these methods here.
        private void showSub ( TreeNode p, int level )
        {                       }

} // class BSTree
```

Step 2: The definition of the BSTree class in the file *BSTree.jshl* does not include the recursive partners of the public methods needed by your implementation of the Binary Search Tree ADT. These recursive partners will be private methods of the BSTree class. Add these recursive methods to the file *BSTree.java*.

Step 3: Save your implementation of all the methods of the Binary Search Tree ADT in the file *BSTree.java*. Be sure to document your code.

Laboratory 12: Bridge Exercise

Name _____

Hour/Period/Section _____

Date _____

Check with your instructor as to whether you are to complete this exercise prior to your lab period or during lab.

The test program in the file *TestBSTree.java* allows you to interactively test your implementation of the Binary Search Tree ADT using the following commands. If you have limited knowledge of reading input from the keyboard in Java, carefully review the *TestBSTree.java* file (and some of the other Java program files provided with this laboratory) and notice the steps that are taken to read in more than one character at a time.

Command	Action
+key	Insert (or update) the element with the specified key.
?key	Retrieve the element with the specified key and output it.
-key	Delete the element with the specified key.
K	Output the keys in ascending order.
E	Report whether the tree is empty.
F	Report whether the tree is full.
C	Clear the tree.
Q	Quit the test program.

Step 1: Prepare a test plan for your implementation of the Binary Search Tree ADT. Your test plan should cover trees of various shapes and sizes, including empty, single-branch, and single-element trees. A test plan form follows.

Step 2: Execute your test plan. If you discover mistakes in your implementation, correct them and execute your test plan again.

Test Plan for the *Operations in the Binary Search Tree ADT*

Test case	Commands	Expected result	Checked

Laboratory 12: In-lab Exercise 1

Name _____

Hour/Period/Section _____

Date _____

Binary search trees containing the same elements can vary widely in shape depending on the order in which the elements were inserted into the trees. One measurement of a tree's shape is its **height**—that is, the number of nodes on the longest path from the root node to any leaf node. This statistic is significant because the amount of time that it can take to search for an element in a binary search tree is a function of the height of the tree.

```
int height ( )
```
Precondition:
None.
Postcondition:
Returns the height of a binary search tree.

You can compute the height of a binary search tree using a postorder traversal and the following recursive definition of height.

$$height(p) = \begin{cases} 0 & \text{if } p = null \text{ (base case)} \\ \max(height(p.getLeft(\,)), height(p.getRight(\,)) + 1) & \text{if } p \neq null \text{ (recursive step)} \end{cases}$$

Step 1: Implement this operation and add it to the file *BSTree.java*. A partial definition for this operation for the BSTree class is included in the file *BSTree.jshl*.

Step 2: Activate the 'H' (height) command in the test program in the file *TestBSTree.java* by removing the comment delimiter (and the character 'H') from the lines that begin with "//H".

Step 3: Prepare a test plan for this operation that covers trees of various shapes and sizes, including empty and single-branch trees. A test plan form follows.

Step 4: Execute your test plan. If you discover mistakes in your implementation of the `height` operation, correct them and execute your test plan again.

Test Plan for the *height Operation*

Test case	Commands	Expected result	Checked

Laboratory 12: In-lab Exercise 2

Name _____

Hour/Period/Section _____

Date _____

You have created operations that retrieve a single element from a binary search tree and output all the keys in a tree. The following operation outputs only those keys that are less than a specified key.

```
void writeLessThan ( int searchKey )
```
Precondition:
None.
Postcondition:
Outputs the keys in a binary search tree that are less than searchKey. The keys are output in ascending order. Note that searchKey need not be a key in the tree.

You could implement this operation using an inorder traversal of the entire tree in which you compare each key with searchKey and output those that are less than searchKey. Although successful, this approach is inefficient. It searches subtrees that you know cannot possibly contain keys that are less than searchKey.

Suppose you are given a searchKey value of 37 and the following binary search tree.

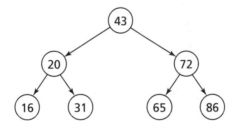

Because the root node contains the key 43, you can determine immediately that you do not need to search the root node's right subtree for keys that are less than 37. Similarly, if the value of searchKey were 67, then you would need to search the root node's right subtree but would not need to search the right subtree of the node whose key is 72. Your implementation of the writeLessThan operation should use this idea to limit the portion of the tree that must be searched.

Step 1: Implement this operation and add it to the file *BSTree.java*. A partial implementation for this operation is included in the definition of the BSTree class in the file *BSTree.jshl*.

Step 2: Activate the '<' (less than) command in the test program in the file *TestBSTree.java* by removing the comment delimiter (and the character '<') from the lines that begin with "//<".

Step 3: Prepare a test plan for this operation that includes a variety of trees and values for searchKey, including values of searchKey that do *not* occur in a particular tree. Be sure to include test cases that limit searches to the left subtree of the root node, the left subtree and part of the right subtree of the root node, the leftmost branch in the tree, and the entire tree. A test plan form follows.

Step 4: Execute your test plan. If you discover mistakes in your implementation of the writeLessThan operation, correct them and execute your test plan again.

Test Plan for the *writeLessThan Operation*

Test case	Commands	Expected result	Checked

Laboratory 12: In-lab Exercise 3

Name

Hour/Period/Section

Date

A **database** is a collection of related pieces of information that is organized for easy retrieval. The set of account records shown below, for instance, forms an accounts database.

Record No.	Account ID	First name	Last name	Balance
0	6274	James	Johnson	415.56
1	2843	Marcus	Wilson	9217.23
2	4892	Maureen	Albright	51462.56
3	8337	Debra	Douglas	27.26
4	9523	Bruce	Gold	719.32
5	3165	John	Carlson	1496.24

Each record in the accounts database is assigned a record number based on that record's relative position within the database file. You can use a record number to retrieve an account record directly, much as you can use an array index to reference an array element directly. The following program from the file *AccountRec.java*, for example, retrieves a record from the accounts database in the file *Accounts.dat*. Notice that both keyboard and file input are used in this program.

```java
import java.io.*;
import java.util.StringTokenizer;

class AccountRec
{
    // Constants
    private static final long bytesPerRecord = 38;   // Number of bytes used to store
                                                     //    each record in the accounts
                                                     //    database file

    // Data members
    private int acctID;                              // Account identifier
    private String firstName;                        // Name of account holder
    private String lastName;
    private double balance;                          // Account balance
```

```java
public static void main (String args[ ]) throws IOException
{
    AccountRec acctRec = new AccountRec( );       // Account record
    long recNum;                                  // User input record number
    String str,                                   // For reading a String
    name;

    // Need random access on the accounts database file; r = read only
    RandomAccessFile inFile =
        new RandomAccessFile("Accounts.dat", "r");

    // Also need tokenized input stream from keyboard
    BufferedReader reader =
        new BufferedReader(new InputStreamReader(System.in));
    StreamTokenizer keybdTokens = new StreamTokenizer(reader);

    // Get the record number to retrieve.
    System.out.println( );
    System.out.print("Enter record number: ");
    keybdTokens.nextToken( );
    recNum = (long)keybdTokens.nval;

    // Move to the corresponding record in the database file using the
    // seek( ) method in RandomAccessFile.
    inFile.seek(recNum * bytesPerRecord);

    str = inFile.readLine( );                      // Read the record

    if (str != null)                               // Is there something in the
                                                   //    string?
    {
        // Need to tokenize the String read by readline( )
        StringTokenizer strTokens = new StringTokenizer(str);

        name = strTokens.nextToken( );             // first String token
        acctRec.acctID = Integer.parseInt(name);   // Convert String to an int
        acctRec.firstName = strTokens.nextToken( ); // 2nd String token -
                                                   //       firstName
        acctRec.lastName = strTokens.nextToken( );  // 3rd String token -
                                                   //       lastName
        name = strTokens.nextToken( );             // 4th String token
        // Convert the String to a double
        acctRec.balance = Double.parseDouble(name);

        // Display the record.
        System.out.println(recNum + " : " + acctRec.acctID + " "
                        + acctRec.firstName + " " + acctRec.lastName + " "
                        + acctRec.balance);
    }
    else
        System.out.println("Reached EOF");

    // Close the file streams
    inFile.close( );
} // main

} // class AccountRec
```

Record numbers are assigned by the database file mechanism and are not part of the account information. As a result, they are not meaningful to database users. These users require a different record retrieval mechanism, one that is based on an account ID (the key for the database) rather than a record number.

Retrievals based on account ID require an index that associates each account ID with the corresponding record number. You can implement this index using a binary search tree in which each element contains the two fields: an account ID (the key) and a record number. Since the binary search tree stores elements of type TreeElem, the class IndexEntry given below can be used to implement this index.

```
class IndexEntry implements TreeElem
{
    int acctID;                         // (Key) Account identifier
    long recNum;                        // Record number

    public int key ( )
        { return acctID; }              // Return key field
}
```

You build the index by reading through the database account by account, inserting successive (account ID, record number) pairs into the tree as you progress through the file. The following index tree, for instance, was produced by inserting the account IndexEntry elements from the database records shown above into an (initially) empty tree.

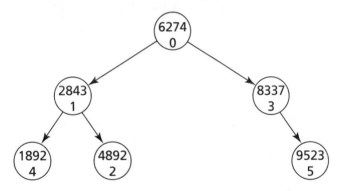

Given an account ID, retrieval of the corresponding account record is a two-step process. First, you retrieve the element from the index tree that has the specified account ID. Then, using the record number stored in the index element, you read the corresponding account record from the database file. The result is an efficient retrieval process that is based on account ID.

Step 1: Using the program shell given in the file *IndexDB.jshl* as a basis, create a program that builds an index tree for the accounts database in the file *Accounts.dat*. Once the index is built, your program should

• output the account IDs in ascending order.

• read an account ID from the keyboard and output the corresponding account record.

Step 2: Test your program using the accounts database in the text file *Accounts.dat*. A copy of this database in given below. Try to retrieve several account IDs, including account IDs that do *not* occur in the database. A test plan form follows.

Record No.	Account ID	First name	Last name	Balance
0	6274	James	Johnson	415.56
1	2843	Marcus	Wilson	9217.23
2	4892	Maureen	Albright	51462.56
3	8337	Debra	Douglas	27.26
4	9523	Bruce	Gold	719.32
5	3165	John	Carlson	1496.24
6	1892	Mary	Smith	918.26
7	3924	Simon	Chang	386.85
8	6023	John	Edgar	9.65
9	5290	George	Truman	16110.68
10	8529	Elena	Gomez	86.77
11	1144	Donald	Williams	4114.26

Test Plan for the *Indexed Accounts Database Program*

Test case	Expected result	Checked

Laboratory 12: Postlab Exercise 1

Name _____

Hour/Period/Section _____

Date _____

What are the heights of the shortest and tallest binary search trees that can be constructed from a set of N distinct keys? Give examples that illustrate your answer.

Laboratory 12: Postlab Exercise 2

Name

Hour/Period/Section

Date

Given the shortest possible binary search tree containing N distinct keys, develop worst-case, order-of-magnitude estimates of the execution time of the following Binary Search Tree ADT operations. Briefly explain your reasoning behind each of your estimates.

retrieve	O( )
Explanation:	

insert	O( )
Explanation:	

remove	O( )
Explanation:	

writeKeys	O( )
Explanation:	

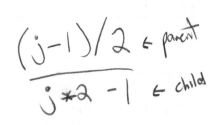

$$\frac{(j-1)/2 \;\leftarrow\; parent}{j*2 \;-1 \;\leftarrow\; child}$$

Heap ADT

OBJECTIVES

In this laboratory you

- create an implementation of the Heap ADT using an array representation of a tree.

- create a heap sort method based on the heap construction techniques used in your implementation of the Heap ADT.

- use inheritance to derive a priority queue class from your heap class and develop a simulation of an operating system's task scheduler using a priority queue.

- analyze where elements with various priorities are located in a heap.

OVERVIEW

Linked structures are not the only way in which you can represent trees. If you take the binary tree shown below and copy its contents into an array in level order, you produce the following array.

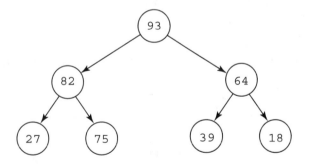

Index	Entry
0	93
1	82
2	64
3	27
4	75
5	39
6	18

Examining the relationship between positions in the tree and entries in the array, you see that if an element is stored in entry N in the array, then the element's left child is stored in entry 2N + 1, its right child is stored in entry 2N + 2, and its parent is stored in entry (N − 1) / 2. These mappings make it easy to move through the tree stepping from parent to child (or vice versa).

You could use these mappings to support an array-based implementation of the Binary Search Tree ADT. However, the result would be a tree representation in which large areas of the array are left unused (as indicated by the dashes in the following array).

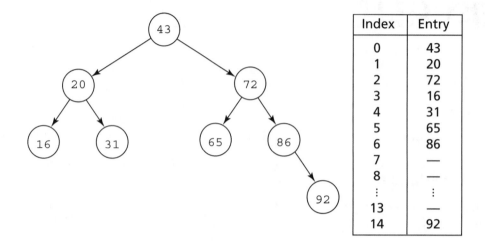

Index	Entry
0	43
1	20
2	72
3	16
4	31
5	65
6	86
7	—
8	—
⋮	⋮
13	—
14	92

In this laboratory, you focus on a different type of tree called a heap. A **heap** is a binary tree that meets the following conditions.

- The tree is **complete**. That is, every level in the tree is filled, except possibly the bottom level. If the bottom level is not filled, then all the missing elements occur on the right.

- Each element in the tree has a corresponding value. For each element E, all of E's descendants have values that are less than or equal to E's value. Therefore, the root stores the maximum of all values in the tree. (Note: In this laboratory we are using a max-heap. There is another heap variant called a min-heap. In a min-heap, all of E's descendants have values that are greater than or equal to E's value.)

The tree shown at the beginning of this laboratory is a heap, as is the tree shown below.

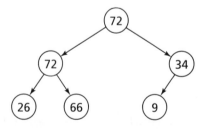

The fact that the tree is complete means that a heap can be stored in level order in an array without introducing gaps (unused areas) in the middle. The result is a compact representation in which you can easily move up and down the branches in a heap.

Clearly, the relationship between the priorities (or values) of the various elements in a heap is not strong enough to support an efficient search process. Because the relationship is simple, however, you can quickly restructure a heap after removing the highest priority (root) element or after inserting a new element. As a result, you can rapidly process the elements in a heap in descending order based on priority. This property combined with the compact array representation forms the basis for an efficient sorting algorithm called heap sort (In-lab Exercise 2) and makes a heap an ideal representation for a priority queue (In-lab Exercise 3).

Heap ADT

Elements

The elements in a heap are of generic type HeapData defined in the file *HeapData.java*. Each element has a priority that is used to determine the relative position of the element within the heap. Elements usually include additional data. Note that priorities are *not* unique—it is quite likely that several elements have the same priority. These objects must support the six basic relational operators, as well as a method called pty( ) that returns an element's priority.

Structure

The elements form a complete binary tree. This is a max-heap. For each element E in the tree, all of E's descendants have priorities that are less than or equal to E's priority.

Constructors and Methods

```
Heap ( )
```
Precondition:
None.
Postcondition:
Default Constructor. Calls setup, which creates an empty heap. Allocates enough memory for a heap containing DEF_MAX_HEAP_SIZE (a constant value) elements.

```
Heap ( int maxNumber )
```
Precondition:
maxNumber > 0.
Postcondition:
Constructor. Calls setup, which creates an empty heap. Allocates enough memory for a heap containing maxNumber elements.

```
void setup ( int maxNumber )
```
Precondition:
maxNumber > 0. A helper method for the constructors. Is declared private since only heap constructors should call this method.
Postcondition:
Creates an empty heap. Allocates enough memory for a heap containing maxNumber elements.

```
void insert ( HeapData newElement )
```
Precondition:
Heap is not full.
Postcondition:
Inserts newElement into a heap. Inserts this element as the bottom rightmost element in the heap and moves it upward until the properties that define a heap are restored. Note that repeatedly swapping array elements is not an efficient way of positioning the newElement in the heap.

```
HeapData removeMax ( )
```
Precondition:
Heap is not empty.
Postcondition:
Removes the element with the highest priority (the root) from a heap and returns it. Replaces the root element with the bottom rightmost element and moves this element downward until the properties that define a heap are restored. Note that (as in insert above) repeatedly swapping array elements is not an efficient method for restoring the heap.

```
void clear ( )
```
Precondition:
None.
Postcondition:
Removes all the elements in a heap.

```
boolean isEmpty ( )
```
Precondition:
None.
Postcondition:
Returns true if a heap is empty. Otherwise, returns false.

```
boolean isFull ( )
```
Precondition:

None.

Postcondition:

Returns true if a heap is full. Otherwise, returns false.

```
void showStructure ( )
```
Precondition:

None.

Postcondition:

Outputs the priorities of the elements in a heap in both array and tree form. The tree is output with its branches oriented from left (root) to right (leaves)—that is, the tree is output rotated counterclockwise 90 degrees from its conventional orientation. If the heap is empty, outputs "Empty heap". Note that this operation is intended for testing/debugging purposes only.

LABORATORY 13: Cover Sheet

Name _____

Hour/Period/Section _____

Date _____

Place a check mark (✔) in the Assigned column next to the exercises that your instructor has assigned to you. Attach this cover sheet to the front of the packet of materials that you submit for this laboratory.

Exercise	Assigned	Completed
Prelab Exercise	✔	
Bridge Exercise	✔	
In-lab Exercise 1		
In-lab Exercise 2		
In-lab Exercise 3		
Postlab Exercise 1		
Postlab Exercise 2		
Total		

LABORATORY 13: Prelab Exercise

Name _____

Hour/Period/Section _____

Date _____

Step 1: Implement the operations in Heap ADT using an array representation of a heap. Heaps can be different sizes; therefore you need to store the actual number of elements in the heap (size), along with the heap elements themselves (element). Remember that in Java the size of the array is held in a constant called length in the array object. Therefore, in Java a separate variable (such as maxSize) is not necessary, since the maximum number of elements our heap can hold can be determined by referencing length — more specifically in our case, element.length.

Base your implementation on the following incomplete definitions from the file *Heap.jshl*. You are to fill in the Java code for each of the constructors and methods where only the method headers are given. Each method header appears on a line by itself and does not contain a semicolon. This is not an interface file, so a semicolon should not appear at the end of a method header. Each of these methods needs to be fully implemented by writing the body of code for implementing that particular method and enclosing the body of that method in braces.

```java
public class Heap
{
    // Constant
    private static final int DEF_MAX_HEAP_SIZE = 10;    // Default maximum heap size

    // Data members
    private int size;                       // Actual number of elements in the heap
    private HeapData [ ] element;           // Array containing the heap elements

    // ——The following are Method Headers ONLY —— //
    // each of these methods needs to be fully implemented

    // Constructors and helper method setup
    public Heap ( )                         // Constructor: default size
    public Heap ( int maxNumber )           // Constructor: specific size

    // Class methods
    private void setup ( int maxNumber )    // Called by constructors only

    // Heap manipulation methods
    public void insert ( HeapData newElement ) // Insert element
    public HeapData removeMax ( )              // Remove max pty element
    public void clear ( )                      // Clear heap
```

```
    // Heap status methods
    public boolean isEmpty ( )              // Heap is empty
    public boolean isFull ( )               // Heap is full

    // Output the heap structure — used in testing/debugging
    public void showStructure ( )

    // Recursive partner of the showStructure() method
    private void showSubtree ( int index, int level )

} // class Heap
```

Step 2: Save your implementation of the Heap ADT in the file *Heap.java*. Be sure to document your code.

LABORATORY 13: Bridge Exercise

Name

Hour/Period/Section

Date

Check with your instructor as to whether you are to complete this exercise prior to your lab period or during lab.

The test program in the file *TestHeap.java* allows you to interactively test your implementation of the Heap ADT using the following commands. If you have limited knowledge of reading input from the keyboard in Java, carefully review the *TestHeap.java* file (and the other test files provided with this laboratory) and notice the steps that are taken to read in more than one character at a time.

Command	Action
+pty	Insert an element with the specified priority.
-	Remove the element with the highest priority from the heap and output it.
E	Report whether the heap is empty.
F	Report whether the heap is full.
C	Clear the heap.
Q	Quit the test program.

Step 1: Prepare a test plan for your implementation of the Heap ADT. Your test plan should cover heaps of various sizes, including empty, full, and single-element heaps. A test plan form follows.

Step 2: Execute your test plan. If you discover mistakes in your implementation, correct them and execute your test plan again.

Test Plan for the *Operations in the Heap ADT*

Test case	Commands	Expected result	Checked

LABORATORY 13: In-lab Exercise 1

Name _____

Hour/Period/Section _____

Date _____

Examining the tree form of a heap rotated 90 degrees counterclockwise from its conventional orientation can be awkward. Because a heap is a complete tree, an unambiguous representation in tree form can be generated by outputting the heap level-by-level, with each level output on a separate line.

```
void writeLevels ( )
```
Precondition:
None.
Postcondition:
Outputs the elements in a heap in level order, one level per line. Only outputs each element's priority. If the heap is empty, then outputs "Empty heap".

The tree shown on the first page of this laboratory, for example, yields the following output.

```
93
82 64
27 75 39 18
```

Step 1:   Implement this operation and add it to the file *Heap.java*. An incomplete implementation of this method is included in the definition of the Heap class in the file *Heap.jshl*.

Step 2:   Activate the 'w' (write levels) command in the test program in the file *TestHeap.java* by removing the comment delimiter (and the character 'w') from the lines that begin with "//w".

Step 3:   Prepare a test plan for this operation that covers heaps of various sizes, including empty and single-element heaps. A test plan form follows.

Step 4: Execute your test plan. If you discover mistakes in your implementation of the writeLevels operation, correct them and execute your test plan again.

Test Plan for the *writeLevels Operation*

Test case	Commands	Expected result	Checked

LABORATORY 13: In-lab Exercise 2

Name _____

Hour/Period/Section _____

Date _____

After removing the root element, the removeMax operation inserts a new element at the root and moves this element downward until a heap is produced. The following method performs a similar task, except that the heap it is building is rooted at array entry root and occupies only a portion of the array.

```
void moveDown ( HeapData [ ] element, int root, int size )
```
Precondition:
The left and right subtrees of the binary tree rooted at root are heaps.
Postcondition:
Restores the binary tree rooted at root to a heap by moving element[root] downward until the tree satisfies the heap property. Parameter size is the number of elements in the array. Remember that repeatedly swapping array elements is not an efficient method for restoring the heap.

In this exercise, you implement an efficient sorting algorithm called heap sort using the moveDown( ) method. You first use this method to transform an array into a heap. You then remove elements one-by-one from the heap (from the highest priority element to the lowest) until you produce a sorted array.

Let's begin by examining how you transform an unsorted array into a heap. Each leaf of any binary tree is a one-element heap. You can build a heap containing three elements from a pair of sibling leaves by applying the `moveDown( )` method to that pair's parent. The four single-element heaps (leaf nodes) in the following tree

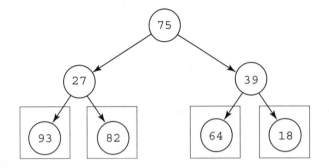

Index	Entry
0	75
1	27
2	39
3	93
4	82
5	64
6	18

are transformed by the calls `moveDown(sample, 1, 7)` and `moveDown(sample, 2, 7)` into a pair of three-element heaps:

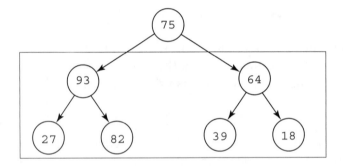

Index	Entry
0	75
1	93
2	64
3	27
4	82
5	39
6	18

By repeating this process, you build larger and larger heaps, until you transform the entire tree (array) into a heap.

```
// Build successively larger heaps within the array until the
// entire array is a heap.

for ( j = (size - 1) / 2; j >= 0; j-- )
    moveDown( element, j, size );
```

Combining the pair of three-element heaps shown previously using the call `moveDown(sample, 0, 7)`, for instance, produces the following heap.

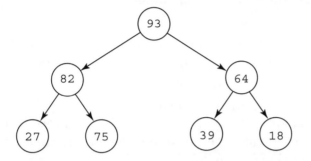

Index	Entry
0	93
1	82
2	64
3	27
4	75
5	39
6	18

Now that you have a heap, you remove elements of decreasing priority from the heap and gradually construct an array that is sorted in ascending order. The root of the heap contains the highest priority element. If you swap the root with the element at the end of the array and use `moveDown( )` to form a new heap, you end up with a heap containing six elements and a sorted array containing one element. Performing this process a second time yields a heap containing five elements and a sorted array containing two elements.

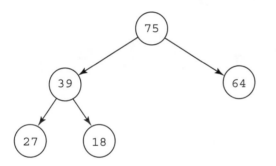

	Index	Entry
	0	75
Heap	1	39
	2	64
	3	27
	4	18
Sorted	5	82
array	6	93

You repeat this process until the heap is gone and a sorted array remains.

```
// Swap the root element from each successively smaller heap with
// the last unsorted element in the array. Restore the heap after
// each exchange.

for ( j = size - 1; j > 0; j-- )
{
    temp = element[ j ];
    element[ j ] = element[ 0 ];
    element[ 0 ] = temp;
    moveDown( element, 0, j );
}
```

A shell containing a `heapSort( )` method comprised of the two loops shown above is given in the file *TestHeapSort.jshl*.

Step 1: Using your implementation of the `removeMax` operation as a basis, create an implementation of the `moveDown( )` method.

Step 2: Add your implementation of the `movedown( )` method to the shell in the file *TestHeapSort.jshl*, thereby completing code needed by the `heapSort( )` method. Save the result in the file *TestHeapSort.java*.

Step 3: Before testing the resulting `heapSort( )` method using the test program in the file *TestHeapSort.java*, prepare a test plan for the `heapSort( )` method that covers arrays of different lengths containing a variety of priority values. Be sure to include arrays that have multiple elements with the same priority. A test plan form follows.

Step 4: Execute your test plan. If you discover mistakes in your implementation of the moveDown( ) and heapSort( ) methods, correct them and execute your test plan again.

Test Plan for the *heapSort() Method*

Test case	Array	Expected result	Checked

LABORATORY 13: In-lab Exercise 3

Name _____

Hour/Period/Section _____

Date _____

A **priority queue** is a linear data structure in which the elements are maintained in descending order based on priority. You can only access the element at the front of the queue—that is, the element with the highest priority—and examining this element entails removing (dequeuing) it from the queue.

Priority Queue ADT

The Priority Queue ADT inherits most of its functionality from the Heap ADT. Therefore, the Priority Queue ADT is a specialized version of the Heap ADT. Thus, Priority Queue is the **subclass** of Heap, and Heap is the **superclass** of Priority Queue.

Elements

The elements in a priority queue are of generic type HeapData found in the file *HeapData.java*. Each element has a priority that is used to determine the relative position of the element within the queue. Elements usually include additional data. These objects must support the six basic relational operators, as well as a method called *pty( )* that returns an element's priority.

Structure

The queue elements are stored in descending order based on priority.

Constructors and Methods

PtyQueue ( )
Precondition:
None.
Postcondition:
Default Constructor. Creates an empty priority queue by calling the default constructor of its superclass. Allocates enough memory for a queue containing DEF_MAX_HEAP_SIZE (a constant value in Heap) elements.

```
PtyQueue ( int size )
```
Precondition:
size > 0.
Postcondition:
Constructor. Creates an empty priority queue by calling the corresponding constructor in its superclass. Allocates enough memory for a queue containing size elements.

```
void enqueue ( HeapData newElement )
```
Precondition:
Queue is not full.
Postcondition:
Inserts newElement into a priority queue.

```
HeapData dequeue ( )
```
Precondition:
Queue is not empty.
Postcondition:
Removes the highest priority (front) element from a priority queue and returns it.

Inherited from Heap

```
void clear ( )

boolean isEmpty ( )

boolean isFull ( )
```

You can easily and efficiently implement a priority queue as a heap by using the Heap ADT `insert` operation to enqueue elements and the `removeMax` operation to dequeue elements. The following incomplete definitions derive a class called PtyQueue from the Heap class. In Java the keyword **extends** is used to specify inheritance (`class PtyQueue extends Heap` means PtyQueue inherits from Heap). Thus, PtyQueue is the subclass and Heap is the superclass. The subclass inherits all of the public and protected instance variables and methods defined by the superclass and adds its own, unique elements as needed.

```
class PtyQueue extends Heap
{

    // Constructor
    public PtyQueue ( )                     // Constructor: default size
    {               }
    public PtyQueue ( int size )            // Constructor: specific size
    {                   }
```

```
    // Queue manipulation methods
    public void enqueue ( HeapData newElement )  // Enqueue element
    {                        }
    public HeapData dequeue ( )                  // Dequeue element
    {                        }

} // class PtyQueue
```

Implementations of the Priority Queue ADT constructor, enqueue, and dequeue operations are given in the file *PtyQueue.java*. These implementations are very short, reflecting the close relationship between the Heap ADT and the Priority Queue ADT. Note that you inherit the remaining operations in the Priority Queue ADT from the Heap class. You may use the file *TestPtyQueue.java* to test the Priority Queue implementation.

Operating systems commonly use priority queues to regulate access to system resources such as printers, memory, disks, software, and so forth. Each time a task requests access to a system resource, the task is placed on the priority queue associated with that resource. When the task is dequeued, it is granted access to the resource—to print, store data, and so on.

Suppose you wish to model the flow of tasks through a priority queue having the following properties:

- One task is dequeued every minute (assuming that there is at least one task waiting to be dequeued during that minute).

- From zero to two tasks are enqueued every minute, where there is a 50% chance that no tasks are enqueued, a 25% percent chance that one task is enqueued, and a 25% chance that two tasks are enqueued.

- Each task has a priority value of zero (low) or one (high), where there is an equal chance of a task having either of these values.

You can simulate the flow of tasks through the queue during a time period n minutes long using the following algorithm.

```
Initialize the queue to empty.
for ( minute = 0 ; minute < n ; ++minute )
{
    If the queue is not empty, then remove the task at the front of the queue.
    Compute a random integer k between 0 and 3.
    If k is 1, then add one task to the queue. If k is 2, then add two tasks.
        Otherwise (if k is 0 or 3), do not add any tasks to the queue.
        Compute the priority of each task by generating a random value of 0 or 1
        (assuming here are only 2 priority levels).
}
```

These steps are similar to the ones used in the simulation program for the Queue ADT in Laboratory 6. Therefore, it may help to review the file *StoreSim.jshl* in the Lab6 Java package/subdirectory. Notice that in *OsSim.jshl* the number of priority levels and the length of the simulation are read in as tokens from the keyboard instead of as arguments entered at the command-line prompt. Review the code in *OsSim.jshl* carefully so you become familiar with how a Java program can be written to read tokens of data.

Step 1: Using the program shell given in the file *OsSim.jshl* as a basis, create a program that uses the Priority Queue ADT to implement the task scheduler described above. Your program should output the following information about each task as it is dequeued: the task's priority, when it was enqueued, and how long it waited in the queue.

Step 2: Use your program to simulate the flow of tasks through the priority queue and complete the following table.

Time (minutes)	Longest wait for any low priority (0) task	Longest wait for any high priority (1) task
10		
30		
60		

Step 3: Is your priority queue task scheduler unfair—that is, given two tasks T_1 and T_2 of the same priority, where task T_1 is enqueued at time N and task T_2 is enqueued at time $N + i$ $(i > 0)$, is task T_2 ever dequeued before task T_1? If so, how can you eliminate this problem and make your task scheduler fair?

LABORATORY 13: Postlab Exercise 1

Name _____

Hour/Period/Section _____

Date _____

You can use a heap—or a priority queue (In-lab Exercise 3)—to implement both a first-in, first-out (FIFO) queue and a last-in, first-out (LIFO) stack. The trick is to use the order in which elements arrive as the basis for determining the elements' priority values.

Part A

How would you assign priority values to elements to produce a FIFO queue?

Part B

How would you assign priority values to elements to produce a LIFO stack?

LABORATORY 13: Postlab Exercise 2

Name _____

Hour/Period/Section _____

Date _____

Part A

Given a heap containing ten elements with distinct priorities, where in the heap can the element with the next-to-highest priority be located? Give examples to illustrate your answer.

Part B

Given the same heap as in Part A, where in the heap can the element with the lowest priority be located? Give examples to illustrate your answer.

Weighted Graph ADT

OBJECTIVES

In this laboratory you

- create an implementation of the Weighted Graph ADT using a vertex list and an adjacency matrix.

- add vertex coloring and implement a method that checks whether a graph has a proper coloring.

- develop a routine that finds the least costly (or shortest) path between each pair of vertices in a graph.

- investigate the Four-Color Theorem by generating a graph for which no proper coloring can be created using less than five colors.

OVERVIEW

Many relationships cannot be expressed easily using either a linear or a hierarchical data structure. The relationship between the cities connected by a highway network is one such relationship. Although it is possible for the roads in a highway network to describe a relationship between cities that is linear (a one-way street, for example) or hierarchical (an expressway and its off-ramps, for instance), we all have driven in circles enough times to know that most highway networks are neither linear nor hierarchical. What we need is a data structure that lets us connect each city to any of the other cities in the network. This type of data structure is referred to as a **graph**.

Like a tree, a graph consists of a set of nodes (called vertices) and a set of edges. Unlike a tree, an edge in a graph can connect any pair of vertices, not simply a parent and its child. The following graph represents a simple highway network.

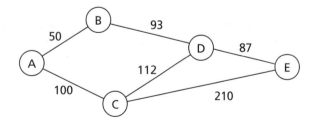

Each vertex in the graph has a unique **label** that denotes a particular city. Each edge has a **weight** that denotes the cost (measured in terms of distance, time, or money) of traversing the corresponding road. Note that the edges in the graph are **undirected**; that is, if there is an edge connecting a pair of vertices A and B, this edge can be used to move either from A to B, or from B to A. The resulting **weighted, undirected graph** expresses the cost of traveling between cities using the roads in the highway network. In this laboratory, the focus is on the implementation and application of weighted, undirected graphs.

Weighted Graph ADT

Elements

Each vertex in a graph has a label (of type String) that uniquely identifies it. Vertices may include additional data.

Structure

The relationship between the vertices in a graph are expressed using a set of undirected edges, where each edge connects one pair of vertices. Collectively, these edges define a symmetric relation between the vertices. Each edge in a weighted graph has a weight that denotes the cost of traversing that edge. This relationship is represented by an adjacency matrix of size $n \times n$, where n is the maximum number of vertices allowed in the graph.

Constructors and Methods

```
WtGraph ( )
```
Precondition:
None.
Postcondition:
Default Constructor. Calls setup, which creates an empty graph. Allocates enough memory for an adjacency matrix representation of the graph containing DEF_MAX_GRAPH_SIZE (a constant value) vertices.

```
WtGraph ( int maxNumber )
```
Precondition:
maxNumber > 0.
Postcondition:
Constructor. Calls setup, which creates an empty graph. Allocates enough memory for an adjacency matrix representation of the graph containing maxNumber vertices.

```
void setup ( int maxNumber )
```
Precondition:

maxNumber > 0. A helper method for the constructors. Is declared private since only WtGraph constructors should call this method.

Postcondition:

Creates an empty graph. Allocates enough memory for an adjacency matrix representation of the graph containing maxNumber elements.

```
void insertVertex ( Vertex newVertex )
```
Precondition:

Graph is not full.

Postcondition:

Inserts newVertex into a graph. If the vertex already exists in the graph, then updates it. If the vertex is new, the entire structure (both the vertex list and the adjacency matrix) is updated.

```
void insertEdge ( String v1, String v2, int wt )
```
Precondition:

Graph includes vertices v1 and v2.

Postcondition:

Inserts an undirected edge connecting vertices v1 and v2 into a graph. The weight of the edge is wt. If there is already an edge connecting these vertices, then updates the weight of the edge.

```
Vertex retrieveVertex ( String v )
```
Precondition:

None.

Postcondition:

Searches a graph for vertex v. If this vertex is found, then returns the vertex's data. Otherwise, returns null.

```
int edgeWeight ( String v1, String v2 )
```
Precondition:

Graph includes vertices v1 and v2.

Postcondition:

Searches a graph for the edge connecting vertices v1 and v2. If this edge exists, then returns the weight of the edge. Otherwise, returns an undefined weight.

```
void removeVertex ( String v )
```
Precondition:

Graph includes vertex v.

Postcondition:

Removes vertex v from a graph.

```
void removeEdge ( String v1, String v2 )
```
Precondition:
Graph includes vertices v1 and v2.
Postcondition:
Removes the edge connecting vertices v1 and v2 from a graph.


```
void clear ( )
```
Precondition:
None.
Postcondition:
Removes all the vertices and edges in a graph.


```
boolean isEmpty ( )
```
Precondition:
None.
Postcondition:
Returns true if a graph is empty (no vertices). Otherwise, returns false.


```
boolean isFull ( )
```
Precondition:
None.
Postcondition:
Returns true if a graph is full. Otherwise, returns false.


```
void showStructure ( )
```
Precondition:
None.
Postcondition:
Outputs a graph with the vertices in array form and the edges in adjacency matrix form (with their weights). If the graph is empty, outputs "Empty graph". Note that this operation is intended for testing/debugging purposes only.

LABORATORY 14: Cover Sheet

Name

Hour/Period/Section

Date

Place a check mark (✔) in the Assigned column next to the exercises that your instructor has assigned to you. Attach this cover sheet to the front of the packet of materials that you submit for this laboratory.

Exercise	Assigned	Completed
Prelab Exercise	✔	
Bridge Exercise	✔	
In-lab Exercise 1		
In-lab Exercise 2		
In-lab Exercise 3		
Postlab Exercise 1		
Postlab Exercise 2		
Total		

LABORATORY 14: Prelab Exercise

Name

Hour/Period/Section

Date

You can represent a graph in many ways. In this laboratory, you use an array to store the set of vertices and an **adjacency matrix** to store the set of edges. An entry (j, k) in an adjacency matrix contains information on the edge that goes from the vertex with index j to the vertex with index k. For a weighted graph, each matrix entry contains the weight of the corresponding edge. A specially chosen weight value is used to indicate edges that are missing from the graph.

The following graph

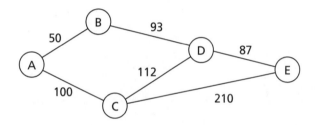

yields the vertex list and adjacency matrix shown below. A '–' is used to denote an edge that is missing from the graph.

Vertex List	
Index	Label
0	A
1	B
2	C
3	D
4	E

Adjacency Matrix					
From/To	0	1	2	3	4
0	—	50	100	—	—
1	50	—	—	93	—
2	100	—	—	112	210
3	—	93	112	—	87
4	—	—	210	87	—

Vertex A has an array index of 0 and vertex C has an array index of 2. The weight of the edge from vertex A to vertex C is therefore stored in entry $(0, 2)$ in the adjacency matrix.

Step 1: Implement the operations in the Weighted Graph ADT using an array to store the vertices (vertexList) and an adjacency matrix to store the edges (adjMatrix). The number of vertices in a graph is not fixed; therefore, you need to store the actual number of vertices in the graph (size). Remember that in Java the size of the array is held in a constant called length in the array object. Therefore, in Java a separate variable (such as maxSize) is not necessary, since the maximum number of elements our graph can hold can be determined by referencing length—more specifically in our case, vertexList.length.

Base your implementation on the following incomplete definitions from the file *WtGraph.jshl*. The class Vertex (for the vertexList) is defined in the file *Vertex.java*. You are to fill in the Java code for each of the constructors and methods where only the method headers are given. Each method header appears on a line by itself and does not contain a semicolon. This is not an interface file, so a semicolon should not appear at the end of a method header. Each of these methods needs to be fully implemented by writing the body of code for implementing that particular method and enclosing the body of that method in braces.

```
public class Vertex
{
    // Data members
    private String label;                    // Vertex label

    // Constructor
    public Vertex( String name )
    {
        label = name;
    }

    // Class methods
    public String getLabel( )
    {
        return label;
    }

} // class Vertex

public class WtGraph
{
    // Default number of vertices (a constant)
    public final int DEF_MAX_GRAPH_SIZE = 10;
    // "Weight" of a missing edge (a constant) — the max int value
    public static final int INFINITE_EDGE_WT = Integer.MAX_VALUE;

    // Data members
    private int size;                        // Actual number of vertices in the graph
    private Vertex [ ] vertexList;           // Vertex list
    private int [ ][ ] adjMatrix;            // Adjacency matrix (a 2D array)
```

```
// ------The following are Method Headers ONLY ------ //
// each of these methods needs to be fully implemented

// Constructors
public WtGraph( )
public WtGraph ( int maxNumber )

// Class methods
private void setUp( int maxNumber )              // Called by constructors

// Graph manipulation methods
public void insertVertex ( Vertex newVertex )         // Insert vertex
public void insertEdge ( String v1, String v2, int wt )// Insert edge
public Vertex retrieveVertex ( String v )         // Get vertex
public int edgeWeight ( String v1, String v2 )    // Get edge wt
public void removeVertex ( String v )             // Remove vertex
public void removeEdge ( String v1, String v2 )   // Remove edge
public void clear ( )                             // Clear graph

// Graph status methods
public boolean isEmpty ( )                         // Is graph empty?
public boolean isFull ( )                          // Is graph full?

// Output the graph structure — used in testing /debugging
public void showStructure ( )

//  Facilitator methods
private int index ( String v )                     // Converts vertex label to an
                                                   //   adjacency matrix index
    private int getEdge ( int row, int col )       // Get edge weight using
                                                   //   adjacency matrix indices
    private void setEdge ( int row, int col, int wt )   // Set edge wt using
                                                   //   adjacency matrix indices
} // class WtGraph
```

Your implementations of the public methods should use your `getEdge( )` and `setEdge( )` facilitator methods to access entries in the adjacency matrix. For example, the assignment statement

```
setEdge(2, 3, 100);
```

uses the `setEdge( )` method to assign a weight of 100 to the entry in the second row, third column of the adjacency matrix and the if statement

```
if ( getEdge(j, k) == WtGraph.INFINITE_EDGE_WT )
        System.out.println("Edge is missing from graph");
```

uses the `getEdge( )` method to test whether there is an edge connecting the vertex with index `j` and the vertex with index `k`.

Step 2: Save your implementation of the Weighted Graph ADT in the file *WtGraph.java*. Be sure to document your code.

LABORATORY 14: Bridge Exercise

Name _____

Hour/Period/Section _____

Date _____

Check with your instructor as to whether you are to complete this exercise prior to your lab period or during lab.

The test program in the file *TestWtGraph.java* allows you to interactively test your implementation of the Weighted Graph ADT using the following commands.

Command	Action
+v	Insert vertex v.
=v w wt	Insert an edge connecting vertices v and w. The weight of this edge is wt.
?v	Retrieve vertex v.
#v w	Retrieve the edge connecting vertices v and w and output its weight.
-v	Remove vertex v.
!v w	Remove the edge connecting vertices v and w.
E	Report whether the graph is empty.
F	Report whether the graph is full.
C	Clear the graph.
Q	Quit the test program.

Note that v and w denote vertex labels (of type String) not individual characters (of type char). As a result, you must be careful to enter these commands using the exact format shown above—including spaces.

Step 1: Prepare a test plan for your implementation of the Weighted Graph ADT. Your test plan should cover graphs in which the vertices are connected in a variety of ways. Be sure to include test cases that attempt to retrieve edges that do not exist or that connect nonexistent vertices. A test plan form follows.

Step 2: Execute your test plan. If you discover mistakes in your implementation, correct them and execute your test plan again.

Test Plan for the *Operations in the Weighted Graph ADT*

Test case	Commands	Expected result	Checked

LABORATORY 14: In-lab Exercise 1

Name _____

Hour/Period/Section _____

Date _____

A communications network consists of a set of switching centers (vertices) and a set of communications lines (edges) that connect these centers. When designing a network, a communications company needs to know whether the resulting network will continue to support communications between *all* centers should one of these communications lines be rendered inoperative due to weather or equipment failure. That is, they need to know the answer to the following question:

Given a graph in which there is a path from every vertex to every other vertex, will removing any edge from the graph always produce a graph in which there is *still* a path from every vertex to every other vertex?

Obviously, the answer to this question depends on the graph. The answer for the graph shown below is yes.

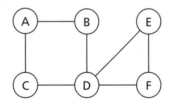

On the other hand, you can divide the following graph into two disconnected subgraphs by removing the edge connecting vertices D and E. Thus, for this graph the answer is no.

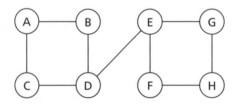

Although determining an answer to this question for an arbitrary graph is somewhat difficult, there are certain classes of graphs for which the answer is always yes. Given the following definitions, a rule can be derived using simple graph theory.

- A graph G is said to be **connected** if there exists a path from every vertex in G to every other vertex in G.

- The **degree** of a vertex V in a graph G is the number of edges in G that connect to V, where an edge from V to itself counts twice.

The rule states:

> If all of the vertices in a connected graph are of even degree, then removing any one edge from the graph will always produce a connected graph.

If this rule applies to a graph, then you know that the answer to the previous question is yes for that graph. Note that this rule tells you nothing about connected graphs in which the degree of one or more vertices is odd.

The following Weighted Graph ADT operation checks whether every vertex in a graph is of even degree.

```
boolean allEven ( )
```
Precondition:
The graph is connected.
Postcondition:
Returns true if every vertex in a graph is of even degree. Otherwise, returns false.

Step 1: Implement the `allEven` operation described above and add it to the file *WtGraph.java*.

Step 2: Save the file *TestWtGraph.java* as *TestWtGraph2.java*. Revise the TestWtGraph class name accordingly. Activate the 'D' (degree) test in the test program *TestWtGraph2.java* by removing the comment delimiter (and the character 'D') from the lines that begin with "//D".

Step 3: Prepare a test plan for this operation that includes graphs in which the vertices are connected in a variety of ways. A test plan form follows.

Step 4: Execute your test plan. If you discover mistakes in your implementation of the allEven operation, correct them and execute your test plan again.

Test Plan for the *allEven Operation*

Test case	Commands	Expected result	Checked

LABORATORY 14: In-lab Exercise 2

Name

Hour/Period/Section

Date

Suppose you wish to create a road map of a particular highway network. In order to avoid causing confusion among map users, you must be careful to color the cities in such a way that no cities sharing a common border also share the same color. An assignment of colors to cities that meets this criteria is called a **proper coloring** of the map.

Restating this problem in terms of a graph, we say that an assignment of colors to the vertices in a graph is a proper coloring of the graph if no vertex is assigned the same color as an adjacent vertex. The assignment of colors (gray and white) shown in the following graph is an example of a proper coloring.

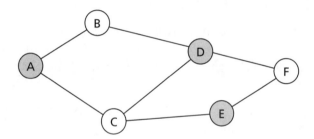

Two colors are not always enough to produce a proper coloring. One of the most famous theorems in graph theory, the Four-Color Theorem, states that creating a proper coloring of any **planar graph** (that is, any graph that can be drawn on a sheet of paper without having the edges cross one another) requires using at most four colors. A planar graph that requires four colors is shown below. Note that if a graph is not planar, you may need to use more than four colors.

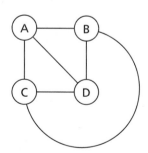

The following Weighted Graph ADT operation determines whether a graph has a proper coloring.

```
boolean properColoring ( )
```
Precondition:
All the vertices have been assigned a color.
Postcondition:
Returns true if no vertex in a graph has the same color as an adjacent vertex. Otherwise, returns false.

Step 1: Add the following data member to the Vertex class definition in the file *Vertex.java*.

```
private String color;    // Vertex color ("r" for red and so forth)
```

Also add the necessary methods to modify and access the vertex color.

Step 2: Implement the properColoring operation described above and add it to the file *WtGraph.java*.

Step 3: Replace the showStructure( ) method in the file *WtGraph.java* with the showStructure( ) method that outputs a vertex's color in addition to its label. An implementation of this showStructure( ) method is given in the file *show14.txt*.

Step 4: Save the file *TestWtGraph.java* as *TestWtGraph3.java*. Revise the TestWtGraph class name accordingly. Activate the 'PC' (proper coloring) test in the test program *TestWtGraph3.java* by removing the comment delimiter (and the characters 'PC') from the lines that begin with "//PC".

Step 5: Prepare a test plan for the properColoring operation that includes a variety of graphs and vertex colorings. A test plan form follows.

Step 6: Execute your test plan. If you discover mistakes in your implementation of the properColoring operation, correct them and execute your test plan again.

Test Plan for the *properColoring Operation*

Test case	Commands	Expected result	Checked

LABORATORY 14: In-lab Exercise 3

Name _____

Hour/Period/Section _____

Date _____

In many applications of weighted graphs, you need to determine not only whether there is an edge connecting a pair of vertices, but whether there is a path connecting the vertices. By extending the concept of an adjacency matrix, you can produce a **path matrix** in which an entry (j, k) contains the cost of the least costly (or **shortest**) path from the vertex with index j to the vertex with index k. The following graph

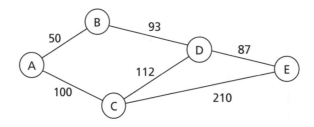

yields the path matrix shown below.

Vertex List	
Index	Label
0	A
1	B
2	C
3	D
4	E

Path Matrix					
From/To	0	1	2	3	4
0	0	50	100	143	230
1	50	0	150	93	180
2	100	150	0	112	199
3	143	93	112	0	87
4	230	180	199	87	0

This graph includes a number of paths from vertex A to vertex E. The cost of the least costly path connecting these vertices is stored in entry (0, 4) in the path matrix, where 0 is the index of vertex A and 4 is the index of vertex E. The corresponding path is ABDE.

In creating this path matrix, we have assumed that a path with cost 0 exists from a vertex to itself (entries of the form (j, j)). This assumption is based on the view that traveling from a vertex to itself is a nonevent and thus costs nothing. Depending on how you intend to apply the information in a graph, you may want to use an alternate assumption.

Given the adjacency matrix for a graph, we begin construction of the path matrix by noting that all edges are paths. These one-edge-long paths are combined to form two-edge-long paths by applying the following reasoning.

```
If there exists a path from a vertex j to a vertex m and
    there exists a path from a vertex m to a vertex k,
then there exists a path from vertex j to vertex k.
```

We can apply this same reasoning to these newly generated paths to form paths consisting of more and more edges. The key to this process is to enumerate and combine paths in a manner that is both complete and efficient. One approach to this task is described in the following algorithm, known as Warshall's algorithm. Note that variables j, k, and m refer to vertex indices, *not* vertex labels.

```
Initialize the path matrix so that it is the same as the edge matrix (all edges are paths).
Create a path with cost 0 from each vertex back to itself.

for ( m = 0 ; m < size ; m++ )
    for ( j = 0 ; j < size ; j++ )
        for ( k = 0 ; k < size ; k++ )
            if there exists a path from vertex j to vertex m and
                there exists a path from vertex m to vertex k,
            then add a path from vertex j to vertex k to the path matrix.
```

This algorithm establishes the existence of paths between vertices but not their costs. Fortunately, by extending the reasoning used above, we can easily determine the costs of the least costly paths between vertices.

```
If there exists a path from a vertex j to a vertex m and
    there exists a path from a vertex m to a vertex k and
    the cost of going from j to m to k is less than entry (j,k) in the path matrix,
then replace entry (j,k) with the sum of entries (j,m) and (m,k).
```

Incorporating this reasoning into the previous algorithm yields the following algorithm, known as Floyd's algorithm.

```
Initialize the path matrix so that it is the same as the edge matrix (all edges are paths).
Create a path with cost 0 from each vertex back to itself.
for ( m = 0 ; m < size ; m++ )
    for ( j = 0 ; j < size ; j++ )
        for ( k = 0 ; k < size ; k++ )
            If there exists a path from vertex j to vertex m and
                there exists a path from vertex m to vertex k and
                the sum of entries (j,m) and (m,k) is less than entry (j,k) in the path
                    matrix,
            then replace entry (j,k) with the sum of entries (j,m) and (m,k).
```

The following Weighted Graph ADT operation computes a graph's path matrix.

```
void computePaths ( )
```
Precondition:
None.
Postcondition:
Computes a graph's path matrix.

Step 1:   Add the data member

```
private int [ ][ ] pathMatrix;    // Path matrix (a 2D array)
```

to the WtGraph class definition in the file *WtGraph.java*. Revise the WtGraph constructors as needed.

Step 2:   Implement the computePaths method described above and add it to the file *WtGraph.java*. You will probably also want to implement facilitator methods for path similar to those used for edge.

Step 3:   Replace the showStructure( ) method in the file *WtGraph.java* with a showStructure( ) method that outputs a graph's path matrix in addition to its vertex list and adjacency matrix. An implementation of this showStructure( ) method is given in the file *show14.txt*.

Step 4:   Save the file *TestWtGraph.java* as *TestWtGraph4.java*. Revise the TestWtGraph class name accordingly. Activate the 'PM' (path matrix) test in the test program *TestWtGraph4.java* by removing the comment delimiter (and the characters 'PM') from the lines that begin with "//PM".

Step 5:   Prepare a test plan for the computePaths operation that includes graphs in which the vertices are connected in a variety of ways with a variety of weights. Be sure to include test cases in which an edge between a pair of vertices has a higher cost than a multiedge path between these same vertices. The edge CE and the path CDE in the graph shown above have this property. A test plan form follows.

Step 6: Execute your test plan. If you discover mistakes in your implementation of the computePaths operation, correct them and execute your test plan again.

Test Plan for the *computePaths Operation*

Test case	Commands	Expected result	Checked

LABORATORY 14: Postlab Exercise 1

Name

Hour/Period/Section

Date

Floyd's algorithm (In-lab Exercise 3) computes the shortest path between each pair of vertices in a graph. Suppose you need to know not only the cost of the shortest path between a pair of vertices, but also which vertices lie along this path. At first, it may seem that you need to store a list of vertices for every entry in the path matrix. Fortunately, you do not need to store this much information. For each entry (j, k) in the path matrix, all you need to know is the index of the vertex that follows j on the shortest path from j to k—that is, the index of the second vertex on the shortest path from j to k. The following graph, for example,

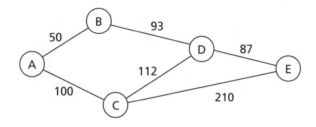

yields the augmented path matrix shown below.

Vertex List	
Index	Label
0	A
1	B
2	C
3	D
4	E

Path Matrix (Cost | Second Vertex on Shortest Path					
From/To	0	1	2	3	4
0	0|0	50|1	100|2	143|1	230|1
1	50|0	0|1	150|0	93|3	180|3
2	100|0	150|0	0|2	112|3	199|3
3	143|1	93|1	112|2	0|3	87|4
4	230|3	180|3	199|3	87|3	0|4

Entry (0, 4) in this path matrix indicates that the cost of the shortest path from vertex A to vertex E is 230. It further indicates that vertex B (the vertex with index 1) is the second vertex on the shortest path. Thus the shortest path is of the form AB...E.

Explain how you can use this augmented path matrix to list the vertices that lie along the shortest path between a given pair of vertices.

LABORATORY 14: Postlab Exercise 2

Name

Hour/Period/Section

Date

Give an example of a graph for which no proper coloring can be created using less than five colors (see In-lab Exercise 2). Does your example contradict the Four-Color Theorem?

Performance Evaluation

OBJECTIVES

In this laboratory, you

- implement a Timer class that you can use to measure the length of time between two events—when a method starts and when it finishes, for instance.

- compare the performance of a set of searching routines.

- compare the performance of a set of sorting routines.

- compare the performance of your array and linked list implementations of the Stack ADT.

OVERVIEW

A routine's performance can be judged in many ways and on many levels. In other laboratories, you describe performance using order-of-magnitude estimates of a routine's execution time. You develop these estimates by analyzing how the routine performs its task, paying particular attention to how it uses iteration and recursion. You then express the routine's projected execution time as a routine of the number of data items (N) that it manipulates as it performs its task. The results are estimates of the form $O(N)$, $O(LogN)$, and so on.

These order-of-magnitude estimates allow you to group routines based on their projected performance under different conditions (best-case, worst-case, and so forth). As important as these order-of-magnitude estimates are, they are by their very nature only estimates. They do not take into account factors specific to a particular environment, such as how a routine is implemented, the type of computer system on which it is being run, and the kind of data being processed. If you are to accurately determine how well or poorly a given routine will perform in a particular environment, you need to evaluate the routine in that environment.

In this laboratory, you measure the performance of a variety of routines. You begin by developing a set of tools that allow you to measure execution time. Then you use these tools to measure the execution times of the routines.

You can determine a routine's execution time in a number of ways. The timings performed in this laboratory will be generated using the approach summarized below.

Get the current system time (call this *startTime*).
Execute the routine.
Get the current system time (call this *stopTime*).
The routine's execution time = *stopTime* – *startTime*.

If the routine executes very rapidly, then the difference between startTime and stopTime may be too small for your computer system to measure. Should this be the case, you need to execute the routine several times and divide the length of the resulting time interval by the number of repetitions, as follows:

Get the current system time (call this *startTime*).
Execute the routine *m* times.
Get the current system time (call this *stopTime*).
The routine's execution time = (*stopTime* – *startTime*) / *m*.

To use this approach, you must have some method for getting and storing the "current system time." One method in Java is to use a System call to get the current time of day, as we have often done in other laboratories to seed the random number generator with a variant value. We can store this information in a variable of the following type:

```
long currTime = System.currentTimeMillis( );
```

This method returns the current time in terms of milliseconds since midnight, January 1, 1970.

In addition to acquiring and storing a point in time, you also need a convenient mechanism for measuring time intervals. The Timer ADT described below uses the familiar stopwatch metaphor to describe the timing process.

Start the timer.
...
Stop the timer.
Read the elapsed time.

Timer ADT

Elements

A pair of times that denote the beginning and end of a time interval.

Structure

None.

Methods

`void start ( )`
Precondition:
None.
Postcondition:
Marks the beginning of a time interval (starts the timer).

`void stop ( )`
Precondition:
The beginning of a time interval has been marked.
Postcondition:
Marks the end of a time interval (stops the timer).

`double elapsedTime ()`
Precondition:
The beginning and end of a time interval have been marked.
Postcondition:
Returns the length of the time interval in milliseconds.

LABORATORY 15: Cover Sheet

Name

Hour/Period/Section

Date

Place a check mark (✔) in the Assigned column next to the exercises that your instructor has assigned to you. Attach this cover sheet to the front of the packet of materials that you submit for this laboratory.

Exercise	Assigned	Completed
Prelab Exercise	✔	
Bridge Exercise	✔	
In-lab Exercise 1		
In-lab Exercise 2		
In-lab Exercise 3		
Postlab Exercise 1		
Postlab Exercise 2		
Total		

LABORATORY 15: Prelab Exercise

Name _____

Hour/Period/Section _____

Date _____

Step 1: Create an implementation of the Timer ADT. Base your implementation on the following incomplete definitions from the file *Timer.jshl*. You are to fill in the Java code for each of the methods where the implementation braces are empty.

```
class Timer
{
    // Data members
    private long startTime,              // Time that the timer was started
                 stopTime;               // Time that the timer was stopped

    // Start and stop the timer
    public void start ( )
    {                                    }
    public void stop ( )
    {                                    }

    // Compute the elapsed time (in milliseconds)
    public long elapsedTime ( )
    {                                    }

} // class Timer
```

Step 2: Save your implementation of the Timer ADT in the file *Timer.java*.

Step 3: What is the resolution of your Timer implementation—that is, what is the shortest time interval it can accurately measure?

LABORATORY 15: Bridge Exercise

Name _____

Hour/Period/Section _____

Date _____

Check with your instructor as to whether you are to complete this exercise prior to your lab period or during lab.

The test program in the program shell file *TimerTest.jshl* allows you to test the accuracy of your implementation of the Timer ADT by measuring time intervals of known duration.

```
//  Test program for the methods in the Timer ADT
import java.io.*;

class TestTimer
{
    static void main ( String args[] ) throws IOException, InterruptedException
    {
        Timer checkTimer = new Timer();      // Timer
        long timeInterval;                   // Time interval to pause

        // Initialize reader - To read a character at a time
        BufferedReader reader =
                new BufferedReader(new InputStreamReader(System.in));
        // Initialize the tokenizer - To read tokens
        StreamTokenizer tokens = new StreamTokenizer(reader);

        // Get the time interval.
        System.out.println();
        System.out.print("Time interval to pause ( in _____ ) : ");
        tokens.nextToken( );
        timeInterval = (long)tokens.nval;

        // Measure the time interval.
        checkTimer.start();                  // Start the timer
        _____(timeInterval);           // Pause for the approximate time interval
        checkTimer.stop();                   // Stop the timer

        System.out.println("Measured time interval (ms) : "
                        + checkTimer.elapsedTime());
    }
} // TestTimer
```

Step 1: Two statements are left incomplete in this program: the call to the method that pauses the program and the string that prompts the user to enter a time interval. Complete the program by specifying the name of a "pause" method supported by your system. Common names for this method include `sleep()` and `wait()`. Add the time unit used by this method to the prompt string. Save the resulting program as *TestTimer.java*.

Step 2: Prepare a test plan for your implementation of the Timer ADT. Your test plan should cover intervals of various lengths, including intervals at or near the resolution of your implementation. A test plan form follows. Please note that due to disparity between system clock interrupts for updating and actual CPU cycles, there may be as much as a 50 ms overrun between the start time plus pause time (*actual time interval*) and the returned stop time (*measured time interval*) for your program.

Step 3: Execute your test plan. If you discover mistakes in your implementation, correct them and execute your test plan again.

Test Plan for the *Operations in the Timer ADT*

Test case	Actual time interval (in milliseconds)	Measured time interval (in milliseconds)	Checked

LABORATORY 15: In-lab Exercise 1

Name _____

Hour/Period/Section _____

Date _____

In this exercise, you examine the performance of the searching routines in the file *Search.java*.

Step 1: Use the program in the file *TimeSearch.java* to measure the execution times of the `linearSearch()`, `binarySearch()`, and `unknownSearch()` routines. This program begins by generating an ordered list of integer keys (`keyList`) and a set of keys to search for in this list (`searchSet`). It then measures the amount of time it takes to search for the keys using the specified routines and computes the average time per search.

The constant `NUM_REPETITIONS` controls how many times each search is executed. Depending on the speed of your system, you may need to use a value of `NUM_REPETITIONS` that differs from the value given in the test program. **Before continuing, you may want to check with your instructor regarding what value of NUM_REPETITIONS you should use.**

Step 2: Complete the following table by measuring the execution times of the `linearSearch()`, `binarySearch()`, and `unknownSearch()` routines for each of the values of `numKeys` listed in the table.

Execution Times of a *Set of Searching Routines*

Routine	Number of keys in the list (`numKeys`)		
	1000	2000	4000
`linearSearch()` O(*N*)			
`binarySearch()` O(Log*N*)			
`unknownSearch()` O( )			

Note: Times shown are in milliseconds.

Step 3: Plot your results below.

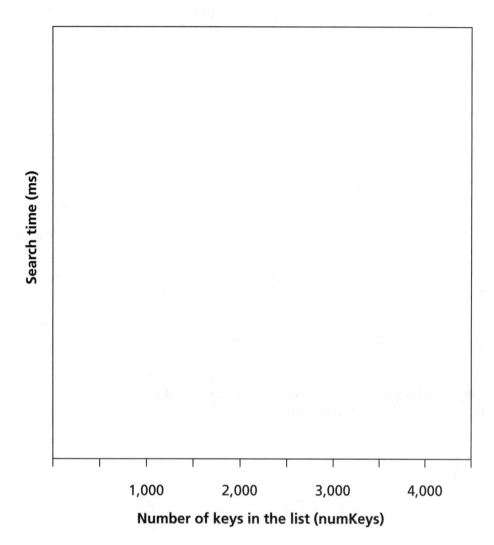

Step 4: How well do your measured times conform with the order-of-magnitude estimates given for the `linearSearch()` and `binarySearch()` routines?

Step 5: Using the code in the file *Search.java* and your measured execution times as a basis, develop an order-of-magnitude estimate of the execution time of the `unknownSearch()` routine. Briefly explain your reasoning behind this estimate.

LABORATORY 15: In-lab Exercise 2

Name

Hour/Period/Section

Date

In this exercise, you examine the performance of the set of sorting routines in the file *Sort.java*.

Step 1: Use the program in the file *TimeSort.java* to measure the execution times of the selectionSort(), quickSort(), and unknownSort() routines. This program begins by generating a list of integer keys (keyList). It then measures the amount of time it takes to sort this list into ascending order using the specified routine.

The constant NUM_REPETITIONS controls how many times each search is executed. Depending on the speed of your system, you may need to use a value of NUM_REPETITIONS that differs from the value given in the test program. **Before continuing, you may want to check with your instructor regarding what value of NUM_REPETITIONS you should use.**

Step 2: Complete the following table by measuring the execution times of the selectionSort(), quickSort(), and unknownSort() routines for each combination of the three test categories and the three values of numKeys listed in the table.

Execution Times of a *Set of Sorting Routines*

Routine	Number of keys in the list (numKeys)		
	1000	2000	4000
selectionSort() $O(N^2)$			
quickSort() $O(N \log N)$			
unknownSort() $O(\ )$			

Note: Times shown are in milliseconds.

Step 3: Plot your results below.

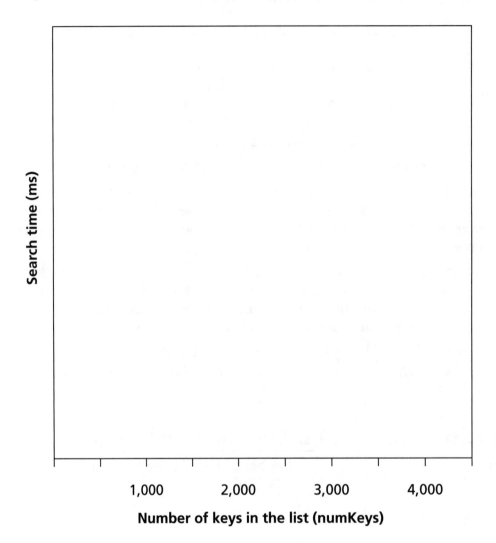

Number of keys in the list (numKeys)

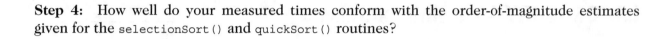

Step 4: How well do your measured times conform with the order-of-magnitude estimates given for the `selectionSort()` and `quickSort()` routines?

Step 5: Using the code in the file *Sort.java* and your measured execution times as a basis, develop an order-of-magnitude estimate of the execution time of the `unknownSort()` routine. Briefly explain your reasoning behind this estimate.

LABORATORY 15: In-lab Exercise 3

Name

Hour/Period/Section

Date

In this exercise, you measure the performance of the array and linked list implementations of the Stack ADT that you created in Laboratory 5.

Step 1: Using the implementation of the Timer ADT that you created in the Prelab as a foundation, write a program that measures the time it takes to completely fill and then empty a 10,000-element stack using the push and pop operations in Stack ADT. Assuming testStack is of type Stack, you can use the following statement to print whether you are testing the class AStack or LStack:

```
System.out.println("Testing the " + testStack.getClass( ));
```

Save your file as *TimeStack.java*. Because these operations execute so rapidly, you may need to fill and empty the stack a number of times in order to produce an accurate measurement of the time it takes to complete a fill/empty cycle.

Step 2: Use your program to measure the time it takes each of your Stack ADT implementations to fill and empty a stack containing 10,000 characters and record the results in the following table.

Step 3: Repeat these measurements using a stack containing 10,000 long integers and record the results below.

Time to Fill and Empty a *10,000-Element Stack*

Stack ADT implementation	Stack Element	
	char	long int
Array implementation		
Linked list implementation		

Note: Times shown are in milliseconds.

LABORATORY 15: Postlab Exercise 1

Name _____

Hour/Period/Section _____

Date _____

You are given another pair of searching routines. Both routines have order-of-magnitude execution time estimates of $O(N)$. When you measure the actual execution times of these routines on a given system using a variety of different data sets, you discover that one routine consistently executes five times faster than the other. How can both routines be $O(N)$, yet have different execution times when they are compared using the same system and the same data?

LABORATORY 15: Postlab Exercise 2

Name _____

Hour/Period/Section _____

Date _____

Using your measurements from In-lab Exercises 1 and 2 as a basis, estimate the execution times of the routines listed below for a randomly generated list of 8,000 integer keys. Do *not* measure the actual execution times of these routines using a list of this size. Estimate what their execution times will be based on the measurements you have already done. Briefly explain your reasoning behind each estimate.

Execution Times of a *Set of Sorting Routines*

Routine	Number of keys in the list (numKeys) = 8000
linearSearch()	Estimated execution time:
Explanation:	
binarySearch()	Estimated execution time:
Explanation:	

Note: Times shown are in milliseconds.

Execution Times of a *Set of Sorting Routines*

Routine	Number of keys in the list (numKeys) = 8000
selectionSort()	Estimated execution time:
Explanation:	
quickSort()	Estimated execution time:
Explanation:	

Note: Times shown are in milliseconds.

Team Software Development Project

OBJECTIVES

In this laboratory, you

- see how a complex problem can be solved by decomposing it into a set of interrelated objects.
- get a feel for the dynamics of a team programming environment.
- learn some object-oriented analysis and design (OOAD) techniques.
- create and implement a program design for a given complex problem.

OVERVIEW

The programs you developed in previous labs solved very specific problems. These programs tended to be relatively short and you were able to create them by yourself directly from the problem descriptions. As problems become more complex, however, team programming efforts and formal program designs become necessary parts of the program development process.

In this laboratory, you work with other students as part a software development team that designs and implements a programming project using established OOAD techniques. This program development process is done over the space of two weeks. During the first week, you work with your teammates to create a program design. In the second week, you implement your design to form a working program.

LABORATORY 16 — Week 1: Prelab Exercise 1

Object-Oriented Analysis and Design Intro

Name _____

Hour/Period/Section _____

Date _____

Given a complex problem, how do you begin to develop a program to solve the problem? Unfortunately, there is no simple answer to this question. How you look at the problem, what form you imagine the solution will take, and what programming language and techniques you intend to use—all of these shape not only the solution but the process of finding a solution.

In this laboratory, you use an object-oriented program development style in which you analyze a problem in terms of the objects in the problem. An **object** is something with a well-defined set of **attributes** and **behaviors**. A statue, a car, a fish, a movie, a party, and a trip—all of these are examples of objects from the real world. We humans are expert at thinking about the world around us in terms of objects. **Object-oriented analysis and design** (OOAD) and **object-oriented programming** (OOP) attempt to apply this ability to the design and creation of programs.

Identifying the object is the most important step in OOAD. Among the recommended techniques for identifying potential objects is the "using nouns" technique of Abbott/Booch.[1] This technique will not find all the objects but is quite simple to apply. In this process the designer identifies all the nouns, pronouns, and noun phrases in the English narrative of the problem. Thus the designer begins to identify potential objects. In like manner, all verbs and predicate phrases are used to help identify object behaviors, and all adjectives are used to help identify object attributes.

Rather than discussing object-oriented design in the abstract, let's try to find the objects in the following problem.

> Part of a child's math education program is a calculator that displays a sad face whenever the number displayed by the calculator is negative and a happy face when the number displayed is positive. The calculator responds to the following commands (where *num* is a floating-point number): +*num*, −*num*, *num, /*num*, and C (clear). In addition, the child can use the Q (quit) command to end the program.

---

[1] Booch, G., "Object-Oriented Development," *IEEE Trans. On Software Engineering*, vol. SE-12, no. 2, pp. 211–21, February 1986.

Based on the "using nouns" technique, one object is obvious: the calculator. What attributes and behaviors are associated with the calculator? That depends on who is doing the associating—different people will produce different results. One possible set of attributes and behaviors is shown below.

Object: Calculator

Attributes: Number displayed (the accumulator)

Behaviors: Performs arithmetic operations

               Displays number

What other objects are there? The problem refers to a display that shows a happy or sad face depending on the number stored in the calculator's accumulator. This face display is another object.

Object: Face

Attributes: Happy or sad

Behaviors: Changes face to happy

               Changes face to sad

               Displays face

Could we have combined the Calculator and Face objects into one object? Yes. The process of finding and using objects is not one with rigid rules. We chose a definition of a calculator that fits a broad range of calculators, not just the one discussed in this problem. Other choices may be equally valid, however.

Finding the final object requires a little more effort. Some object should coordinate the actions of the Calculator and Face objects based on the command input by the child. This object is commonly called the interface.

Object: Interface

Attributes: Calculator

               Face

               Command

Behaviors: Coordinates the calculator and face displays

               Reads a command

               Executes the command

Now that we have identified a set of objects, we need to develop a Java class for each object. As a general rule, an object's attributes become data members of the object's class and its behaviors become class methods. Keep in mind, however, that in program design there are no inflexible rules, only guidelines.

Let's start with the Face object. This object has an attribute that indicates whether the face is a happy face or a sad one. It has behaviors that display the face and change it to *happy* or to *sad*. We represent the Face object using a Java class called Face in which the happy/sad attribute is represented by an integer data member `state` and the behaviors are represented by the class methods `display()`, `makeHappy()`, and `makeSad()`. An incomplete definition/implementation for the `Face` class and the specifications for its class methods are shown below. Note that we have included a constructor that initializes a face to happy when it is declared (constructed).

```
class Face
{
    // Data members
    private int state;           // Face state (1=happy, 0=sad)

    // Class Methods
    public Face ( )              // Constructor
    public void makeHappy ( )    // Set face to happy
    public void makeSad ( )      // Set face to sad
    public void display ( )      // Display face
}
```

Face ( )
Precondition:
None.
Postcondition:
Default Constructor. Creates a face and initializes it to happy.

void makeHappy ( )
Precondition:
None.
Postcondition:
Changes a face to happy.

void makeSad ( )
Precondition:
None.
Postcondition:
Changes a face to sad.

void display ( )
Precondition:
None.
Postcondition:
Displays a face.

Continuing with the Calculator object, we represent this object's accumulator attribute by a double-precision floating-point data member `accum` and its behaviors by the class methods `add()`, `subtract()`, `multiply()`, `divide()`, and `display()`. We complete the set of class methods by adding a constructor and an access method, `value()`. The constructor initializes the accumulator to zero and the `value()` method communicates the accumulator's value to other classes. An incomplete definition/implementation for the `Calculator` class is shown below.

```
class Calculator
{
    // Data members
    private double accum;                    // Accumulator

    // Class Methods
    public Calculator ( )                    // Construct calculator
    public void add ( double num )           // Add to accumulator
    public void subtract ( double num )      // Subtract from accum
    public void multiply ( double num )      // Multiply accumulator
    public void divide ( double num )        // Divide accumulator
    public void clear ( )                    // Clear accumulator
    public double value ( )                  // Return accumulator
    public void display ( )                  // Display calculator
}
```

Calculator ( )
Precondition:
None.
Postcondition:
Default Constructor. Creates a calculator and initializes the accumulator to zero.

void add (double num)
Precondition:
None.
Postcondition:
Adds num to the accumulator.

void subtract (double num)
Precondition:
None.
Postcondition:
Subtracts num from the accumulator.

void multiply (double num)
Precondition:
None.
Postcondition:
Multiplies the accumulator by num.

```
void divide ( double num )
```
Precondition:
The value of num is not zero.
Postcondition:
Divides the accumulator by num.

```
void clear ( )
```
Precondition:
None.
Postcondition:
Clears the accumulator (sets it to zero).

```
double value ( )
```
Precondition:
None.
Postcondition:
Returns the value stored in the accumulator.

```
void display ( )
```
Precondition:
None.
Postcondition:
Displays a calculator.

We create the Interface class in much the same way we did the Calculator and Face classes. In this case, we represent the calculator, face, and command attributes by three data members: calc, smiley, and userCmd.

```
class Interface
{
  ...
    // Data members
    private Calculator calc;    // Calculator object
    private Face smiley;        // Face object
    private Command userCmd;    // User command


    .....
}
```

All the data members in the Interface class are objects in other classes rather than one of Java's predefined data types. We have already defined two of these classes. The userCmd data member stores the last command the user entered along with the command's argument (if any) in the class Command. The Command class is defined below. Note that its data members are not declared private, so they are treated as public by other classes in this Java package or sub-directory.

```
class Command
{
    // Data Members
    char cmd;                          // Command name (letter)
    double arg;                        // Command argument
}
```

We represent the `Interface` object's behaviors by the class methods `generateDisplay()`, `getCommand()`, and `executeCommand()`. To these we add a constructor that initializes the data members and a `done()` method that indicates when the child has entered the Q (quit) command. The incomplete definition/implementation for the `Interface` class and the specifications for its class methods are given below.

```
class Interface
{
    // Data members
    private Calculator calc;           // Calculator object
    private Face smiley;               // Face object
    private Command userCmd;           // User command

    // Class Methods
    public Interface ( )               // Constructor
    public void generateDisplay ( )    // Generate interface display
    public void getCommand ( )         // Get user command
    public void executeCommand ( )     // Process user command
    public boolean done ( )            // Exit interface

}
```

Interface ( )
Precondition:
None.
Postcondition:
Constructor. Creates an interface and initializes its data members.

void generateDisplay ( )
Precondition:
None.
Postcondition:
Generates an interface display consisting of a calculator and a happy/sad face.

void getCommand ( )
Precondition:
None.
Postcondition:
Prompts the user for a command, reads in a command from the keyboard, and stores it in userCmd.

```
void executeCommand ( )
```
Precondition:
None.
Postcondition:
Executes the user's last command (in userCmd).

```
boolean done ( )
```
Precondition:
None.
Postcondition:
Returns true if the user has entered the Q (quit) command. Otherwise, returns false.

We now have a set of well-defined classes for the child's calculator problem. Taken together, these object descriptions, class definitions, and method specifications provide a **design** for one solution to this problem. With a good design, developing an implementation is an easy task. With a bad design, implementation is a difficult, if not impossible, job. That is why the design development process is so important—in many ways, it is the art that defines computer science. Creativity and insight in the design phase lead to programs that are easy to implement and maintain. More important, they result in programs that are enjoyable to use. Mistakes made in the design phase, on the other hand, are costly to fix and often yield a poor product.

FOLLOW-UP EXERCISE

A stoplight is a familiar object on our roadways. Define the attributes and behaviors for a stoplight below.

Object: Stoplight

Attributes:

Behaviors:

LABORATORY 16 — Week 1: Prelab Exercise 2

OOAD REVISITED

Name _____

Hour/Period/Section _____

Date _____

DESCRIPTION OF THE OOAD/PROGRAMMING PROJECT

Overview

Many people use a calendar to keep track of assignments, parties, appointments and the like. In this project, you create a program that takes a set of dated notes and generates an HTML note-board consisting of a set of monthly calendars and associated notes. The contents and appearance of the HTML noteboard are specified by a noteboard file and a set of user-controlled content filters and appearance properties. This HTML noteboard is to be viewed using a web browser. For those unfamiliar with writing HTML, there are several tutorials and the like readily available on the Internet.

You are to view the following description as the program specifications provided by the user. Therefore, as in a real workplace situation, you must make every effort to concisely satisfy each of these program specifications.

Noteboard File Format

The noteboard (*.nbd*) file consists of three parts: the calendar year, the names of 12 image files (one for each month, in month order), and an unordered set of notes of the following form

   month day category text

where

- *month* and *day* identify the month and day to which the note applies.

- *category* identifies the category to which the note belongs (e.g., "personal", "school").

- *text* is the note's narrative text.

A sample noteboard data file is shown below. Notice that while the image file names are listed in month order, the notes are unordered. This data is provided in the file *sample.nbd*. This file includes data for all 12 months of a single year.

```
2002                                 ⌉ Year
january.jpg
february.jpg                           Image file names for all 12 months
march.jpg
...
december.jpg                         ⌉
4 1 holiday April Fool's Day
1 1 holiday New Year's Day             Notes
4 15 personal Taxes due
2 14 holiday Valentine's Day
5 20 school Final exams
10 21 personal My birthday
...                                  ⌋
```

Content Filters

Which months and which notes appear in the HTML display of the noteboard is determined by the following filters.

Content filter	Description
start *month*	The first month to display, where *month* is in the range 1-12. Default: 1
end *month*	The last month to display, where *month* is in the range 1-12. Default: 12
category *filter*	Only the notes in the specified category are included when the noteboard display is generated. The category filter all indicates that all of the notes should be included. Default: all

Appearance Properties

The appearance of the HTML version of the noteboard is determined by the following properties.

Appearance property	Description
background *color*	Background color (bgcolor) for the noteboard display, where *color* is an HTML color constant (e.g., red, white, blue). Default: white
text *color*	Text color for the noteboard display, where *color* is an HTML color constant. Default: black
layout *style*	Layout of the noteboard display, where *style* is either horizontal or vertical. The corresponding layouts are illustrated below. horizontal <table><tr><td>January calendar</td><td>January notes</td></tr><tr><td>February calendar</td><td>February notes</td></tr><tr><td>. . .</td><td>. . .</td></tr><tr><td>December calendar</td><td>December notes</td></tr></table> vertical <table><tr><td>January calendar</td></tr><tr><td>January notes</td></tr><tr><td>February calendar</td></tr><tr><td>February notes</td></tr><tr><td>. . .</td></tr><tr><td>December calendar</td></tr><tr><td>December notes</td></tr></table> In either layout, each month's calendar consists of an image and a calendar day grid. In addition, the notes for each month are output in **ascending order based on day.** Default: horizontal

User Interface

Your program begins by prompting the user for the name of a noteboard (*.nbd*) file. It then reads in the calendar year, the calendar image file names, and the entire set of notes, grouping the notes by month as they are read in. You can assume that there are no more than 15 notes per month.

The user controls your program via a simple command-line interface. The current state of the content filters and appearance properties is displayed (see the example below) and the user is prompted to enter a command.

```
----------------------------------------------------------
Filters
   start:       1
   end:         12
   category:    all
Appearance
   background:  white
   text:        black
   layout:      horizontal
   interactive  true
----------------------------------------------------------
Enter command (enter help to show command list):
```

The set of user commands is listed below with the first word (e.g., start) being the specific command followed by its parameter (e.g., *mm*).

Command	Description
start *mm*	Sets the first month to display, where *mm* is in the range 1–12.
end *mm*	Sets the last month to display, where *mm* is in the range 1–12.
category *filter*	Sets the category filter, where *filter* is a text string (without whitespace).
background *color*	Sets the background color (bgcolor) of the noteboard, where *color* is a text string containing a valid HTML color constant.
text *color*	Sets the text (foreground) color of the noteboard, where *color* is a text string containing a valid HTML color constant.
layout *style*	Sets the noteboard layout, where *style* is either horizontal or vertical.
html *filename*	Generates an HTML calendar noteboard file named *filename* for the filtered months and notes, using the specified colors and layout.
print *mm*	Outputs to the screen the calendar noteboard for the specified month (*mm*) including the month's display along with its filtered notes.
help	Displays this list of commands along with a short description of each command.
quit	Terminates the program.

If the user enters a command other than one of the keyboard commands listed above, your program should output the message "Invalid command." See the OPTIONAL FEATURES section later in this laboratory for additional suggested command options.

The framework of the noninteractive (static) HTML noteboard that you are required to implement for this project follows. This HTML file will produce a *vertical* layout. (The HTML framework given in the OPTIONAL FEATURES section of this laboratory will produce a *horizontal* layout. Also included, of course, are the HTML tags that make it interactive.) Depending on the current setting of the noteboard's layout (horizontal or vertical), it is required that your program accordingly produces a static HTML noteboard file that displays the noteboard in the specified layout.

```
<html>
<head>
<title>Noteboard</title>
</head>
<body bgcolor=white text=black>
<hr width=100%>
<table cellspacing=10>
<tr><td>
<img src=january.jpg align=left hspace=20>
<pre>
January          2002
 S  M  T  W  T  F  S
       01 02 03 04 05
06 07 08 09 10 11 12
13 14 15 16 17 18 19
20 21 22 23 24 25 26
27 28 29 30 31
</pre>
</td></tr>
<tr><td>
1/1Happy New Year<br>
1/2Recover<br>
1/15MLK Day<br>
</td></tr>
</table>
<hr width=100%>
<table cellspacing=10>
<tr><td>
<img src=february.jpg align=left hspace=20>
<pre>
... Calendar and notes for February ...
</td></tr>
</table>
...
... Calendar and notes for December ...
</td></tr>
</table>
<hr width=100%>
</body>
</html>
```

Optional Features

(Check with your instructor before including this in your project.)

This program can be designed with many other enhancements. For example, additional user commands might include the following:

- year *yyyy*—to change the calendar year,

- addNote—to add a note to the set of notes for the calendar, (also gives the user the option of appending the new note to the end of the *.nbd* file that was read in at the beginning of the program),

- delete—to remove a note from the noteboard and/or the *.nbd* file,

- edit—to revise an existing note rather than having to use *delete* and *addNote*.

These and other enhancements you may consider useful should be discussed with your teammates (and, in a real programming project, with the user) to determine their practicality and feasibility.

Another interesting program enhancement is to create an interactive noteboard. When the interactive property setting is *true,* it is intended that the program will produce an interactive HTML noteboard consisting of the following:

- A menu bar listing the months that can be displayed.

- The calendar and notes for the month the user selected from the menu bar.

A sample interactive noteboard is illustrated below. If the user clicks "June," then the calendar and notes for June are displayed. On the other hand, if the user clicks "September," then the calendar and notes for September are displayed.

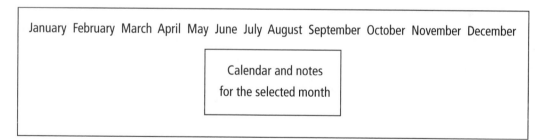

The `interactive` property is defined as follows:

Appearance property	Description
`interactive` true/false	Indicates whether the HTML file is interactive (`true`) or static (`false`). Default: `true`

The following HTML framework will produce the interactive noteboard. Please note that besides being interactive, this HTML will have a *horizontal* layout.

```
<html>
<head>
<title>Noteboard</title>
<script src=menu.js></script>
</head>
<body bgcolor=white text=black>
<table width=100%>
<tr>
<td><a style='color:black;text-decoration:none' href=#
      onclick=select('month1')>January</a></td>
<td><a style='color:black;text-decoration:none' href=#
      onclick=select('month2')>February</a></td>
...
<td><a style='color:black;text-decoration:none' href=#
      onclick=select('month12')>December</a></td>
</tr>
</table>
<hr width=100%>
<div id=month1
    style='position:absolute;left:0;top:60;visibility:hidden'>
<table cellspacing=10>
<tr>
<td valign=top>
<img src=january.jpg align=left hspace=20>
<pre>
January        2002
  S  M  T  W  T  F  S
        01 02 03 04 05
06 07 08 09 10 11 12
13 14 15 16 17 18 19
20 21 22 23 24 25 26
27 28 29 30 31
</pre>
</td>
<td valign=top>
1/1Happy New Year<br>
1/2Recover<br>
1/15MLK Day<br>
</td>
</tr>
</table>
<hr width=100%>
</div>
<div id=month2
    style='position:absolute;left:0;top:60;visibility:hidden'>
 ... Calendar and notes for February ...
</div>
 ....
```

```
<div id=month12
     style='position:absolute;left:0;top:60;visibility:hidden'>
... Calendar and notes for December ...
</div>
</body>
</html>
```

Note that the contents of the noteboard (months and notes) are still specified by the content filters and the noteboard's appearance (colors and layout) is still specified by the appearance properties.

Generating the interactive HTML noteboard is similar to generating the static noteboard. The HTML file still contains *all* of the calendars and notes. The difference is that each month's calendar and note set are grouped into an identifiable `<div>` element. One `<div>` element is generated for each month, as in the following example.

```
<div id=month1
     style='position:absolute;left:0;top:60;visibility:hidden'>
... Calendar and notes for January ...
</div>
<div id=month2
     style='position:absolute;left:0;top:60;visibility:hidden'>
... Calendar and notes for February ...
</div>
...
```

Note that all the months have the same position (one on top of the other) and that all the months are initially marked as hidden (not visible).

The menu bar at the top of the interactive noteboard display consists of a simple HTML table of the following form. This code appears near the beginning of the interactive HTML file.

```
<table width=100%>
<tr>
<td><a style='color:black;text-decoration:none' href=#
    onclick=select('month1')>January</a></td>
<td><a style='color:black;text-decoration:none' href=#
    onclick=select('month2')>February</a></td>
...
<td><a style='color:black;text-decoration:none' href=#
    onclick=select('month12')>December</a></td>
</tr>
</table>
```

Clicking the name of a month on the menu bar activates the JavaScript `select()` function for the corresponding month. This function, in turn, reveals the selected month's `<div>` element. The file *menu.js* contains the required JavaScript code. You include this code near the beginning of the HTML file as follows:

```
<head>
...
<script src=menu.js></script>
</head>
```

LABORATORY 16 — Week 1: Bridge Exercise

Project Development Phases 1, 2, and 3

Name _____

Hour/Period/Section _____

Date _____

The development phases of this team project will span across Week 1 and Week 2. In Week 1 you will analyze and design the calendar/noteboard project using the OOAD techniques illustrated in the child's calculator problem presented in Prelab Exercise 1. In Week 2 you will implement and test the final calendar/noteboard project system.

Phase 1: Project Design

Step 1: Individually identify the objects in the calendar/noteboard project discussed in Prelab Exercise 2. Begin by applying the "using nouns" technique to find potential objects. In addition be sure to look for objects that are not described explicitly in the problem statement but that are implicitly part of the problem. Examples of these kinds of "hidden" objects are

- Objects that are collections (sets or lists) of other objects.

- Objects that provide the means (information or actions) through which other objects interrelate—the role played by the Interface object in the child's calculator problem, for instance.

Step 2: List each object's attributes and behaviors. Recall that all verbs and predicate phrases can be used to help identify object behaviors and that all adjectives can be used to help identify object attributes. A blank project cover sheet for listing these object characteristics is given at the end of this section.

Step 3: Review the sets of objects produced by you and your teammates. Focus your discussion on the similarities and differences in how each of you saw the problem and created objects. Did you produce different numbers of objects? If so, why? How do the objects differ in terms of their attributes and their behaviors? Are these differences serious or merely cosmetic?

Remember that there are no rigid rules for the design process. Different people see problems in different ways. These diverse perspectives, in turn, shed considerably more light on a problem than does a single view.

Step 4: Combine your team's efforts and create *one* set of objects/classes for the programming project. Remember that while there are no rigid rules for the design process, it is important to consider how the various classes (objects) in your design will interact with one another. Some questions to consider include the following:

- Does the class provide the functionality needed by the other classes?

- Is it clear what each class method does and how it is to be used?

- Is the class missing methods or does it have extra (unused) class methods?

- Does the class maintain the information needed by other classes? If so, do these classes have a way of accessing this information?

- Do the classes in your design collectively provide the functionality required to solve the problem?

Produce a document listing the objects, their attributes, and their behaviors similar to the format used in the Prelab Exercise 1 in this laboratory.

Step 5: Assign each object to a team member. Each team member will design (and later implement) a Java class for each object, so try to balance the projected workload equitably among team members.

Step 6: For each Java class, the designated team member is to provide the following information:

- A brief description of the class focusing on what the class does and how it is used.

- A detailed specification for each class method similar to the method specifications presented in each laboratory in this textbook.

- An incomplete/skeleton Java class definition, including data members and class methods.

- A list of the other classes that use this class (its **clients**).

- A list of the other classes that this class uses (its **collaborators**).

Phase 2: Project Test Plan

Step 1: As a team, create a test plan for each class in your design. A blank class test plan form is given at the end of this section.

Step 2: Create a test plan for the complete project. A blank project test plan form is given at the end of this section.

Phase 3: Document Team's Project Plan

Complete documentation is an essential part of any programming project. The program's design must be carefully documented so that before writing any code, each team member is aware of the configuration of entire project. Therefore, you are to combine your team's efforts to produce a team design document for this programming project. Base the organization of your design documentation on the following outline.

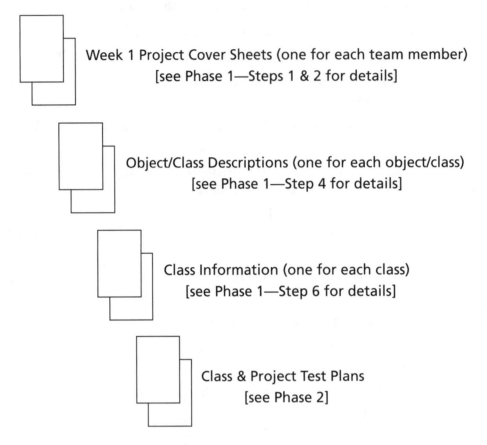

Week 1 Project Cover Sheets (one for each team member)
[see Phase 1—Steps 1 & 2 for details]

Object/Class Descriptions (one for each object/class)
[see Phase 1—Step 4 for details]

Class Information (one for each class)
[see Phase 1—Step 6 for details]

Class & Project Test Plans
[see Phase 2]

LABORATORY 16 — Week 1: Project Cover Sheet

Name

Hour/Period/Section

Date

Each team member is to individually identify the objects/classes in the OOAD calendar/note-board project introduced in Prelab Exercise 2. Individual lists of objects will be reviewed by the whole team and used to ultimately create one set of objects/classes for this project. For each team member, attach one copy of this sheet to the front of your Team's Project Plan (for Week 1). Use an additional sheet of paper if necessary.

Team member (name):	
Proposed object/class:	
Attributes:	
Behaviors:	

Team member (name):	
Proposed object/class:	
Attributes:	
Behaviors:	
Proposed object/class:	
Attributes:	
Behaviors:	

Test Plan for the *class*

Test case	Sample data	Expected result	Checked

Test Plan for the *Calendar/Noteboard Programming Project*

Test case	Sample data	Expected result	Checked

LABORATORY 16 — Week 1: In-lab Exercise

Implement the Child's Calculator

Name _____

Hour/Period/Section _____

Date _____

Having completed the design of the child's calculator program, our next task is to implement the methods in the `Calculator`, `Face`, and `Interface` classes—as well as the calculator program's `main()` method. We will store our implementations for the `Calculator`, `Face`, and `Interface` classes in the files *Calculator.java*, *Face.java*, and *Interface.java,* respectively. The implementation for the `Command` class may also be placed in the *Interface.java* file.

Let's start the implementation process with the `Calculator` class. The methods of this class are quite simple—no surprises here. The `display()` method forms the calculator using standard ASCII characters. This approach allows for generality of use—every environment supports ASCII text output—at the price of visual pizzazz. Because formatting is not always easily done in Java, the `display()` method calls a private method that formats the value in `accum` within precisely 12 spaces.

```
public void display ()
// Displays a calculator.

{
    System.out.println("----------------");
    System.out.print("|");
    System.out.print(strRight(new Double(accum), 12));
    System.out.println("  |");
    System.out.println("|             |");
    System.out.println("|  1  2  3  +  |");
    System.out.println("|  4  5  6  -  |");
    System.out.println("|  7  8  9  *  |");
    System.out.println("|    0  C  /   |");
    System.out.println("----------------");
}

private String strRight( Object output, int minimumWidth )
// Creates a String using a specified width and right justification
// Works like setw(minimumWidth) in C++
{
    int i;
    StringBuffer s = new StringBuffer( output.toString( ) );
    StringBuffer add = new StringBuffer( );
```

```
        // Create any leading spaces and then the Object itself.
        for ( i = s.length( ); i < minimumWidth; i++ )
            add.append(" ");
        s.insert(0, add);
        return s.toString( );
}
```

Implementing the `Face` class is an equally straightforward task. In this case, the `display()` method outputs the smiley face discussed in the design phase, using both its "happy" and "sad" incarnations that are commonly used in textual e-mail messages.

```
public void display ( )
// Displays a face.
{
    if ( state == 1 )
        System.out.print ( ":-)");
    else
        System.out.print(":-(");
}
```

Implementing the `Interface` class is a little trickier. Recall that this class has three data members: `calc`, `smiley`, and `userCmd`. The `Interface` class constructor must correctly initialize all these data members including setting the command name (`userCmd.cmd`) to the null character.

```
public Interface ()
// Default Constructor. Creates an interface and initializes its
//   data members.

{
    calc = new Calculator( );
    smiley = new Face( );
    userCmd = new Command( );
    userCmd.cmd = '\0';
}
```

The `generateDisplay()` method uses the `display()` methods in the `Face` and `Calculator` classes to display the smiley face followed by the calculator. Note that additional formatting is done to center the smiley face above the calculator.

```
public void generateDisplay ( )
// Generates an interface display consisting of a happy/sad face and
// a calculator.

{
    System.out.println();
    System.out.print("        ");
    smiley.display( );
    System.out.println( );
    calc.display( );
}
```

User commands are read from the keyboard by the `getCommand()` method. If a command has a numeric argument, this argument is read in as well. The input command and argument (if any) are stored in `userCmd`.

```java
public void getCommand ( )
// Prompts the user for a command, reads in a command from the
// keyboard, and stores it in userCmd.
{
    .....
    System.out.print("Enter command: ");
    userCmd.cmd = (char)System.in.read( );
    while ( Character.isWhitespace(userCmd.cmd) )
        userCmd.cmd = (char)System.in.read( );

    if ( userCmd.cmd == '+'  ||  userCmd.cmd == '-'  ||
          userCmd.cmd == '*'  ||  userCmd.cmd == '/'     )
    {
        tokens.nextToken();
        userCmd.arg = tokens.nval;
    }
}
```

The `executeCommand()` method processes the user's last command. This method must rely on the methods of the `Face` and `Calculator` classes to modify the `smiley` and `calc` objects.

```java
public void executeCommand ( ) throws IOException
// Executes the user's last command (in userCmd).

{
    switch ( userCmd.cmd )
    {
        case '+' :  calc.add(userCmd.arg);        break;
        case '-' :  calc.subtract(userCmd.arg);   break;
        case '*' :  calc.multiply(userCmd.arg);   break;
        case '/' :  if ( userCmd.arg != 0 )
                        calc.divide(userCmd.arg);
                    else
                        System.out.println("Cannot divide by 0");
                    break;
        case 'C' :
        case 'c' :  calc.clear();  break;
        case 'Q' :
        case 'q' :  break;
        default  :  System.out.print("Invalid command");
    }
    if ( calc.value() < 0 )   // Update the face
        smiley.makeSad();
    else
        smiley.makeHappy();
}
```

Finally, using the `done()` method, clients of the `Interface` class test whether the user has input the Q (quit) command.

```
public boolean done ()
// Returns true if the user has entered the Q (quit) command.
// Otherwise, returns false.

{
    return ( userCmd.cmd == 'Q' || userCmd.cmd == 'q' );
}
```

After completing the implementation of the `Face`, `Calculator`, and `Interface` classes, all that is left to do is create a `main()` method that moves the interface through repetitions of the following three-step cycle:

```
generate display,
get command, and
execute command.
```

See the file *KidCalc.java*.

At this point, we have completed development of the child's calculator program. The question that now arises is: How do we test and debug our program? One approach would be to throw everything together and test the entire program as a whole. The problem with this approach is that testing and debugging an even moderately large program can easily become overwhelming, with errors compounding errors and everything falling into chaos. A better approach is to test and debug our program using the same strategy that we used to develop it. First, we test each class. Once we've worked out the bugs in the individual classes, we combine them and test the complete program.

We start by testing the classes that do not depend on other classes and work our way up through the class hierarchy. Let's start with the `Calculator` class. We begin by developing a simple test program that provides us with the ability to check each method using various input values. A simple interactive test program for the `Calculator` class is given below (and available in the file *TestCalc.java*).

```
import java.io.*;

class TestCalc
{
    public static void main (String args[]) throws IOException
    {
        Calculator calc = new Calculator();      // Calculator object
        char oper;                               // Input operator
        double num;                              // Input number

        BufferedReader ins =
                new BufferedReader(new InputStreamReader(System.in));
        StreamTokenizer tokens = new StreamTokenizer(ins);
```

```
// Test the arithmetic methods and the value() method.
System.out.println();
System.out.println("Start of testing");

do
{
    calc.display();
    System.out.println();
    System.out.print("Enter operator ( Q 0 to end ) : ");
    oper = (char)System.in.read( );
    while ( Character.isWhitespace(oper) )
        oper = (char)System.in.read( );
    tokens.nextToken();
    num = tokens.nval;

    switch ( oper )
    {
    case '+' :  calc.add(num);       break;
    case '-' :  calc.subtract(num);  break;
    case '*' :  calc.multiply(num);  break;
    case '/' :  calc.divide(num);    break;
    }

    System.out.println("Calculator value : "
                         + calc.value());

} while ( oper != 'Q'  &&  oper != 'q' );

// Test the clear() method.

calc.clear();
System.out.println();
System.out.println("Calculator cleared");
calc.display();
    }

} // class TestCalc
```

Testing the `Face` class is equally straightforward (see the file *TestFace.java*).

Once the `Calculator` and `Face` classes have been thoroughly tested and debugged, we can begin testing the `Interface` class, which depends on these two classes. Note that testing the `Interface` class before we are sure that the `Calculator` and `Face` classes work properly is just asking for trouble. Adding a simple method such as `showCommands( )` to the `Interface` class is all that is needed to check that the `getCommand( )` method is reading in user commands correctly using the file *TestIntf.java*.

```
public void showCommands( )
// For testing/debugging purposes only
{
    // Echo the command read
    System.out.println("Command:   " + userCmd.cmd);
    // Echo the argument read
    System.out.println("Argument:   " + userCmd.arg);
}
```

Next, we test the executeCommand( ) method by uncommenting the rest of the statements in the *TestIntf.java* program and perhaps commenting out the showCommands( ) statement. Finally, we run a systematic test of the entire program using the file *KidCalc.java*.

Follow-Up Exercise

The following files will contain the class implementations and test programs for the classes developed above.

Class	Implementation	Test program
Face	*Face.java*	*TestFace.java*
Calculator	*Calculator.java*	*TestCalc.java*
Interface	*Interface.java*	*TestIntf.java*

Step 1: Informally test (no test plan required) the implementation of the Face class in the file *Face.java* using the test program in the file *TestFace.java*.

Step 2: Informally test the implementation of the Calculator class in the file *Calculator.java* using the test program in the file *TestCalc.java*.

Step 3: Informally test the implementation of the Interface class in the file *Interface.java* using the test program in the file *TestIntf.java*.

Step 4: Having completed the testing of these classes, informally test the child's calculator program using the class implementations in the files *Face.java*, *Calculator.java*, and *Interface.java* and the main( ) method in the file *KidCalc.java*.

LABORATORY 16 — Week 2: Project Cover Sheet

Name _____

Hour/Period/Section _____

Date _____

List the members in your software development team and the class (or classes) each team member implemented in the following In-lab Exercise for Week 2. Attach one copy of this sheet to the front of your team's implementation documents for Week 2.

Team member (name)	Classes implemented	Completed

LABORATORY 16 — Week 2: In-lab Exercise

Implement the Calendar/Noteboard Program

Name _____

Hour/Period/Section _____

Date _____

During the first week of this laboratory, you and your teammates developed a design and test plan for this calendar/noteboard programming project by completing development Phases 1, 2, and 3. This week in development Phases 4 and 5, each team member implements and tests the classes that they designed last week. These efforts are then combined to produce a complete program.

Some Preliminary Implementation Notes

In order to produce a calendar for a given month, you need to know on which day of the week the first day of the month occurs. In addition, you need to know if a particular year is a leap year. To facilitate these operations, you may want to include Java's built-in class `GregorianCalendar` in your implementation either as a superclass or as a data member of one of your class definitions.

You may also find the built-in `Vector` class useful for implementing dynamic arrays in your programming project. A **vector** is essentially a variable-length array of object references.

To create an InputStream object connected to a file, you need to use a statement that creates an instance of the `FileInputStream` class for a specified file. For example, the following creates a FileInputStream object called `inFile`, which is attached to the file *sample.nbd*:

```
FileInputStream inFile = new FileInputStream("sample.nbd");
```

To create a BufferedReader for an InputStreamReader object connected to this FileInputStream, you need to use a statement similar to the following:

```
BufferedReader finReader = new BufferedReader(new InputStreamReader(inFile));
```

Remember a BufferedReader is used to provide optimum reading efficiency.

Last, as in several previous laboratory exercises, you may want to insert a tokenizer (either the `StreamTokenizer` class or the `StringTokenizer` class) in your program so you can process complete numbers, words, or strings. Also, you may want to consider using the `StreamTokenizer` method `lowerCaseMode( )` or the `String` method `toLowerCase( )` so the user's input will not be case sensitive.

Writing to a file is very similar to reading from a file. First, you connect to an output file by creating an instance of the `FileOutputStream` class for a specified file. For example, the following statement creates a FileOutputStream object called `htmlFile`, which is attached to the file *notebd.html*:

```
FileOutputStream htmlFile = new FileOutputStream("notebd.html");
```

To write characters and strings to this stream rather than a byte at a time, you must create an instance of `PrintWriter` from the `FileOutputStream` instance as follows:

```
PrintWriter writer = new PrinterWriter(htmlFile);
```

Once you have an instance of `PrintWriter`, you can write strings to the stream, using the `print` and `println` methods similar to those used with `System.out`. For example, the following statement will write the string `<html>` to the file output stream declared above:

```
writer.println("<html>");
```

As a matter of good programming practice, you should always close files using the `close` method once they are no longer needed.

Phase 4: Project Implementation and Testing

Step 1: Implement the methods for each of your assigned classes in your team's design. The team member whose class manages the user interface should also implement the program's `main()` method. Be sure to document your code.

Should you make any changes to a class—by adding a data member or a class method, for instance—be certain to inform your teammates in a timely manner.

Step 2: Test the classes you implemented by creating test programs to run the class test plans you developed in Step 1 of Phase 2. For each class, check each case in the class's test plan and verify the expected result. If you discover mistakes in a class implementation, correct them and execute the class's test plan again.

Step 3: Combine your tested class implementations with your teammates' efforts to produce a complete program. Test your complete project. Check each case in your project test plan and verify the expected result. If you discover mistakes in your program, correct them and execute the project test plan again.

Step 4: Create an implementation document that contains the source code and test plans for your team's program. Base the organization of your document on the following outline.

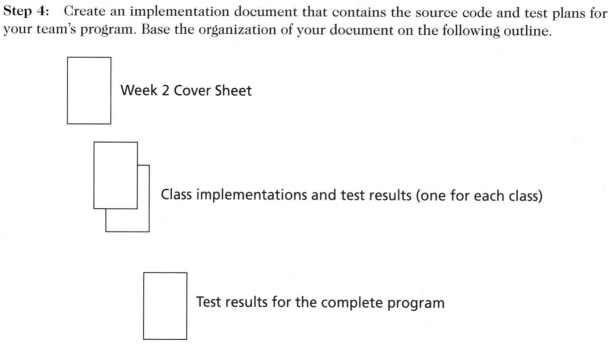

Week 2 Cover Sheet

Class implementations and test results (one for each class)

Test results for the complete program

LABORATORY 16 — Postlab Exercise

Name _____

Hour/Period/Section _____

Date _____

Phase 5: Project Analysis

What problems did your team face in implementing your class designs? What caused these problems? How would you avoid these kinds of problems in future programming efforts?